climbing australia
the essential guide

greg pritchard

NEW
HOLLAND

ACKNOWLEDGMENTS

I would especially like to thank Innigo Montoya and Simon Mentz for their drawings and advice; Pete Steane for his help with the Tasmanian section; Sam Latz and Damian Auton for help with the Northern Territory; Chris Jones for Western Australia; Simon Carter for allowing the use of his excellent photographs; Jon Bassindale, Al Stephens, Roxanne Wells, Garn Cooper, Richard Smith, Brigitte Muir, Phil and Korry, Malcolm Matheson and Steve Monks and everyone else who has helped me.

I would also like to thank all the guidebook editors, web page writers and editors, and article writers whose work has been of invaluable help in compiling this book. Without your tireless efforts, 'best of' guidebooks like this one would never be possible.

First published in Australia in 2002 by
New Holland Publishers (Australia) Pty Ltd
Sydney • Auckland • London • Cape Town

14 Aquatic Drive Frenchs Forest NSW 2086 Australia
218 Lake Road Northcote Auckland New Zealand
86 Edgware Road London W2 2EA United Kingdom
80 McKenzie Street Cape Town 8001 South Africa

National Library of Australia Cataloguing-in-Publication Data:

Pritchard, Greg, 1960–.
Climbing Australia: the essential guide.

Includes index.
ISBN 1 86436 694 X.

1. Rock climbing – Australia – Guidebooks. 2. Rock climbing – Australia. I. Title.

796.52230994

Publishing Manager: Anouska Good
Editor: Sophie Church
Designer: Nanette Backhouse
Layout: Saso Content and Design
Photographer: Simon Carter/Onsight Photography
Cartographer: Ian Faulkner
Map references: Innigo Montoya and Greg Pritchard
Production Controller: Wendy Hunt
Reproduction: Sang Choy International, Singapore
Printer: Times Offset

This book is typeset in Oranda BT 9.5/12pt and Futura Condensed Light 9.5/12pt.

10 9 8 7 6 5 4 3 2 1

Front cover: Frey Yule and Brendan Junge on *Supertrance 2000* 23, Pierce's Pass (see page 40), another superb Blue Mountains' sandstone arête.

contents

To Glen and Ruby,
for their patience and love.

INTRODUCTION

This book is intended as a guide to the best cliffs in Australia. It is designed for climbers, both novices and experts, who want to travel around the country and experience as much of the great climbing in Australia as possible, whether they are from Australia or overseas.

How to use this book

The first part of this book deals with the technicalities of climbing in Australia—our grading system, our cliffs and environment—as well as the abbreviations and route jargon adopted for this book. The second part lists climbing areas in Australia, and provides the route descriptions, access and camping information for each listed area.

The common criticism of general climbing guidebooks is that they are useless without the relevant area guides and are therefore of limited appeal. Although it is impossible to accurately describe every climb in a book of this format, I have tried to provide route descriptions for enough climbs (in fact several hundred) to enable you to do some climbing with this guide alone, regardless of what grade you climb. If you find you like the area and want to do more, I have listed further recommended climbs but to find them you'll have to ask other climbers, or use the relevant guidebook for the area.

With this guide I have tried to give you the best of both worlds. Hopefully, using this book only, you should be able to find some climbs in more than 70 areas, ranging in grade from 2 to 33. (I have tried to give a grade range at each cliff, understanding that not everyone climbs over grade 25, but that some do.) These climbs are not just a selected best of the most fashionable areas. I have tried to include modern classics but, since there are people of all ages who are still keen to experience all that climbing has to offer (bouldering, sport climbing and traditional climbing), I have also included many traditional classics. (You don't *have* to go climbing in the Warrumbungles or at Frenchmans Cap, but I have given you the necessary information if you are interested.) When I was unable to include a climb (and this includes some three-star absolute classic climbs), I hope the brief description that comes with the area information will be enough to captivate your curiosity, and to inspire you to seek out more detailed area guides to find further information. I have also awarded each area either one, two or three stars to denote the rock quality. This is, at best, a very rough guide to provide comparison with other areas. Within areas, and between climbs, quality can vary greatly.

Wherever possible, make sure you check with local climbers, rangers or cliffcare groups about the current access status of the cliff you are planning to climb. Some cliffs are closed to climbing during nesting seasons, while other cliffs are placed under temporary or permanent bans. Check before you climb.

Finally, remember that climbing is dangerous. It should only be done with adequate training and experience, using the right equipment and taking great care. The information in this guide should not be treated as infallible. Above all, use your common sense and always follow correct safety procedures.

Australian travel tips for climbers

If you are planning a trip to, or around, Australia you should check out one of the travel guides, such as Australia's own Lonely Planet guides, for information on visas, customs, culture and places to visit.

This book provides transport details for each area, but travel guides give more detailed information on public transport, which will usually get you to the nearest large town or city to the cliff you are planning to climb. If you are planning a long trip (say two or three months) contemplate buying a car, a fairly cheap option among a few friends. You should be able to find something reasonably reliable for about $2–3000. Check out the notice boards in backpackers' hostels or look in the *Trading Post*. There are often climber's cars for sale in Natimuk or at Arapiles.

Camping is one of the joys of climbing in Australia, and can reduce the cost of your trip. Pay special attention to the 'Taking care of the cliffs' chapter. Accommodation details for each area are provided in this book, but travel guides will give more detailed information.

For more information on climbing, I have listed climbing shops, gyms and instruction companies in each state in Appendices 1 and 2. These are great places to contact other climbers, get instruction or buy equipment. Very few cliffs are guaranteed to have climbers at them all the time. The exceptions are Arapiles, some of the Blue Mountains' cliffs (including Piddington) and Frog in Queensland. In Tasmania, local climbers go to Cataract Gorge in Launceston on Thursday nights during the summer months.

part one

how to climb in australia

ROUTES

Firstly, I have assumed that people who buy this book know, or are learning, how to climb. The aim is to get you to the base of as many climbs as possible, with an idea of where the route goes. Rather than editorialising the route descriptions—that is, telling you how to climb—I have left it up to you to decide whether you want to climb 'with difficulty' or 'easily up'.

Secondly, I am assuming that you have adequate knowledge on how to place protection and what to carry. I have rarely listed the gear you will need for a climb. On most climbs you can probably work it out from the ground. If you are not experienced with lead climbing then you should take extreme care, get some experience on grades you are comfortable with or perhaps stick to top-roping. In some areas, including the very popular Arapiles, there are few sport climbs and some leading experience is necessary. Take it easy.

Each route has been awarded either one, two or three 'triangles'. These relate to the quality of the route—a three-triangle route is of better quality than a one- or two-triangle route. However, triangles are relative to each area and do not compare throughout the book (a one-triangle route on Taipan might get three triangles if it were in another area). Almost all of the climbs are recommended by climbers and guidebooks editors and I am not responsible for the quality of the routes—hopefully there are no real horrors! I have tried not to waste too many words on gushy superlatives, leaving you to discover the enjoyment of each climb for yourself. All routes are graded using the Ewbank grading system—refer to p. 6 for more information.

Since it has been necessary to keep route descriptions brief, it is advisable to read the information on access, as well as the route descriptions on either side of the route you intend to do, in order to get the full picture of where the climb starts and ends, and where the descent is. Don't just take my word for it though—always use your own judgement.

Example route description

▲▲▲   23   65m   (2) [22,23] 1963 {1985}

I am an Example — Start 4m L. 1. (13m) Up to and up flake. 2. (21m) Diagonally R and through roof. BB at ledge. Move R to chains.

Each description begins with four boxes which summarise the essential infomation for the route, followed by the route name:

▲▲▲	quality of route
23	grade of route
65m	length of route in metres
(2)	number of pitches, if more than one
[22,23]	grades of pitches, if known
1963	date route was originally climbed
{1985}	date route was freed
I am an Example —	route name

The route is then described, using the following abbreviations (see below for additional bolt abbreviations):

L	left	N	north	RHV	right hand variant
R	right	S	south	LHV	left hand variant
FI	facing in	E	east	Trav	traverse
FO	facing out	W	west	FFA	first free ascent*

* Where multiple dates are given, e.g. {1985–87}, the climb may have been freed over a period of time, or may be a composite of two or more routes. Top-roped free ascents are not acknowledged. This of course gives no indication of how much aid was originally in a route. Look at the date it was done, and the date it was freed. In more historically important cliffs the longer these dates are apart the greater the chance that it had a lot of aid.

BOLTS

There are a number of bolting technologies used in Australia. Older bolts are generally called carrots. A 'carrot' is a $\frac{3}{8}$ in bolt (rarely stainless steel) that was filed down and hammered into a $\frac{3}{8}$ in hole. When done well they are extremely strong. Be careful of carrots that are bent down or have a mushroomed head (a sign they have been overdriven). To use a carrot you need to carry (in your chalkbag) some bolt plates (sometimes referred to as RP plates or hangers). These have a keyhole in them which slips over the carrot head. The carabiner stops the plate from coming off the carrot. Sometimes a keyhole plate (or non-keyhole) is put on the bolt before it is hammered in, making a fixed hanger.

A wire can be used to clip awkward sized bolts (or ones out of reach). Slide the head down a little to get it over the bolt, then slide the head up snug. However, this method should only be used in emergencies because they can flip-off during a fall.

A batman move, specified in some Blue Mountains areas and Nowra, involves clipping into the first bolt (stick-clip) and hauling yourself up the rope—used to avoid an impossible start, or M0 (see page 6).

In this book, the following bolt abbreviations are used:

BR	bolt runner *	2BB	double bolt belay
FH	fixed hanger **	HBB	hanging bolt belay
PR	peg runner or piton	semi-HBB	semi hanging bolt belay
BB	bolt belay	rap	a rap point ***

* May be a carrot or something more modern but unspecified. If you can't see it you are advised to carry a plate. (Also check the date of the climb and note the nature of the area.)

** May be a bolt (carrot or other) with fixed hanger or plate, or alternatively a ring bolt or glued in U-bolt.

*** May be two rings, fixed hangers or a chain. If I have known there is a chain on a route I have generally mentioned it. If a route says rap from slings then you should consider taking new slings to rap off. The Australian sun is quite strong and you should be very wary of any old slings or rope.

GRADING SYSTEMS

Australia uses the Ewbank free grading system (designed by Australian climber John Ewbank in the 1960s). It is an open-ended numerical system, currently ranging from 1 to 33. If used well it can be very descriptive, and should take into account both technical and head difficulty, including protection. (The 'other' grading system is campsite drum, which Americans call 'beta'—i.e., get as much information from other climbers as possible, and watch out for people with big smirks on their faces or, worse, who are doing a little jig. They are usually sandbaggers, but you can trust me, I'm not a sandbagger—ask anyone…)

The aid grading system used in Australia is more confusing. Not a lot of climbers go aid climbing and few understand the aid grades. It has been proposed that we change to the American A system and some climbs are graded thus. To complicate matters there is the grade of MO (only used in Australia), proposed for climbs with a rest, tension and pendulum (or single aid point!) Victorians never really warmed to the idea and although the MO grade is accepted in New South Wales, such things as 'batman starts' (see p. 5) are not given such a grade.

Until recently the only bouldering grades used in Australia were the exquisite B1, B2 and B3 systems or local esoteric systems. With the recent huge surge in popularity of bouldering, there has been common usage of the American V system (invented by John 'Vermin' Sherman and styled on the Ewbank system) although European superstars have also used European grades in Australia.

Bouldering grades comparison

Font	6a+	6b	6b+	6c	6c+	7a	7a+	7b	7b+	7c	7c+	8a	8a+	8b	8b+
V	0	1	2	3	4	5	6	7	8	9	10	11	12	13	14

Aid grades comparison

Aus	MO	M1	M2	M3	M4	M5	M6	M7	M8	M9
US	AO	A1	A1+	A2		A3		A4		A5

Free grades comparison

Route Grades					
Aus	UK Trad	UK Tech	French	USA	UIAA
18	VS	4c	5a	5.8	6-
19	HVS	5a	5b	5.9	6
20	E1	5b	5c	5.10a	7-
			6a	5.10b	
21	E2	5c	6a+	5.10c	7
			6b	5.10d	
	E3		6b+	5.11a	
			6c	5.11b	
23	E4	6a	6c+	5.11c	8-
24			7a	5.11d	8
25	E5		7a+	5.12a	8+
26			7b	5.12b	
27	E6	6b	7b+	5.12c	9-
			7c	5.12d	9
28			7c+	5.13a	9+
29		6c	8a	5.13b	
30			8a+	5.13c	10-
31			8b	5.13d	10-
32	E8	7a	8b+	5.14a	10
33			8c	5.14b	11-
34	E9	7b	8c+	5.14c	11
35	E10		9a	5.14d	11+

TAKING CARE OF THE CLIFFS

Nearly all the cliffs in Australia are located in national parks or on private land. If we are not discreet and careful when we climb, we may lose access to even more cliffs. Whether on private property or in national parks make every effort to remember the basic courtesies and rules of bush camping and coexistence.

▲ Dogs, other pets and firearms are forbidden in national parks. Do not take them onto private land without permission.

▲ Keep to tracks and take note of path restrictions. When driving through private land make sure you leave all gates as you find them.

▲ Observe fire restrictions. Fires are forbidden on total fire ban days. Even in parks where firewood collection and fire lighting is allowed, be vigilant. It is best to take a gas or fuel stove, and in some areas these are mandatory. Never leave a fire unattended. Keep flammable material clear of the fireplace and make sure the fire is *completely* out before you go to bed or leave the campsite.

▲ Be responsible for your waste. In areas that do not have toilets, or when at the cliff-face, faeces should either be carried out (perhaps invest in a tube) or well buried at a depth of at least 10cm, and not in water catchment areas or within 100m of a water source. Toilet paper (and this applies equally to women and men) should be carried out and disposed of sensibly. It should not be buried as animals dig it up again. The practice of burning the paper, though sensible in other areas, can be close to suicide in some of Australia's tinder-dry environments, and is not recommended.

▲ Carry out all your rubbish. When in camp, retrieve any plastic bags etc. that blow away. At the cliff, take care of rubbish, particularly cigarette butts (pack a tin and carry them out), hand tape, chalk wrappers etc. Citrus peel degrades slowly so take that with you too.

▲ Do not disturb or remove any plants, animals or rock structures.

▲ Be culturally sensitive and aware that some rocks are important to Aboriginal people. Do not disturb art sites.

▲ Often camp sites come with the local resident pest species. They may be cute and cuddly but generally get to be a nuisance. Please do not feed rosellas, possums or other wildlife as it upsets the natural ecological balance as well as encouraging them to hang around. Possums, though a feral nuisance in New Zealand, are a protected species in Australia. Snakes are also protected. If you come across one, avoid it. They are generally not aggressive and will go away if left alone. Most people get bitten trying to kill or capture snakes.

▲ Respect the ethics of the area. Some areas, such as Girraween in Queensland and the Gap in Albany, are non-bolting areas. Retro-bolting (certainly of adequately protected climbs) and chipping are generally considered to be the activities of weak-minded people. Despite the fact that national park authorities have pointed out the illegallity of bolting in national parks, the future will probably see more bolt-protected routes. How this is seen by both climbers and national park authorities will depend to a large extent on how discreet or blatant it is, and how much respect climbers are seen to have for the environment generally. Just because it's blank doesn't mean it has to be bolted or even climbed. Suppress your ego; respect the rock. Leave some challenges for climbers in ten or fifty years time.

▲ Be considerate of other cliff and camp users, both in the daytime and at night. If you must play music, try and make it interesting. Regardless of their talent, Pink Floyd is currently banned in all Australian camp sites and The Beatles will get you stoned to death anywhere (near me at least!)

▲ Above all, look after the environment in every way. Me, here, now is not all there is to life.

TAKING CARE OF YOURSELF

Many Australian cliffs are quite remote and rescue is not always an immediate option. You should always take extreme care, wear a helmet and be prudent with protection. It is a good idea to learn first aid, particularly cardiopulmonary resuscitation (CPR). The golden rule of first aid is **DRABC**: remove the **D**anger, check the patient's **R**esponse, keep the **A**irway clear, check for **B**reathing, check the **C**irculation (find a pulse) and if necessary start CPR.

The emergency number throughout Australia is 000. An operator will put you through to the emergency service you require—ambulance, police, fire or other rescue groups. Keep calm, answer clearly and stay on the line until told otherwise. Mobile phone coverage is not complete throughout Australia, depending on the phone and the network, and mobile phones do not always work.

Dangerous wildlife

The good news is that few animals that live around Australian cliffs will actually eat you. The bad news is that Australia is home to a large percentage of the world's most venomous snakes, along with a couple of venomous spiders. Although it is unlikely that you will come into contact with snakes and spiders, you should be aware of their presence, and if you do come across one treat it with respect. Try not to be scared.

The most common venomous snakes are the taipan, tiger, king brown, brown, and black snakes. Some of these snakes are found all over Australia, while others are only found in certain areas (the taipan, for example, is native to Queensland). Snakes generally get out of your way long before you reach them, but take care stepping over rocks and logs, or anywhere where you can't see your feet, such as in long grass. Wear strong footwear, and long trousers are also a good idea. If bitten by a snake, follow the instructions on the following page and seek immediate medical attention.

Australia is also home to a number of harmless snakes, such as carpet snakes or children's pythons (which are found particularly in Queensland). These snakes are constrictors and have no venom. Goannas (large lizards) and other lizards are harmless, but it is still best to keep your distance.

The two most venomous species of spider are redbacks and funnelwebs. The redback is the most common and tends to live under timber and iron. You are probably more at risk of being bitten by a redback in the backyard than at the cliff. They are shy, shun the light and are non-aggressive. Funnelwebs, found in areas such as Sydney, the Blue Mountains, Kaputar and Nowra, are large, dark brown or black spiders which can be aggressive. Be especially careful when putting on clothes and shoes which have been lying on the ground. If bitten by a spider, treat as for snakebite and seek medical help immediately.

A danger to watch out for in the sea is the box jellyfish or 'stinger'. These are found in northern waters at all times of the year, but particularly in summer (Oct–May). The sting is extremely painful and can be fatal. If you are stung, *do not* remove the sting, but douse the area in vinegar (often available on beaches) and treat as for snakebite.

Australian mosquitoes do not carry malaria (yet) but in some areas (including Arapiles) they can carry the Ross River virus, which is similar to glandular fever. However, mosquitoes and sandflies are mostly just annoying. If you are susceptible to bites, buy some mosquito repellent ('Rid' is about the best) and cover up as much as possible.

What to do if bitten by a snake or spider

1. DRABC (see p. 9).
2. Rest and reassure the casualty.
3. Apply a wide (15cm) pressure immobilisation bandage to the afflicted limb. Bandage as much of the limb as possible, above (firstly) and below the bite area. It should be tight enough to compress tissue but not tight enough to restrict blood flow. Apply a splint with another bandage to immobilise the limb.
4. Try to identify the snake, but do not try to catch it. Do not wash or tamper with the wound.
5. Seek medical attention immediately.

The Australian climate—a note to mad dogs, Englishmen and other crazies

The climate varies greatly throughout Australia. Generally, in the southern states summer lasts from Dec–Feb and can be very hot (up to 40°C). Winter lasts from June–Aug and temperatures can reach 0°C, or just below, at night. It can be colder in Tasmania and alpine areas. (The outback can also be surprisingly cold at night.) Generally, spring (Sept–Nov) and autumn (Mar–May) are good months climatically. The further north you go, the closer to tropical Wet and Dry seasons you get. In Brisbane, climbing in winter is ideal because it is mild and dry, whereas summer is hot, humid and often wet. Special climatic conditions are listed where necessary in area descriptions.

The sun is very hot in Australia. Try not to climb in the heat of the day in summer, and at any time cover up. Shirts, hats and sunscreen are all necessary to stop painful sunburn and to prevent skin cancer. Carry lots of water and drink plenty of it. Heat exposure and heat stroke can occur if you get too hot, and can be fatal.

On the flip side, at many alpine cliffs in Australia (including many Tasmanian cliffs and Buffalo) the weather can change suddenly. Be prepared for rain and cold, and take adequate clothing.

part two

where to climb in australia

CLIMBING AREAS OF AUSTRALIA

For a climber, standing in the middle of the vast Australian desert can be an unnerving experience. There is no vertical, instead a seemingly endless horizontal. Here the night sky is big and close, as if someone had just tipped a bag of diamonds onto a black velvet cloth. Somewhere far off, the all too mournful sound of a howling dingo hangs in the cool air. Otherwise it is quiet—quiet and flat.

Australia is the oldest continent on earth. Through geological ages it has been worn down and eroded. What has remained is a little stub of a country, the lowest continent, the only one without any decent mountains. Our highest mountain is Mt Kosciuszko, a meagre 2228m, one you can walk up with relative ease. With the exception of the coastal fringes and the south-east corner, Australia is mostly flat (and largely unpopulated). If the cross section of Australia was the line of an ECG machine you would think the patient close to death. The redeeming feature of Australian climbing, however, is that for the most part our cliffs are situated in beautiful bushland, often in the sort of wilderness that many countries no longer have.

With a shortage of mountains Australia has become a nation of crag climbers. We have some great crag areas including the Blue Mountains and the Grampians, both huge areas of bushland and long sandstone escarpments. And we have Arapiles, arguably the greatest crag on the planet. By far the majority of Australian routes fall between 10m and 100m (though some reach upwards of 600m) and most climbers are probably more comfortable at these heights.

There is good climbing in every state of Australia and, as with anywhere, the number of routes and developed areas is directly proportional to the population. Hence many of Sydney's close crags, including the sea cliffs that fringe the city, have been visited, whereas climbers in the remote Northern Territory have hardly scratched the surface.

In Victoria there are three great areas: the quartzite Arapiles with close to 3000 climbs; the seemingly endless Grampians with its immaculate orange sandstone wall, Taipan; and the alpine granite area of Mt Buffalo, home to Australia's longest aid routes and some of the most perfect slabs on the planet.

New South Wales has an incredible diversity of areas. Historically, the most important and popular are the sandstone walls of the Blue Mountains which boast long sandstone adventure routes and cutting edge sport climbs. In the north of the state there is a smaller pocket of diversity, a number of different cliffs clustered around the university town of Armidale in New England, as well as the grand volcanic plugs of the Warrumbungles and Kaputar. South of Sydney there is the sport climbing Mecca on the sandstone cliffs of the rivers and creeks around Nowra and, nearby, the spectacular Point Perpendicular. Not far inland the giant gorge of Bungonia has Australia's best limestone climbing.

The nation's capital, Canberra, in the Australian Capital Territory, sits on a bedrock of granite stronger than the principles of many of its politicians, and in places like Booroomba this rock allows some very fine climbing, including some of the country's best slabs.

South Australia has the most limited amount of rock, but is compensated by the quality of its premier crag, Moonarie—a jewel of red sandstone in a beautiful arid landscape. Climbing at Moonarie is one of the most Australian of climbing experiences.

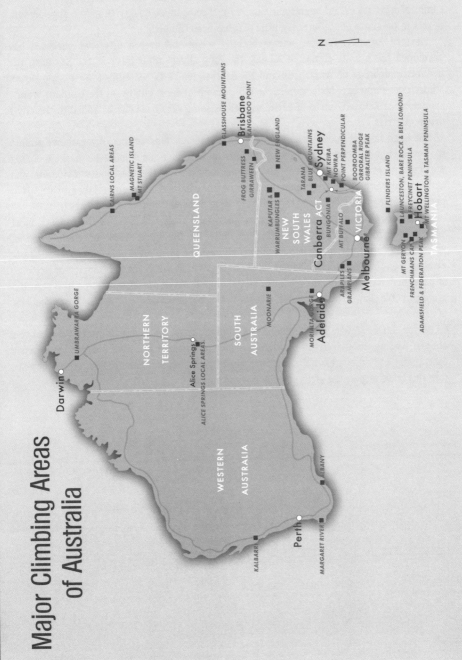

Major Climbing Areas of Australia

The cliffs clustered around Alice Springs in the south of the Northern Territory are matched by the landscape, but the low numbers of climbers there has not produced the quantity of climbs of other states, although some climbs are of comparable quality. Despite a huge amount of rock in the north of the Territory, little of it has been climbed.

Western Australia has an active climbing scene and over a fifty-year period it has developed the granite climbs of Albany, the long adventurous faces of the Stirlings, the hedonistic delights of Willyabrup and the marvellous black sea cliff of West Cape Howe. Modern developments have seen the establishment of sport climbs on the brilliant orange sandstone of Kalbarri, north of Perth, as well as some very hard climbs added to the city's urban quarries.

The large state of Queensland has many excellent cliffs. Most of them are gathered around the southern population centre of Brisbane, and these include the rhyolite 'jamnasium' of Frog Buttress, the granite of Girraween and the volcanic cliffs of the Glasshouse Mountains and Maroon. Further north in the tropics there are the fine climbs of Mt Stuart and the tropical island paradise of Magnetic Island, and the climbing around the northern centre of Cairns.

Tasmania is completely different again. The island state has some of the longest, most adventurous routes in Australia including those on the huge white quartzite lump of Frenchmans Cap. There are dolerite columns all over the place with unfashionable cracks par excellence on the Ben Lomond Plateau and hanging right above the city of Hobart. For a change of pace there are the hundreds of climbs in and around the centre of Launceston, the beautiful granite of Coles Bay on the east coast, and the new sport pump-outs on the weird conglomerate of Adamsfield.

As you can see, Australia has hundreds of climbing areas, on all sorts of rocks. Whether you are just passing through from other lands, or live in Australia and have a desire to see what other states and other areas have to offer, there is something out there for you. Grab your gear, take this book, respect the areas you climb—and enjoy.

Index to climbing areas

Queensland

Western Australia

The Northern Territory

NEW SOUTH WALES

New South Wales has the largest population of any state or territory, the largest climbing population and, as a result, the greatest number of developed crags. Many of the climbers live in Sydney and are spoiled by the amount of sandstone in and around the city. In fact, along the eastern edge of Sydney, where it abuts the Pacific Ocean, is a series of famous beaches and not-so-famous (outside climbing circles) sandstone headlands—the Sydney sea cliffs. The hills that fringe the western edge of the city, barely visible through the smog, are the Blue Mountains, with hundreds of crags and thousands of climbs.

Just to the north of Sydney, there is climbing on the cliffs along the Hawkesbury River and at Port Stephens (near Newcastle) as well as isolated crags in the hinterland of Kempsey and other coastal towns. There is even a weird little cliff near Murrurundi on the New England Highway south of Tamworth. West of Tamworth is the historically important giant volcanic plugs of the Warrumbungles, their not so well known neighbour, Kaputar, and slightly to the east the collection of cliffs on the New England plateau gathered around the university town of Armidale. Further north again is the volcanic plug of Mt Warning, the first point on the Australian mainland to get the sun. This is not a climbing area, but it is home to a giant route by Malcolm Matheson and Tim 'Tadpole' Balla:

24 M1   **568m**   (15) [20,21,21,23,19,17,23,23,20M1,24,23,19,23M1,23,15]

The Lost Boys — see *Rock* 24, Spring 1995 for topo.

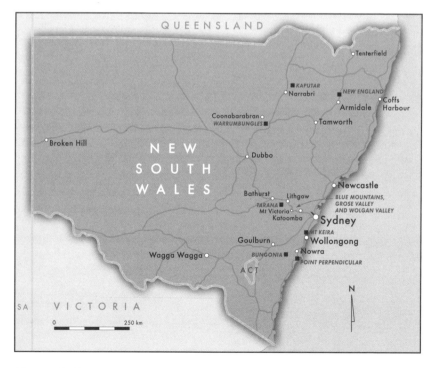

In the south of the state there is the sport climbing Mecca of Nowra and the atmospheric Point Perpendicular. These areas have largely usurped the popularity of The Big K (the cliffs of Mt Keira) that hover over the industrial town of Wollongong. Inland there is the almost forgotten Perpendicular Rock and the climbs on the Gib above Mittagong, and down the Hume Highway is the giant limestone gorge of Bungonia. There is limited developed climbing in the Snowy Mountains though lots of potential. At the most developed area, the nice granite climbs of Blue Lake in the Kosciuszko National Park, the official policy is that climbing 'is not preferred'. And deep in the south of the state there are the climbs on the aptly named Rock, near the town of the same name 50 kilometres north of Albury.

Sydney Metropolitan

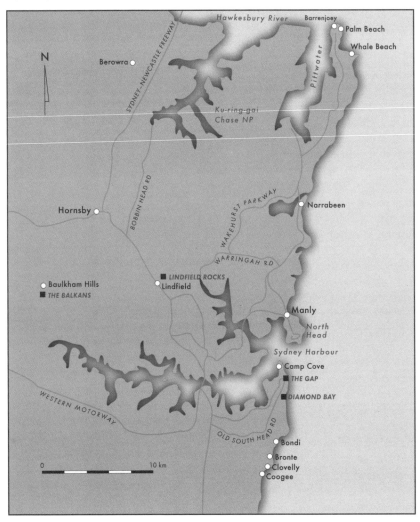

Long before anyone I know could spell cappuccino, the climbers of Sydney, inspired by Mike Law, decided that climbing shouldn't just be a rural activity and imbued it with a certain urban blackness, caffeine depravity, and café-racer fashionability. Here you could jump on your bike (a Ducati of course), rip off to do a steep, scary route and hit the cafés on your way home. Like so much that has 'post-modern sensibility', these climbs are more modern than sensible, but the sea-drenched sandstone does offer a unique urban climbing experience. Pick up some cheesecake on your way home? Included under this rubric are the areas of Berowra, Mandalay Cliff, Narrabeen, Pyrmont Slab, Lugano and other almost suburban cranking not described in the book.

Be warned that these cliffs are not just play areas, however. Climbing here can be very serious. Take care with your protection. Like all sea cliffs, keep one eye on the sea and your escape route.

Because there are lumps of sandstone lying around all over the place, there is also a lot of good bouldering in and around Sydney. Most of the non sea-based cliffs have potential for bouldering. By far the most popular, and famous, is the bouldering and small climbing area of Lindfield Rocks, in the suburb of Lindfield. It is a worthwhile place to spend an afternoon, or a year. (To get to Lindfield, which is past Chatswood N of the city, walk 1km down Tryon Rd from Lindfield Station. After Archibold Rd turn L and walk behind the tennis courts for 50m.) The Balkans is a recently fashionable area with 150 problems ranging from V0 to V11 (including *L'homme obu* aka *Rocket Man* sit start V11 by Fred Nicole). The Balkans is in north-western Sydney (Baulkham Hills) in Excelsior Park within the Cumberland State Forest, on either side of the Darling Mills Creek.

Geology/type of rock/quality: Sandstone **

Grades: Up to 29 (SPK). Treat all grades with suspicion.

Height: Up to 100m, usually shorter.

Number of routes: Hundreds.

Climbing style. Up. Natural gear and suspect bolts. Don't trust anything that's not stainless steel.

Brief history: As mentioned in the introduction, the area had been largely ignored until the late '70s/early '80s when Mike Law and a host of suckers (including Greg Child, Warwick Baird and Giles Bradbury) started putting up routes here. It was extremely fashionable for a while to bag ascents of classics such as *The Fear* 17 and *The Bolt Ladder* 20, which are now sadly both illegal. Some time later Law added *SPK* 29 at South Coogee, the hardest route here to date (if you don't count some of the more extravagant grades such as 100 that were given at North Coogee in the past).

Season: All year round, but perfect when the mountains can't be seen for a veil of rain (not that you can see them through the smog anyway). Of course, if it's raining in Sydney (which it often is) you'll have to do something steep, or head straight to a café.

Location/access: (See map, p. 19.) There are climbs at Coogee, Clovelly, Bronte, Bondi, Rosa Gully, Camp Cove, Whale Beach, Palm Beach and Barrenjoey, among other areas. Go to the place of the same name and you'll find the rock. To find the climbs you'll need to pick up a sea cliffs guide (see below). Among the better areas are The Gap and Diamond Bay.

Camping and local amenities: You're joking, aren't you?

Transport: Car, taxi, motorbike, train and bus.

Guidebooks: *Sydney and the Sea Cliffs: A Rock Guide*, Mike Law, Wild Publications, Melbourne, 1991; *Sydney Bouldering*, Peter Balint, Sydney Bouldering, 2001.

Information: Sydney climbing shops (see Appendix 1).

The Gap

To get to The Gap find your way to the suburb of Watson's Bay, east of the CBD (along New South Head Rd). The Gap is not hard to find, backed by lookouts and parks. Walk about 15m N from the main lookout and rap in off a big triangular block (perhaps leave a rope fixed and take ascenders down). The big line is *Cruise or Bruise*. If you walk S from the lookout, take a look over when the fence and the cliff converge and you should see a classic corner on orange rock, *Poet's Corner*.

Big Dipper — 40m R of *Cruise or Bruise* is a little corner round R arête of the wall. 1. (20m) Climb up corner, trav R past BRs, across roof and up to BR. Up to another ledge. 2. (35m) Go 4m L, diagonally L and up.

Cruise or Bruise — The obvious line. 1. (30m) Up to BR on L arête, into corner and up to slot (Belay). 2. (12m) Up, or trav R, round arête and up easy wall.

Poet's Corner — (See access description for area.) Rap in. Climb out (2BR).

Lost in Space — 12m S of *Poet's Corner* is a big scary roof. Rap off the cable down small corner and trav R under the roof to 2BB (and gear). Climb up to roof and through it to ledge, then up and R, BR, R to arête and up.

100m S of *Lost in Space* the **Duelling Biceps** area can be seen. Here there are the classic routes (L>R):

▲▲	23	40m	**Duelling Biceps**
▲▲	24	40m	**Fat Action**
▲▲	28	18m	**Doggit**
▲	26	75m	**Fish Fingers**
▲▲	23	95m	**Boyzone**
▲	24	60m	**Why Me**

Diamond Bay

I've included Diamond Bay because of the grade range here. To get to Diamond Bay, head S from The Gap on Old South Head Rd, turn L into Diamond Bay Rd, and then Craig Ave. Park here. There is a small reserve between you and the ocean with two gullies/coves, the N most being Rosa Gully (Trendies Corner is about 500m N again) and the square S gully is Diamond Bay. To get into Diamond Bay scramble down a dubious collection of holds and ladders on the S side (scope from N side first).

LP — Just R of the descent ladders is a short corner.

Sleazy Mission — The blunt arête 3m R of LP (2BR). Step L at ledge and follow corner.

▲ `23` `10m`

Small Pox — 2m R of *Sleazy Mission*. Climb wall past BR to ledge, L and up.

`19` `10m`

Thin — Sport. Up the thin crack R of *Small Pox*, L and up.

▲ `16` `18m`

The Corner — The corner on the N side of the cove.

▲▲ `23` `18m`

What'll The Neighbours Think — Up *The Corner* for 5m and trav R. There is a 'big move' to the scoop, then back L to corner. Up, past 3BR. Can finish R.

▲▲ `25` `18m`

Ordeal by Fur — Start at *The Corner*. Trav R 2m and up wall. 7BR + cams.

▲▲ `26` `18m`

Moore — 'Reachy, sustained, strenuous and misspelt.' Start 6m R of *The Corner*. Up R and over roof (BR) then up wall past 5BR.

▲▲ `20/21` `18m`

Acute What — Spectacular position. Start 8m R of *The Corner* (on a big boulder at the arête). Up wall (BR), around arête and up 5m, trav R and out to arête. 8BR. Walk back to BB on mainland.

The Blue Mountains

The Blue Mountains is not one cliff but a whole area, a wonderland of sandstone cliffs, like a park with too many playgrounds—and every playground is different (of course, it don't mean a thing if it ain't got that swing): short monkey bar cliffs whose goal in life is dislocation; long traditional cracks and corners; savage loose faces.

At a more prosaic level, the Blue Mountains is an immense area of escarpment and deep gullies that sprawl to the west of Sydney. The cliffs offer a myriad of differing experiences, from short, dogged pumps where the latte is only a minute away, to long climbs where you might wish you'd never heard the word 'adventure'.

There are a large number of cliffs in the Blue Mountains and unfortunately it is not within the scope of this guide to describe them all. Areas include the Three Sisters, Pindari, Boronia Point, Mt Piddington, Narrowneck, Mt York, Porters Pass, Echo Point, Shipley (Lower and Upper), Centennial Glen, Bowens Creek, and the large areas of The Wolgan and Grose Valleys. Off Bells Line of Road lie the great areas of Cosmic County, The Freezer, The Dam Cliffs, the Railway Cliffs and Bowens Creek.

Geology/type of rock/quality: Sandstone, up to ***
Grades: Up to 33.
Height: Up to 300m.
Number of routes: Many thousands.

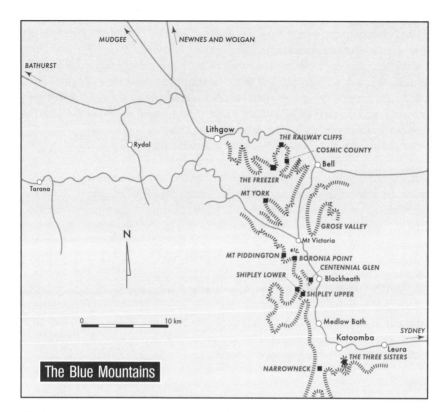

The Blue Mountains

Climbing style: Naturally protected cracks and bolted walls. There is a great range of styles, including loose aid faces, classic adventure routes, consumer cracks and modern bolts cranks on steep walls.

Brief history: The history of Blue Mountains climbing is the history of Australian climbing, from the earliest pioneers—the members of the Katoomba Suicide Club in the '30s (including Dr Eric Dark and Dot Butler)—through the early mastery of John Ewbank and Bryden Allen, the teenage renaissance of Kim Carrigan and Mike Law among others (including Greg Child and Chris Peisker), the tireless development and exploration by Giles Bradbury and John 'Crunch' Smoothy, and the embracing of the '90s with some of the best sport cliffs in Australia.

Numerous climbers have pioneered routes and areas all through the mountains. In the late '60s Ewbank put up the country's first 19, 20, and 21 routes here with ascents of *Colosseum Corner* (1965) at Sublime Point, *Solomon* at Piddington (1965) and *King Kong* at Narrowneck (1967). The Sydney Rockclimbing Club has been active since the '50s, with member Kevin Westren credited with the discovery of Piddington in 1964 and the first ascent of *Hocus Pocus*.

Andrew Penney anticipated the future with his bolting of *Exhibition Wall* 21 at Mt York in 1979, though some of his later endeavours will perhaps be judged more harshly by history. Warwick Baird set standards of grace and boldness that have not been repeated. In the '90s Mark Baker set the standard, only to be overwhelmed by the remarkable Garth Miller who has again brought the cutting edge back to the mountains with ascents like *Grey Area 33* and *Theda Bara 33* at Diamond Falls.

Season: Bloody rain! I've spent days sitting in the cafés and pubs in the area watching the drizzle.

Everyone has similar experiences in the Blueys. However, the more modern cliffs like Centennial Glen are generally steep enough not to catch too much rain. Autumn and spring are generally good but winter (June–Sept) can be pretty bleak in the area, and it does snow up here occasionally. The older cliffs often face north or west and on a nice winter's day areas like Piddington can be wonderful. The inverse is true in summer and only the stupid venture out of the more shaded areas after about 11am. Corroboree Walls, the Railway Cliffs and the Freezer are good for hot days. The Wolgan can be nice when it is wet at the higher cliffs, and Tarana cooler in summer.

Location/access: See map, p. 23. Further details under individual areas.

Camping and local amenities: See under various areas below.

Transport: The Blue Mountains are one of the few climbing areas in Australia that are readily accessible by public transport, in this case by train. People commute from here to Sydney so trains run regularly. You can catch a train to Blackheath, Mt Victoria or Katoomba. To get to more remote areas like the Wolgan you will need your own vehicle.

Guidebooks: There are a number of guidebooks to the Blue Mountains, including: *The Blue Mountains*, Mike Law, Wild Publications 1994; *Blue Mountains—Selected Climbing Areas*, Martin Pircher and Simon Carter, 2nd ed., November 1999, Onsight Photography and Publishing, Blackheath, NSW; *Rockclimbs in the Grose Valley*, Warwick Williams, Sydney Rockclimbing Club, 1997; *Rockclimbs in the Upper Blue Mountains*, 2nd ed., Sydney Rockclimbing Club, 1996.

Information: Sydney Rockclimbing Club, see Appendix 3; Blue Mountains Cliffcare tel: (02) 4787 1727; Sydney and Katoomba climbing shops and schools, see Appendix 1; Blue Mountains National Park tel: (02) 4787 8877; some online material, see Appendix 3.

Katoomba

Katoomba is the hub of the Blue Mountains tourist industry, where every second person has a 'label' pile jacket, more as a fashion statement than for need. The most famous area here, though not necessarily to climbers, is the Three Sisters. More popular with climbers is the area of Diamond Falls, especially with the hardcore as it is home to the highest concentration of Australia's hardest routes. There are the big serious climbs of Echo Point (up to 200m), the scary horrors of Dogface (mostly aid) and the historical and moderate routes of the Narrowneck.

Geology/type of rock/quality: Sandstone, up to ***

Grades: Up to 33 (Diamond Falls).

Height: Up to 200m (Echo Point).

Number of routes: Many hundred.

Climbing style: Naturally protected cracks and bolted walls. The Katoomba area has a great range of styles including loose aid faces on Dogface, classic adventure routes at Narrowneck and Echo Point, and modern bolt cranks on steep walls at Narrowneck and Diamond Falls.

Brief history: Refer to guidebooks.

Season: As for Blue Mountains, see p. 23.

Location/access: The cliffs are all easily accessible from Katoomba. The Three Sisters (Echo Point) are S down the main street (Katoomba St), L into Waratah St and R into Lurline Street (which turns into Echo Point Rd). They are about 2.5km from the Railway Station.

To get to Diamond Falls and Narrowneck, drive S down Katoomba St for 1.5km and turn R into Katoomba Falls Rd (becomes Cliff Dr.). After 700m and just past the kiosk turn L (this is still Cliff Dr.). This takes you past the top of Dogface. After 1.5km turn L (dirt) onto the road to Narrowneck (Glenn Raphael Dr.). Follow this to the end at a locked gate (keep clear) and small parking area. From the parking area head R (W) down a faint track heading towards a little rock platform (not down towards the falls). The path leads down into a gully and onto a large ledge. Turn L and follow the walls along (past dozens of routes) until you come to the steepest section, covered in bolts—Mr Wall.

To get to Narrowneck, park at the small turnout 1km down Glen Raphael Drive at locked gate (leave gate clear). Walk along the track to a pumping station where a small track leads down to a gully and to a series of rusty ladders, the infamous Dixon Ladders.

Camping/local amenities: All available in Katoomba. At Narrowneck, there is camping in the famous Psyncaves (upper and lower).

Transport: Train to Katoomba Station, or own vehicle.

Guidebooks: See p. 24.

Information: See p. 24.

The Three Sisters

You can't not find this cliff. Just go to Katoomba and follow the million odd tourists down to the cliff edge—it is the three pinnacles. The ▲ *West Wall* 12 290m (11) is the classic here, but from 1 July 2000 the NPWS has imposed a **ban on all climbing and abseiling on the Three Sisters**. A rehabilitation programme is planned and the situation will go under review during the next five years. Other climbs at Echo Point are not closed.

Narrowneck

Another older style cliff with classic, easy to moderate grade routes, although there are a few more modern, hard routes as well. Narrowneck is largely out of vogue now and is a good place to escape the crowds. If you sift through the rubbish you'll find a few gems. It's a relatively big cliff and the easy climbs offer good exposure for the grades, an aspect of Blue Mountains climbing not readily available at other cliffs.

Must do classics include:

▲▲	18	65m	(3) 1978	**On Both Sides of the Glass**
▲▲	13	68m	(3) 1962	**Cave Climb**
▲▲	13	94m	(5) 1962	**Tal**
▲▲	16	55m	(2) 1967	**Toll**

For something harder try:

| ▲▲ | 25 | 45m | 1990 | **008** |

or the more recent:

| 32 | | | **Mr Manilow** |

Diamond Falls

This is a modern area among cliffs reeking with Australian climbing history. Diamond Falls is where history is being made. The climbs of Diamond Falls' Mr Wall are the vanguard of difficulty in Australia. Rob Le Breton showed what was possible with his ascent of *Some Kind of Bliss* and more recently Garth Miller has been pushing the boundaries with his modern routes like *Theda Bara* and *Grey Area*. It is mostly a sport area with ring bolts but you may need natural gear for the easier lines. This area is within the Blue Mountains National Park, so behave.

The routes L>R (not all recommended) are:

	27	8m	1997	**Impossible Princess**
	26	12m	1999	**Rhythm Method**
▲	27	20m	1999	**Mr Magoo**
				Project
				Project
▲▲	26	15m	1997	**Super Weak**
				Project
				Project
▲	33	20m	1999	**Theda Bara**
				Open Project
▲▲	31	18m	1997	**Mr Carpet Burn**
▲	33	20m	2000	**Grey Area**
▲▲	27	18m	1994	**Hairline**
	26	10m	1997	**Runt**
	26	20m	1997	**You Did It Again**
▲▲▲	31	20m	1998	**Some Kind of Bliss**

Blackheath

Around Blackheath there are a number of brilliant climbing areas: Centennial Glen, Shipley Lower and Upper, Logan Brae, and Porter's Pass, among others. There is access to the amazing Grose Valley and routes at the spectacular Hanging Rock. Unfortunately, the stupid behaviour of some climbers (trashing the environment and using loud, offensive language) has upset local residents who live above the cliff, and the Glen and Shipley Upper are under access threats. Take it easy here.

Geology/type of rock/quality: Sandstone, up to ***
Grades: Up to 32.
Height: Up to 90m (Centennial Glen up to 20m).
Number of routes: Many hundred.
Climbing style: Varies from long, sandstone traditional routes to the steep sport climbs of Centennial Glen.
Brief history: Largely unrecorded. Refer to guidebooks.
Season: As for Blue Mountains, see p. 23.
Location/access: Blackheath is on the railway line, and close to the Great Western Hwy (32) between Katoomba and Mt Victoria.

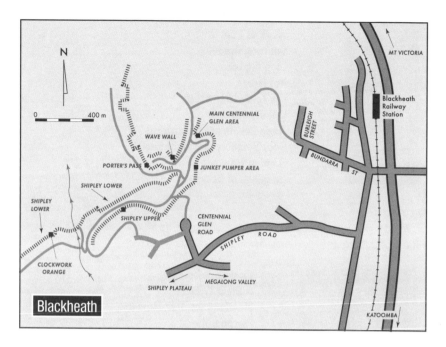

Camping/local amenities: There are a couple of caravan parks in Blackheath, a national park campsite at Acacia Flat in the Grose Valley (or camp at Perrys Lookdown car park) and a variety of other accommodation options. Many supplies are available in Blackheath, or try Katoomba.

Transport: Train to Blackheath Station, or own vehicle.

Guidebooks: See p. 24.

Information: See p. 24.

Shipley Upper

A popular modern crag, with easy access and excellent quality rock on the (mostly) sport routes. Some of the classics date back to the mid '80s with first ascentionists' names like Chris Peisker, Martin Scheel and J. Smoothy. Its aspect (NW) makes it a nice crag on cooler days. In the last few years a lot of the routes here (including a lot of new classics) have been ringbolted.

To get there, turn L (at lights) in Blackheath (across railway line) to Shipley Plateau (and Megalong Valley), then L again and follow back along railway line. When possible turn R into Shipley Road and a few streets down R again (dirt) into Centennial Road. Park at parking area. On foot now, go through the locked gate and walk along dirt road. After a couple of minutes a track heads off R. Follow this down and you will come to the R end of the cliffs. It is possible to walk around here (past Porters's Pass) from Centennial Glen. The classics—many of which require a batman move (see p.5) off the deck—are (L>R):

▲	28	15m	1995	**Equaliser**
▲▲	29	20m	1999	**Decodyfier**
▲	26	25m	1999	**Supercallousfragileextradosage**

▲	22	22m	1999	Weak as I am
▲	23+	22m	1999	Golliwog Grading
▲▲	25	22m	1986	Loop the Loop
▲▲	23	25m	1985	Hot Flyer
▲	23	25m	1997	The Lardy Lady s Lats
▲	19	18m	1985	Country Special
▲▲	22	15m	1985	These People are Sandwiches
▲▲	18+	5m	1985	Giles Bradbury Memorial Stretch
▲	24	25m	1985	Flaming Flamingo
▲▲	24	25m	1985	Language of Desire

Shipley Lower

A larger, grander cliff, with more difficult access involving an abseil down below Shipley Upper (below R end of cliff). Nevertheless there are some classics down here:

▲▲▲	20	61m	(2) 1972	Clockwork Orange
▲▲	24	45m	(2) [23,24] 1986	Nuclear Winter
▲▲	23	55m		St Valentines Day Massacre
▲▲	25	35m	1989	Psycho Killer

Centennial Glen

The Blue Mountains' first real sport crag, and after certain ethical problems and clean up campaigns, it is still one of the best and most popular. It is very sheltered in here and good for many conditions. Very little here is easy so if you are not up to steep, pumpy things I suggest you go elsewhere.

Wave Wall

1. *The Tube* 24
2. *Hang Five* 21
3. *Cold Water Classic* 25
4. *Shore Break* 24
5. *Split Wave* 23 (classic)
6. *Jacqueline Hyde* 24
7. *Sea Air* 28
8. *Smoked Mussels* 25
9. *Tsunami* 29 (classic)
10. *Blame it on the Moon* 31
11. *Microwave* 29
12. *Rubber Lover* 25
13. *Off the Lip* 23
14. *Jaws* 21
15. *Nappies Patrique?* 26
16. *Better than Chocolate* 23

Main Wall

1. *Touch and Go* 28
2. *Open project*
3. *Unplugged* 27
4. *Disintegrator* 23
5. *Acceptably Cosmic* 23
6. *Acceptably Hairy* 23
7. *Hairy Horace* 23
8. *Horrace Herrod* 25
9. *Pad'ngton* 25
10. *Apraxia* 25
11. *Bernie Loves Sausages* 27
12. *Better than Life* 31 (classic)
13. *August 1914* 29
14. *Bare Essentials* 26
15. *Trix Roughly* 26 (classic)
16. *Madge MacDonald* 25 (classic)
17. *Iona* 24
18. *Mostly Harmless* 29

19. *Nev Herrod* 23
20. *Ernest in Africa* 25
21. *Chase the Lady* 23
22. *Ratcat* 24
23. *Ruddy Norry* 22

Junket Pumper Area

1. *Running of the Bowells* 25
2. *Roof Raider* 29
3. *Project*
4. *Project*
5. *Project*
6. *Brutal Movements* 27
7. *Wrong Movements* 27 (classic)
8. *Glad Ingram* 24
9. *Glad Ingram Direct Start* 27
10. *Junket Pumper* 24
11. *Alpha Leather* 32
12. *Billy Bunter* 19

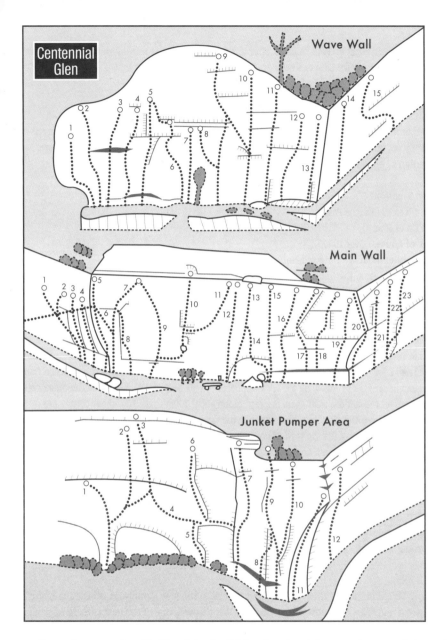

To get there, turn into Blackheath (as for Shipley above) and down to the car park. Instead of going through the gate a track leads off the end of the car park. About 200m down the track, down a set of steps, turn R at boulder (L goes to Shipley Upper) and walk along under the cliff line (past Porter's Pass). If you have come by train it is quicker to walk down Bundarra St and down the track at its end, which brings you in at the L end of the Main Wall. The cliff is divided into six areas of which (L>R) Area 2 Wave Wall and Area 4 Main Wall are the most popular and have the best routes.

On Area 5 (Junket Pumper Wall, named after a classic 24) there is the infamous *Alpha Leather*, climbed originally by Mike Law but now graded 32 after a better ascent by Garth Miller in 1999.

See map on previous page and key on p.28 for routes.

Mt Victoria

Clustered around the small hamlet of Mt Victoria are a number of fine cliffs. The most famous is Mt Piddington, but there are also the areas of Zig Zag, Corroboree Walls, Boronia Point, Ikara, Mt York, Barden's Lookout and New York.

Geology: Sandstone ***
Grades: Up to 30 (Boronia Point).
Height: Up to 60m.
Number of Routes: Over 1000.
Climbing style: Naturally protected cracks and bolted walls (carrots mostly).
Location/access: From the Imperial Hotel in Mt Victoria (up the hill from the railway station) turn S along Hooper St. At Victoria Ave turn R and then L into Innes Rd for the Zig Zag and Corroboree Walls. Or turn L and follow Victoria Ave (which becomes Carlisle Pde) around the curve until you come to a turn L (dirt) to Hornes Point and Mt Piddington. It is about 300m to the summit of Mt Piddington (car park) then another 800m down the R-hand track (sharp R down the steep rough track after 60m) to Hornes Point. Walk down to the L side of the lookout block, turning R (N) at the bottom for Wirindi (70m) and L for Pindari. There is a path along the top of the cliffs and this can also be reached from the summit car park by following a track W and down (creek bed) past some trashed camping caves. When you hit the cliff top track there is a rap station about 300m to the L(S), above *Curtain Call*.
Camping/local amenities: It is possible to camp in the caves (Sundeck, Possum) down from the summit car park, or even along the top road (if not full). There's also a good camping spot in the bush just above Zig Zag, near the track on the way in—you can even get cars to it. There are more luxurious options in Blackheath and Katoomba caravan parks, or there are a number of hostels, hotels etc. in the area, including the civilised 'Imperial' in Mt Victoria. There is a glut of cafés etc. in the area and Katoomba has large supermarkets, expensive cinnamon toast and climbing shops.
Transport: Train to Mt Victoria Station, or own vehicle.
Guidebooks: See p. 24.
Information: See p. 24.

Mt Piddington

Wirindi or Mt Piddington ('Piddo') is the grand old cliff of the Blue Mountains, steeped in history, blood, sweat and tears. For most of the '60s and '70s this was one of the best cliffs in Australia, with some of the best sandstone cracks around on which the push into the 20s was made. Since then it has merely been a very popular area for beginners and those who enjoy older styles of climbing. The climbs here are immaculate, very clean and obvious, and the access is good. This is where you want to come to do easy climbs.

Many of the classic climbs here are marked. From the S end (R–FI) walk N (L–FI). About 30m along there is a short wall (Helen Boulder) down left (W). On the wall facing out (W) there is a thin diagonal (*Zany*).

| ▲ | 23 | 20m | 1992 |

The Loch Ness Whippet – 6m L of *Zany*. 5BR and #2cam to Rap point.

| ▲ | 18 | 22m | 1978 |

Salem Super Direct – 4m L of *Zany*, up R-edge of blunt arête past PR and BR to break. R (BR) and up.

| ▲ | 19 | 23m | 1978 |

Zany – Take crack past PR and past roof (2BR).

| ▲ | 20 | 22m | 1978 |

Pandemonium – 1m R of *Zany*—up to BR, and over roof (2BR).

100m around from walk down is a chimney (L-facing) about 10m above track. This is:

| ▲ | 8 | 40m | (2) 1964 |

Chimney and Wall – Take chimney and then wall.

| ▲▲ | 16 | 50m | (3) 1965 |

Spartan – A further 20m along there is a short corner in the R of a small alcove, underneath big orange roofs. 1. (16m) Up corner then L to base of L-hand corner. 2. (24m) Up wide crack in corner, then trav out L under roof into alcove. 3. (10m) Up.

| ▲▲ | 23 | 40m | 1980 |

The Plunge – Feeling a little bold? 25m L of *Spartan* is a big wall with a rotten groove down low. Up groove and L to old PRs, then past 3BR to small bulge. Hand trav 4m L and mantle to BR, then up wall and corner.

| ▲ | 14 | 56m | (3) 1964 |

Joseph – L of *The Plunge* is a gully and then a little further some easy stuff, including a horrible grade 5 chimney (*Valhalla*). 1. (10m) 1.5m L of this, take corner to ledge. 2. (24m) Up corner to next ledge. 3. (22m) Crack and corner.

| ▲▲ | 19 | 26m | (first pitch) 1967 |

Eternity – Continue L (30m L of *The Plunge*) until you notice a searing clean crack splitting a dark wall. This is one of the Mountains' old classics. Walk off L (Fl) 50m to chains above *Angular Crack*. There is a 2nd pitch up the wall at 20.

The next routes (up to *Flake Crack*) finish at the same ledge and descend via chains above *Angular Crack*.

| ▲ | 23 | 20m | 1978 |

SSCC3 23 – Starts as for *SSCC1* (below) but stays to R of arête past 3BR.

| ▲ | 14 | 33m | 1966 |

SSCC1 – L of *Eternity* is a wide crack (*Pharoh* 15) and *SSCC1* starts 4m to L on L of arête, climbing past BR at 14m before going R and up crack to top of block. Up arête to ledge.

▲▲ **15** **33m** 1966

The Carthaginian – Old time corner classic 2m L of *SSCC1*.

▲▲▲ **17** **28m** 1966

Psychopath – Don't let the name fool you. This climb has been rehabilitated. Crack 5m L of *The Carthaginian*, with step R into next crack, before continuing up.

▲▲ **15** **31m** (2) [13,15] 1965

The Phantom – The impressive corner 5m to L. 1. (21m) Undercut start into corner leads to R wall into skull cave. Hand trav L to ledge. 2. (10m) Up steep arête and wall. Can belay before or after hand trav.

▲▲▲ **15** **30m** (2) 1965

Tombstone Wall – Walk L 40m until you get to this classic, starting at a thin crack low on a black wall (R of big square corner—abseil and *Angular Crack*). Up thin crack, mantle, trav R and up to break, R again to arête and up wall, then L and up past BR to top wall.

11 **25m** 1964

Angular Crack – Block and corner. Not bad but watch out for down traffic.

▲▲ **22** **28m** 1977

On Edge – Starts on L of arête 5m L of *Angular*. Up to PR, then arête past BRs to BB. R to descend off chains.

▲▲▲ **17** **34m** (2) [15,17] 1964

Flake Crack – Start 4m L. 1. (13m) Up to and up flake (*Saxby's*). 2. (21m) Diagonally R and through roof. BB at ledge. Move R to chains.

The following four climbs finish at a lower rap chain.

▲ **8** **15m** 1964

Faith – Corner 4m L of *Flake Crack*. Can add 2 pitches by continuing up (37m).

▲ **14** **15m** 1966

Hope – Finger crack 4m L.

▲ **14** **15m**

Sincerity – 4BR up wall to L, going R to chain.

▲ **10** **15m** 1964

Charity – Corner 2m L.

▲ **20** **64m** (4) 1967

Foreword – Contender for the first 20 in Australia. A very obvious grand corner line 10m L of marked *TOTGSDS* (*Traverse of the Gods Direct Start*). 1. (21m) Corner to PR then through roof and up. 2. (9m) Trav R to blocks. 3.

(18m) Up wall. 4. (21m) Up weakness past BRs, then trend L and up.

| ▲▲▲ | 22 | 44m | 1978 |

Psychodrama — Aptly named when it was done. Still superb. Starts on black R wall of obvious corner (*Amen Corner* 18) which is 10m above track and about 90m L of *Flake Crack*. Starts up thin crack in centre of wall, past small roof and up to BR. Go L and up flake, then up R to BR. Then PR and BR to small ledge. Up slab, small roof (BR) and final wall. *Direct 23* goes straight up wall instead of going L.

| ▲▲ | 19 | 49m | (2)[18,19] 1966 {FFA later} |

Minotaur — 9m L of *Psychodrama* and 2.5m R of *Amen Corner*. 1. (27m) Up 3m to trav line then R to PR and up flake and past BR. Diagonally R to trav line then R to arête. Up to 2BB. 2. (22m) Up L to crack.

| ▲ | 21 | 27m | 1966 {FFA later} |

Janicepts — A historical classic (claimed as first 21 in Oz) but perhaps too wide to be pleasant now. The obvious crack 3m L of *Amen Corner* (L fork).

| ▲ | 27 | 25m | 1991 |

Whores du Combat — The line defined by 10BR 6m L of *Janicepts*.

| ▲▲ | 24 | 25m | 1990 |

Désirée — Start 20m L at thin flake, which is climbed then diagonally R and up through overlap past BRs and gear.

| ▲▲ | 22 | 20m | 1978 |

Thin Time — Start as for *Désirée* but go L and through roof (instead of R) and thin corner, past BRs.

| ▲ | 21 | 23m | 1978 |

Starkosis — 7m L on wall R of arête. Use cairn and technique to gain 'spinning' BR. Then up arête (BR) going around L when easier. Over roof and up (BRs).

| ▲▲ | 21 | 40m | (2) 1967 {1972} |

Kraken — Start in corner 10m L of *Janicepts*. Corner then chimney.

| ▲ | 8 | 49m | 1964 |

Hocus Pocus — An up–down route with an almost tidal bolt count. Starts 120m L of *Amen Corner* on flat saddle between big (*Cottage*) boulder and cliff. Up black slab 5m R of thin crack heading for vague corner at R end of roofs. R on jugs (PR) and up to ledge. Can belay or head up, going R at first, up, and diagonally L into corner.

| ▲▲ | 18 | 49m | 1967 |

Curtain Call — Thin crack up slab to L.

On the steep orange N wall of the *Cottage Boulder* (below *Curtain Call*) scramble down R (FO) or S to find the climbs. L>R (FI or E) they are:

▲▲ 21   45m   (2) 1978

Disinclined — Start of trav line, off cairn. 1. (20m) Up off cairn, trav R to 2nd BR, jug (BR) and a drop down/swing across to scoop to BR (joins *Flaming Youth*). R to arête (2BB). 2. (20m) Unprotected slab, up and R.

▲▲ 23   35m   1980

Flaming Youth — Start on wall 9m R of *Disinclined*. Climb 10m up flakes past 4 BR and trav R and up to 2BB.

▲▲ 24   30m   1982

Leanings — More of the same—excellence. Up to *Flaming Youth* trav line and move L, up and R, then jugs to arête and up. 8BRs and BB at top.

Back on the main cliff:

▲▲ 20   61m   (3) 1965 {1973}

Solomon — Another of the grand old classics. Arguably Australia's first 20. Right-angled corner and cracks 40m L of *Curtain Call*. Starts in small corner with diagonal crack in L wall (*Gemini* 19).

▲▲ 22   54m   (2) 1978

Flight Line — Start 6m L of *Solomon*. 1. (23m) Left of arête to BR, then to pedestal. 2. (31m) Arête.

▲ 17   42m   (2) [16,17] 1966 and 1970

Genesis/Cardiac Arête — A good link. Start 10m L of *Solomon*. 1. (24m) diagonal twin cracks to ledge. 2. (18m) Move L around arête and up to BR, then back R and up (BR).

Corroboree Walls

If you continue around the cliff from Wirindi you come to the tall and impressive Corroboree Walls (though they are best reached from Innes Rd and then walking down past Pulpit Rock to rap in). There are a couple of absolute classics down here, and some other good routes as well. The must do routes are:

▲▲ 24   65m   (2)[24,23] 1988   I was a Teenager for the CIA
▲▲ 25   70m   (3)[25,23,-] 1983   It Came From Outer Space

Boronia Point

On the other side of the headland of Piddington is the modern sport area of Boronia Point with good routes in the 17–30 bracket. The older routes have carrot bolts. Boronia Point is reached from the summit car park by following the Cox Cave walking path from the SE side of turn-around, but turn R from this and down to cliffs. This will take you down a (usually) dry creek bed. When you see the rocks to your R follow the trail around to the climbs—this brings you out at the R (FI) of the main area (there are some climbs the other way). Or alternatively follow a track L from halfway down the Hornes Point track (at sandy patch) which will bring you down to L (FI) end of the cliffs. The climbs (L>R) are:

▲ 21 10m 1992

Cowboy Clip – L end of cliff, up to chain.

▲▲ 17 10m 1992

Mr Curly – 12m R. 3FH to chain.

▲ 21 10m 1994

Diana Ross – 2m R and 1.5m L of arête. Up, L, up past 4BR.

▲ 19 10m 1994

Ancient Mariner – Start just L of arête (as for *Albatross* 19) but climb up and R, up arête past 4BR to chain.

▲ 25 10m 1989

Sydney Rose – Wander R a little until you find a cheat cairn, just R of the roof. Off cairn and up past 4BR to big ledge and chain.

▲▲ 23 22m 1989

Euchre – 3m R. Jump to pocket (BR) then L to shallow diagonal groove. Up this (3FH) to ledge, R and up groove to top past BRs. L to rap.

▲▲▲ 23 23m 1989

Lyptus – 3m R. Up to BR, ledge, R through small roof and straight up to rap. 6FH.

▲▲ 25 22m 1994

Grape Hour – 2m R. Marked 'Project'. 8BR to rap.

▲ 26 20m 1989

Grey Power – R of *Grape Hour*, trending L to almost meet that route before heading back R and then L again to same rap.

▲▲▲ 28 20m 1997

Veteran's Affairs – Superb. Start as for *Grape Hour*, then swing R and up to rap.

▲▲ 27 20m 1989

Onions – R of *Grey Power* and L of roofs, and up to chain. Originally 26M1 and still that grade with a batman start. Direct finish goes straight up (not R) at 27.

▲▲ 29 30m 1993

Don't Believe the Tripe – Start as for *Onions* but trend R above the roof then up past 5BR, then L and up to rap. *Tripe* 30 20m continues R and up and *Green Eggs and Ham* 28 35m even further R and up.

▲▲ 30 27m 1994

Big Wednesday – Climbs flake through roof in the grotto, ending (rap) below *Green Eggs* rap.

Mt York

A consumer classic. In the early '80s this was the place to hang. The area can be crowded so watch out for adventure abseilers flooding over you. From the Imperial Hotel in Mt Vic head W along the highway for 1km before turning R to Mt York. There is a turning circle about 5kms along, toilets and a picnic shelter ('The Tin Tent'—a popular doss spot).

There are 14 gullies down the cliff. The first (L most—FI) is Gilroy's Gully—walk down the track (Cox's Rd) past the 'three heads' statue (now smashed, they once were Blaxland, Wentworth and Lawson—early Blue Mountains' explorers) for about 130m to a fork. Go L for 65m to another fork (plaque), L again, 24m, L again, 15m, L again (FO) to the top of the gully. At the bottom turn L (FO). If you wander R (FI) along the bottom of the cliff (140m) you eventually go past the next access gully, Echo Gully. R of this is a steep corner, *The Obituary*.

There are so many good routes here I suggest you get a guidebook (see p. 24) and make a week of it. Absolute classics include (L>R):

▲▲▲   19   27m   1974

Auntie Jack — Follow the cliff along R from Gilroy's gully for 40m until you get to an undercut slab and smooth wall—marked AA (and RR). Get onto slab, then L and up past 2BR. L again to thin flake and up wall.

▲▲▲   14   20m   1974

The Obituary — The corner as described above.

▲▲▲   20   20m   1983

Atomic Punk — 2m R. Up rib and slab on L then up walls. 5BRs and other gear.

▲▲▲   21   30m   1979

Exhibition Wall — Lays claim to Australia's first sport climb and an excellent one at that. 40m R of *The Obituary* is a smooth bowed wall (cairn). Follow line of 12 FH and 1BR to top.

▲▲   23   30m

The Rage This Season — Starts 5m R and warily climbs up into *Exhibition Wall*.

▲▲   24   30m

The Age of Rubber — Another 5m R. Up to break, then up L to BR. Up to FH, BR and L into *Exhibition Wall*.

▲▲   23   30m

Software Freak — Starts as for *Age of Rubber* and climbs up past two breaks then trav R to 2BR. Up past break to BR, L and up to flake then past BR.

▲▲   25   40m   1985

Ashes to Ashes — Right around to the R of the cliff—come down the Blaxland Gully W of the 'Tin Tent'—is this old classic. It starts 17m R of gully (L of smooth orange wall and 6m L of easy corner—*Venturi* 8) and follows 6BR to chain.

R still further is the dark side of Mt York, an area now called Barden's Gully, with quite a few excellent routes. Many have been ringbolted and there is a fine selection in the 18–22 range, as well as ▲▲▲ *Way of All Flesh* 26—a pump city mountain classic.

Bells Line of Road

There are a number of cliffs along Bells Line of Road, which runs from Lithgow to Richmond through Bell (you can cut into it from Mt Victoria along the Darling Causeway). To the E are the areas of Pierces Pass (see Grose Valley below) and Bowens Creek and to the W the Dam Cliffs, Railway Cliffs, Tunnel Cliff, Cosmic County and The Freezer. Bowens Creek in particular has matured into one of the better sport cliffs in the Blueys (note: there is not much under 20 there). Though all these cliffs are excellent there are continuing access issues. Check out the Blue Mountains Cliffcare web site (see Appendix 3) for the latest access status before you climb.

Geology/type of rock/quality: Sandstone, up to ***

Grades: Up to 30+

Height: Up to 250m.

Number of routes: Many hundred.

Climbing style: There are older traditional lines here as well as a number of excellent new sport areas like Bowens Creek and The Freezer. At Pierces Creek are the megatrips like *Disco Biscuit* 23 and *Bladderhozen* with its 60+ carrots. Cosmic County is another historically classic cliff which underwent most development during the '80s.

Brief history: Largely unrecorded. Refer to guidebooks.

Season: As for Blue Mountains, see p. 23.

Location/access: There are a variety of ways to get to get to the Dam Cliffs, Railway Cliffs, Tunnel Cliff and Cosmic County. Drive 6.3km from Bell (towards Lithgow) and turn R onto a dirt road just before you cross the railway line (bridge). Note that it is recommended not to drive into this area but instead walk or ride. Be discreet. The cliffs are on crown land but access is through State Rail Authority land and the installation of a locked gate has complicated matters. It is now about a half-hour walk to Cosmic, and The Freezer is a bit further. For the Dam Cliffs follow the dirt road for 1.3km and turn L (before the grey signal box) onto a rough track which is followed to a parking area. A 2 min walk to the dam will reveal the cliff. For the other cliffs, continue along the dirt road for another 2km to a multiple intersection with a big tree, at which point you need to take the obvious L leading road and follow for 400m to another track veering L. Go down this and on ahead to a car park. There is a walking track from the R (as you come in to the parking area) which leads to Greenhouse Gully (230m and down R) and after this The 39 Steps (295m), Memory Lane (90m), Stateline Gully (250m) and finally to Osirus Gully (300m). From the base of Greenhouse Gully you can walk R (FI) to the County. About 60m along where the climbs start a small cairn shows the point from where you head down across the creek and up to the Railway Cliffs.

For The Freezer, go ahead at the big tree and work your way along tracks until you come to a cairn by the track (above the cliff). From here follow the path down to the cliff.

To get to Bowens Creek, take Bells Line of Road. There is a locked gate on a track R 12.7km after Bell or 7.9 km after Mount Tomah (coming from Richmond). Just N of this is a small parking area on the E side of the road. The cliff is a fair walk along the track through the gate. 25 min will get you to a faint track that leads down the R end of the cliff, down a short fixed rope. Another 10min along main track brings you to its end from where another track and fixed rope takes you to near the L end, to the L of the Main Wall. The Aliens Domain (one separate sector) is reached by an elaborate flying fox.

Camping/local amenities: As for other Blue Mountains areas.

Transport: Own vehicle.

Guidebooks: See p. 24.

Information: As for Blue Mountains, p. 24.

The Freezer

▲▲	24	20m	1992	**Good Big Dog**
▲▲	25	23m	1992	**Gruntled**
▲▲	26	28m	1992	**Lactitoc**

The Railway Cliffs

▲▲	25	115m	(3) [25,22,23] 1991	**I Must Go Down to the Sea Again**
▲▲	22	75m	1982	**The Five Forty Five**
▲▲	22	45m	1991/92	**The Belles, The Belles**

Cosmic County

▲	21	28m	1981	**Mid Life Crisis**
▲▲	23	40m	1992	**In the Flesh**
▲▲	25	30m		**Aesthetic Images Direct**
▲▲	23 or 21M1	45m	1980	**Alhelal**
▲▲	25	30m		**Toyland**
▲▲	25	30m		**Toyland Direct**
▲	23	28m	1979	**Gentleman's Drag**
▲	27	35m	1987	**Hollow Men Direct**
▲▲	19	40m	1980	**I'd Rather Be Sailing**
▲▲	22	45m	1980 (serious)	**Razor Blade Alley**
▲▲	21	25m	1980 (serious)	**Comfortably Numb**
▲▲	23	20m		**Walking Wounded**
▲▲	18	30m	1980	**The Eighty Minute Hour**
▲▲	21	20m	1981	**Mindblower**
▲	17	35m	1979	**Interstate 31**
▲	21	40m	1987	**Barbarossa**
▲	16	25m	1980	**Allied Chemical News**
▲	19	30m	1979	**Crunch's Corner**
▲	19	30m	1980	**Touchstone**
▲▲	22	30m	1981	**Fear in the Western World**

Bowens Creek

▲▲	21	15m	1997	**Mr Pink**
▲▲	28	28m	1999	**Hoofmeister Blue**
▲▲	27	25m	1999	**Lloyd of the Rings**
▲▲	25	20m	1997	**97% Fart Free**
▲▲	27	27m	1999	**Beef Cake**
▲▲	26	25m	1999	**The Big Bang is On**

The Grose Valley

The wild and untamed Grose is one of Australia's most amazing climbing areas, though not that often frequented, despite being close to many Blue Mountains' towns. It is another large cliff-ringed gorge that takes up a large area of the Blue Mountains north of Katoomba, Mt Victoria and Blackheath. The reasons it is not as frequented are the perceived access problems (climbs often involve long committing abseils in), the varying quality of the rock and the height and seriousness of some routes. It is such a large area, however, with so many different cliffs, that it is difficult to make generalisations. If you are after adventure, this is the place for you. (Note that the Grose Valley overlaps with most other Blue Mountains areas.)

Geology/type of rock/quality: Sandstone, up to ***
Grades: Up to 30.
Height: Up to 300m.
Number of routes: Several hundred.
Climbing style: Mostly long, traditional sandstone routes up classic lines, although there are now some sportily bolted excursions up the walls.
Brief history: Refer to guidebooks.
Season: As for Blue Mountains, see p. 23.
Location/access: As for Blue Mountains, see map, p. 23.
Camping/local amenities: See details for Katoomba, Blackheath and Mt Victoria, depending on which part of the Grose you plan to climb in.
Transport: As above.
Guidebooks: See p. 24.
Information: See p. 24.

Ikara Head

Ikara Head, close to Mt Victoria, has classic crack lines up to 100m:

▲	22	90+m	1976	**Jezebel**
▲▲	22	40m	1980	**Aladinsane**
▲▲	22	100+m	1979	**Blast Off**
▲▲	19	85m	1975	**Telstar**
▲▲	20	65m	1975	**Kaladan**

Or more modern sport routes by Mikl Law and co:

▲▲	24	50m	1992	The Mooing
▲▲	24	87m	1992	The Squealing
▲▲	21	85m	1992	Splattergram

Pierces Pass

This area, off Bells Line of Road, has excellent long adventure climbs.

▲▲	23	250m	(7)[19,6,19,20,23,22,21]	Disco Biscuit 2000
▲	25	40m	1990	Non-Stop Disco Party
▲	23	35m	1997	Supertrance 2000
▲	25	200m	1996 {1999}	Samarkand
▲▲	23	110m	(3)[21,21,23]	Bladderhozen – Carrot sport line route.
▲▲▲	24	200m	(5)	Weaselburger

Hanging Rock/Burramoko Buttress

This area, accessed from Blackheath, has the extremely photogenic ▲ *Black Rose* 27 and some better routes:

▲▲	24	45m	1990	Oranges Poranges – Sporty.
▲	19	150m	(4)[19,19,16,17] 1995	Burramoko Buttress – Alpine.

Medlow Bath

If you're up for a big (loose) day, this area has daunting adventure routes:

24	200m	Carnivore Corner
21M5	215m	Big Loose Corner

The Wolgan Valley

It is unfortunately not within the scope of this guide to describe the Wolgan Valley in detail. Suffice it to say it is a magical sandstone escarpment-ringed valley, which can be quiet and idyllic mid-week (the opposite on weekends and public holidays). It can also be warmer and more sheltered than some of the higher Blue Mountains' cliffs. The main areas here are the Coke Ovens, the Coal Mine Cliffs, the grand 100m routes on Old Baldy, with good routes at Eldorado, the Exploding Galaxies and Firecat Wall.

Geology/type of rock/quality: Sandstone, up to ***
Grades: Up to 31.
Height: Up to 250m (routes near Rocky Creek). Big Glassy is one of the largest faces in the Blue Mountains but both these cliffs involve long walk ins. Routes between 40–100m are more common.
Number of routes: Many hundreds.
Climbing style: The Wolgan has all the variety of climbing of the Blue Mountains with some longer climbs on Old Baldy, as well as shorter classic crack, flakes and wall on other cliffs.
Brief history: Refer to guidebooks and article in *Rock* 45 (see below).

Season: As for Blue Mountains (see p. 23). The Wolgan, however, is a little further W and lower and can be quite nice on a winter's day as it stays warmer and drier than other areas. In summer, north facing cliffs (including the Coke Ovens) are unbearable.

Location/access: Part of the Wolgan's attraction is its remoteness. There is only one dirt road into the valley. Drive W along the Great Western Highway (32) from Lithgow for 7km and then turn L into Mudgee Road. About 6km further (past power station) the road forks and the Wolgan Rd (turns to dirt after 10km) splits off (straight ahead/R). It is 35km to the locality of Newnes in the valley though only 28km to the Coal Mine Cliffs.

Camping/local amenities: The camping in the Wolgan (when it's not busy) is one of its nicest attractions. The area is within national park. Follow the road in past the old wooden hotel (now tourist information centre) to the camping area of Little Capertree, a large grassy paddock accessible by 2WD vehicles. To escape the crowds (by 4WD) cross the ford a further 250m on and take a sharp L. Climbers mostly head for the last campsite on the L before the barricades.

Transport: Own vehicle.

Guidebook: *The Wolgan Valley*, Wade Stevens, Sydney Rockclimbing Club, 2000. There is also an informative article, 'The Wolgan Experience', by the late Wade Stevens and Greg Claire in *Rock* 45, Jan–March 2001.

Information: As for Blue Mountains (see p. 24). There is an information office in Lithgow at the visitor's centre, tel: (02) 6353 1859; Blue Mountains National Park, tel: (02) 4787 8877.

The Coke Ovens

▲	13	**Sod**
▲	15	**Organ Grinder/Monkey Business**
▲	18	**Sizzler**
▲▲	18	**Mirrorman**
▲▲	19	**Cactus**
▲	19	**The Knuckle**
▲▲	22	**The Righteous Brothers**
▲	31	**Microcosm**

The Coal Mines

▲	20	**Khe Sanh**
▲▲	21	**Tranzister**
▲▲	22	**Red Hot and Blue**
▲▲	23	**Chrysalis**
▲▲	23	**Corregidor**

Old Baldy

▲	18	**Excalibur**
▲	18	**Scimitar**
▲	19	**Liquid Sky (Lower Cliff)**

Tarana

If you have worked your way through all the cliffs in the Blue Mountains you'll be getting fairly sick of steep, pumpy sandstone. Out past the Blueys and Lithgow is the almost forgotten area of Tarana with its balancy granite slabs, some of which are very run out. It's a long way to go, but it is a pleasant spot (cooler in summer than the Blueys) and if you're passing…

Tarana is a reserve and climbing has been banned at various times. **Check the current status of the cliff with the Ranger before you climb.** Bolting and the extreme wire brushing that occurred here in the past are not encouraged.

Geology/type of rock/quality: Granite ***

Grades: Up to 26.

Height: Up to 75m.

Number of routes: Over 100.

Climbing style: Predominantly granite slabbing.

Brief history: After a start by Dave Tanner and Bathurst climbers in 1971, Tarana languished until Joe Friend and others started climbing here in the mid '70s. Routes included *Barad Dur* 18 in 1975 by Joe Friend, and *Brian Savage* 21 and *Chain Mail Crack* 21 by Mike Law. Law also added *Bilbo Baggins* 18, the first route on Googleplex Crag. In the late '80s, John Smoothy took Mark Colyvan here for a visit and ushered in a period of intensive development in which most the classic climbs were done. These included Giles Bradbury's *Dr Marten's Boots* 21 and *Roller Disco* 23, Colyvan's *Six Days on the Toad* 21 and *The Howling* 23, and Smoothy's *This One's for Evelyn* 22. Paul 'Animal' Colyvan took the area's climbing to new levels of difficulty and scariness with his ascents of *Finger Tight* 23 and *Rubber Nuns* 26 (one of the hardest slabs in Australia).

Season: As for Blue Mountains, however, like the Wolgan, Tarana is further W and lower and as a result, when it is raining (or snowing) up in the Blueys it can be better down here.

Location/access: Turn onto the Rydal Rd (at roadhouse) about 1km after Lithgow (coming from Sydney) and follow it to a T at 11km. Go R then L straight away onto Tarana Rd. After 10km turn L onto Honeysuckle Falls Rd and follow this for 2km. There is a sign 'Evan's Crown Nature Reserve' and a stile. A track (250m) leads up to the granite tors and brings you out at the R (N) end, near Deckout Buttress. Walking L will take you along the main long Googleplex Crag. Descents are easily off the back and down gullies.

Camping/local amenities: Camping is not allowed. Accommodation and supplies are available in Lithgow.

Transport: Own vehicle.

Guidebooks: 'Evan's Crown, Tarana', Mark Colyvan, *A Rock Guide*, 1990; *The Blue Mountains*, Mike Law, Wild Publications, 1994.

Information: Tel: (02) 6331 9777 for the Ranger.

▲▲	21	25m	1987, Deckout Buttress	**Dr Marten's Boots**
▲▲▲	20	45m	1987, Googleplex Crag	**Six Days on the Toad**
▲	22	55m	1989, Googleplex Crag	**Laughing Boy Morris**
▲	18	75m	(2) 1987/8, Googleplex Crag	**Fuzzy Navel**
▲	26	35m	1989, Googleplex Crag	**Rubber Nuns**

Bungonia

An eon is a long time in the rock world, long enough to carve a deep gorge (200m high on the N side, 300m of the S side) through the limestone of Bungonia. Limestone is rare in Australia, and good limestone even rarer. The climbing at Bungonia is the best on offer, and at its best is great. The gorge is a unique climbing area that can be a place as warm as climb names like *Overture to the Sun* suggest, and it can also be a cold, dark hole. The routes here are long and sustained, superb monuments to the climbers that conceived them, pushing their way up orange rock, past perfect pockets, stalactites and lovingly placed protection.

Geology/type of rock/quality: Limestone, of varying quality **
Grades: Up to 31 (with Lee Cossey's new *Teflon* 31).
Height: Up to 300m.
Number of routes: About 50.
Climbing style: Limestone face climbing. There is nothing very easy here. Many of the routes have long sections of natural gear. There are bolts, both carrots (carry hangers) and fixed hangers, on some routes.
Brief history: Climbing at Bungonia is really only a phenomena of the last two decades. Sydney climbers such as Giles Bradbury (*Strangeness and Charm*) started to push routes up the walls at the same time that Canberra climbers like Mike Law-Smith, Tony Barten and Mike Peck, bored with granite, discovered that it offered a relatively close option. Glenn Tempest and Richard Smith were among Victorian climbers who put it on their 'must drop in' list and did just that, grabbing a part of the new route action—*Critical Mass* 24. Andrew Bull and Andrew McAuley are among more local developers. The person who has probably done the most to develop the cliff is the eternal Canberra powerhouse John Fantini with lines like *Siblings of the Sun*, making the place his own with many of his scary pitches still unrepeated.
Season: Same as for most Sydney areas. Winter (June–Sept) can be cold. Because the walls are N–S it is possible to pick which wall to climb on, depending if you want shade or sun. In spring and winter be prepared for retreat if need be. In summer carry lots of water on the longer routes.
Location/access: Bungonia is about 200km SW of Sydney off the Hume Hwy (31). About 30km E of Goulburn and just S of Marulan turn off L and head S to the town of Bungonia. From here a signposted road leads to the gorge (13km). An entry fee of $6 per vehicle per day is charged. Park before the lookout in the David Reid car park and take the Red Efflux track into the gorge. It is also possible to rap in to some sport climbs from the Cooee Point lookout. Take care on the long and steep walk to the gorge bottom.
Camping and local amenities: There is a campground with hot water, toilets etc. at the top of the gorge (fee is $5 per night plus vehicle entry fee per day). Many climbers camp in the gorge (water is available from Efflux stream and there is even a swimming hole). It's best to take a fuel stove as there is limited firewood. The most popular campsite in the gorge is called Camp Pritikin.
Transport: Own vehicle or hitch (difficult).
Guidebooks: *Strangeness and Charm, Climbing in Bungonia Gorge*, Mike Law-Smith, (self-published), 1995.
Information: National Parks info line tel: (02) 4844 4341 or (02) 4844 4277.

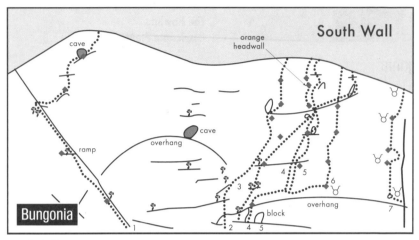

South Wall

1. *Red Supergiant* 21
2. *Red Meat* 22
3. *Reason for Man* 19

4. *Overture to the Sun* 26
5. *Siblings of the Sun* 24
6. *Albino* 24

7. *Solar Flare* 21

North Wall Western End

1. *Solar Wind* 21
2. *Strangeness and Charm Direct* 23
3. *Critical Mass* 24
4. *Comet Chaser* 22 A1
5. *Strangeness and Charm* 22
6. *Galactic Wonderer* 21 A1
7. *Cosmos* 22

North Wall Eastern End

1. *Morgan Mortimer* 21
2. *Jewel Box* 23

The 200m long super routes *Siblings of the Sun* with its 54 bolts (7 pitches with grades of 21, 23, 22, 21, 23, 26 and 18) and its sibling *Overture to the Sun* (7 pitches with grades of 25, 21, 22, 24, 23, 25 and 26) are two of the most sustained and superb routes in Australia, for those up to the challenge.

There are a number of good new one pitch sport routes (approached by climbing *Polenta Pumper* on the 'Phantom Menace Wall') including Andrew Bull's 27 and Le Breton's *Sith Lord* 27.

Nowra

Feeling strong? Then a visit to the area that introduced sport climbing to Australia might be in order: solid, sandstone, dank, steep, pumpy sport climbing. The weathered cliffs that hide in the lush scrub around the town of Nowra are not the prettiest climbs in Australia, but they are certainly some of the hardest and most powerful. And though there are possibly greater sport areas now (arguably), Nowra will always remain the spiritual home of Australian sport climbing. It's just such a modern sort of place: trashed cliffs, rubbish, McDonalds and coke, thieves, and bolts—lots of bolts.

If you are sick of concentrating your way up long trad routes and feel like a flirtation with the cult of the move, welcome home.

Geology/type of rock/quality: Nowra rock is sandstone of varying quality, from hard orange and grey to almost sand ***
Grades: Up to 32.
Height: Up to 25m.
Number of routes: Over 600.

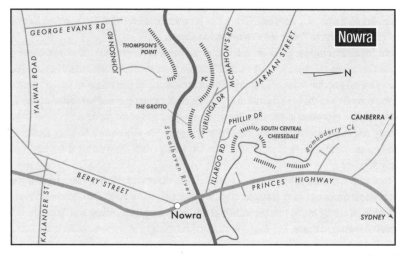

Climbing style: Steep, pumpy walls are the name of the game. Sport, though there is the odd naturally protected climb around (very odd here). Climbs end at chains and rarely top out. There is some excellent bouldering areas with some of the best found at Cheesedale and Lot 33.

Brief history: Climbing started here in the '70s with locals bagging a few easy cracks. Despite pronouncing it worthless on an early visit, Wollongong climber Graeme Hill returned in 1984 with Steve Bullen and started bolting routes at areas like Ben's Walk. Word got out in the late '80s and development of the Grotto showed what was possible in the area. Hill put up *Avocado Queens of Death* and *Belgium Tourists* and Rod Young added *Alien Monsters*. In 1989 attention shifted across the river to Thompson's Point, with Ant Prehn and Giles Bradbury getting involved.

Bullen's *Married and Mortgaged* 28 was the hardest thing done during this period. In the '90s development shifted to the secret PC (Planet Cock), the Bombaderry Creek areas of South Central, Cheesedale and Rosies. There are more hard than easy routes here. As well as the prolific Hill, his wife Veronique, Bullen (*No More Gaps* 30), other climbers such as Prehn (*Conehead and the Barbituates* 28), Bradbury, Dave Filan, Paul Westwood (*Sperm Bitches* 30), Graeme Fairburn, George (*Dungeon Master* 31) and Sarah Fieg, Rod and Sue Young (many of the Thompson Point routes), Stuart Wyithe (*Ain't No Sunshine* 28), Tony Barton (ACT), Brogan Bunt (ACT), Andrew Bull (*Frosty* 29) and Rob Le Breton (*Sexy is the Word* 31, *El Maco* 31, *Attack Mode* 32) started to push development. In 1992 Steve Bullen turned his head to serious bouldering at areas like Cheesedale, establishing some of the hardest boulder problems in Australia.

Season: It is possible to climb all year at Nowra (April–Sept is best) but summer can get hot so you'll need to avoid the hottest part of the day (go swimming in the river) and find some shade. Winter is better for friction etc. but can be wet so you'll need to hide under something steep (South Central or areas at Thompson's Point). It can be windy as well. Thompson's Point is one of the warmer cliffs (facing NW) and the Grotto and PC are cooler.

Location/access: (See map, p. 45.) The city of Shoalhaven (with Nowra and Bombaderry on either side of the Shoalhaven River) is a large town on the S coast of NSW (about 2hrs S of Sydney and 1hr S of Wollongong). It is about 10km inland from the sea and there are many beautiful beaches in the area.

South Central, Cheesedale (walk L or NE), the Bakery, Bartondale, Rosies, Mortein Wall and Lot 33 and 34 (walk R or SE and E) are all along Bombaderry Creek and are accessed from the end of Jamieson Rd (take Phillip Dve off Illaroo Rd, L into Castle Glen, R into Jamieson) or the N end of Walsh Cres (off Illaroo). See below for access to Thompson's Point and The Grotto.

Camping and local amenities: There are a few caravan parks in Nowra, but the closest to most cliffs is the Ski Park on the river, tel: (02) 4423 2488 or the Nowra Animal Park, tel: (02) 4421 3949. Both places are off Rockhill Drive, off Yurunga Dve or McMahons Rd (see access to P.C. and Grotto below). You can camp in the bush upstream if you want but **camping is not permitted at any of the crags with the exception of Babylon**. There is more luxurious accommodation in Nowra and Bombaderry and supermarkets etc. for most of your needs. You should buy or bring mosquito repellent because there are lots of these little guys (especially when the weather is warmer) and they really suck!

Transport: Own vehicle or train or bus to Bombaderry and then either walk, hitch or taxi around. If you camp at the ski park, a form of water transport can take you straight across the river to Thompson's Point. Note: Car break-ins are rife in this area, particularly at the Thompson's Point parking area. Take care.

Guidebooks: *Rockclimbing at Nowra*, Rod Young, Australian Rockclimber Publications, Wollongong, 2000.

Information: National Parks office, tel: (02) 4423 2170; information centre, tel: 1800 024 261.

Bouldering: Nowra has long been one of Australia's best bouldering areas, thanks largely to the work of Steve Bullen. Currently the hardest problems here are *Un-named*, Lot 33, V12/13 by Paul Westwood, *Bumpy Boys*, Cheesedale, V12, by Sam Edwards and *Drawback* at Cheesedale, a V11 by Bullen. There are a swag of other V11s here as well.

Thompson's Point

To get to Thompson's Point, turn R down Berry St (just W of river) and follow this all the way through town, turning R into Albatross Rd at the end, then R again into Yalwal Rd, and R again into George Evans Rd. Turn R off this into Jonnson Rd and after 300m L onto a dirt road and follow this down to the river and the Thompson's Point Reserve (watch out for thieves in the car park). Walk between three power poles, turn R (FO) and walk along cliff top for 100m to find descent gully. Turn L at bottom, and you should come out at base of Descent Gully Walls (to L–FO), which have some of the easier lines at Nowra. Walk R(FI) for Orca Wall, Alley Wall, Butterfly Wall (in front of car park), Pocketed Wall and Grease Caves

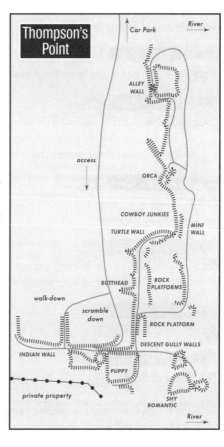

▲	21	12m	1990

Alex the Kid – 2m R of arête of descent gully chimney. 4BR to FH up right.

▲▲	20	15m	1995

Layoff – 6m R—L and past 5FH to U-bolt BB.

▲▲▲	18	15m	1994

Samurai Pizza Catz – Start as for *Layoff* going straight (ish) up past 4BR, FH and rap anchors.

▲	17	15m	1994

Woderwick – 3m to R at L of cave. 5FH and 2 ring-BR rap.

▲▲	11	15m	1994

Lucifer – The R arête of buttress. 4FH to anchors.

▲▲▲	15	15m	1997

Santa's Little Helper – 1.5m R of arête. Up wall , step L over cave, up. 6FH to anchors.

▲▲ 17 15m 1994

Butt Head – 2m R. 6FH to 2 ring-BR anchors.

The flake is the naturally protected *Barbie Twins* 16.

▲▲ 20 15m 1994

Beavis – 2m R of the flake past 6BR to anchors.

▲▲▲ 17 15m 1991

Hang On – 2m R, just R of arête. Up and through bulge at BR (3rd) to reach R. Up arête to anchors.

▲▲▲ 25 15m 1990

Cowboy Junkies – R of the above routes is a slabby (Turtle) wall and R again an undercut arête forming a large roof. There is a small (mini) wall in front of it. There are 2 ring-BR at the start of this climb. Out roof past 3 ring-BR, then R to horn on flake. Then L to arête and up. 5 ring-BR to anchors.

▲▲ 24 10m 1999

Potato Junkies – Start as for *Cowboy Junkies* but go straight out 'bowl' where *Cowboy Junkies* goes R (past FH). Over lip and exit L to anchors.

▲▲▲ 18 25m 1991

Orca – R of the above roof (past Mini Wall) is an arête with a corner crack on it (*Ceiling Your Fate* 24, natural). Start on ledge 2m L of arête, climb up orange wall and arête, then to top wall and chain. Mostly ring-BR.

▲▲ 18 24m 1999

Korca – 2m R. Up arête and R-side of arête (3FH) to join *Orca*, stepping L at top wall and up to anchors.

▲▲ 19 24m 1990

The Money or the Box – 2m R. Wall, BRs and chain.

Continue R pass two lichen-infested buttresses, and the steep black slab of **Alley Wall**, then a tall black buttress and a large white gum tree, then **Vanderholics Wall**.

▲▲ 22 20m 1994

Freak Magnet – 7m L of corner chimney follow 8FH to 2 ring-BR rap, passing L of cave. Take care clipping 2nd ring-BR.

▲▲ 18 25m 1990

Vanderholics – 3m R. Up wall L of crack and up to cave. Exit R and up to anchors. The line to the R is *Gina Hardface* 18.

▲▲ 24 20m {1993}

Butterfly Wall Direct – 3m R of narrow chimney. 7FH to ring-BR rap. To the R is a project.

▲▲▲   **26**   **18m**   1990

Stone Roses – One of the area's early classics. Hard move onto overhung wall, going R at 2nd FH and up to L edge of cave, then back R to FH and up to chain. The route that comes straight up line of bolts to chain is Steve Bullen's *No More Gaps* 30 which only received its 2nd ascent in 1999 (Tara Sutherland).

▲▲▲   **28**   **15m**   1991

Concrete Petunias – Start as for *Stone Roses* but go R from 3FH then up L of arête to chain below R from cave.

▲▲▲   **18**   **24m**   1996

Diddy Kong – The next wall R (*Gun Barrel Highway*) has a couple of classics. *Diddy Kong* starts at weakness 3m R of arête on L and climbs up 2m steeping L at flake, then follows bolts to chains. The ▲ *Direct Start* 20 starts 2m L and climbs flake to 3FH and then R to join original at ledge.

▲▲▲   **19**   **25m**   1992

Gun Barrel Highway – Starts as for *Diddy Kong* and follows crack through bulge and up (9FH) to chain.

Other classics at Thompson's Point include (L>R):

▲▲	22	10m	1991, The Very Nice Wall	**Killer Boas**
▲▲	22	12m	1992, The Pocketed Wall	**Murdoch the Horse Fucker**
▲▲	21	30m	1996, Little Grease Cave	**Mosquito Slap**
▲▲	27	15m	1992, Grease Cave	**Top One Thommo**
▲▲	30	17m	1994, Grease Cave	**Say You Don't Want To Slip It In**
▲	31	10m	1992, Grease Cave	**Sexy is the Word**
▲▲	23	12m	1992, Grease Cave	**Pulling on the Porcelain**
▲▲	21	15m	1992, Betty Blue	**Shifting Sands**
▲▲	21	15m	1992, Betty Blue	**A Day at the Beach**
▲▲	26	20m	1990, Betty Blue	**Still Life with Chalkbag**
▲▲	24	22m	1998, Vine Wall	**Spank the Donkey**
▲▲	16	23m	1994, Fossil Cave area	**Sloth**

The Grotto

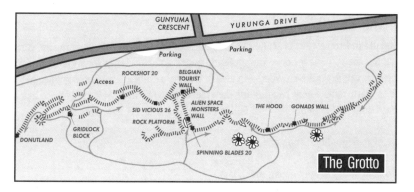

new south wales   ▲   49

To get to PC and the Grotto turn N off the Princes Highway up Illaroo drive (just E of the river) and follow this, forking L at the North Nowra Shops (McMahon's Road) then L again towards the river (down Jarman St to Yurunga Drive). Off Yurunga Dve there is a fenced lookout (opposite no. 240) and to the L of this (FO) a series of glued rungs down a slab. This brings you to the R(FI) end of the P.C. cliffs. The other Grotto areas are accessed by various chimneys and gullies off Yurunga Dve, although the Grotto proper (including the *Belgium Tourists*, *Gonads* and *Alien Space Monsters* walls) are accessed from the walkway from a small parking area just N of Gunyuma Cr.

Belgium Tourist Wall (L>R)

▲▲	23	20m	1989	**Avocado Queens of Death**
▲▲	24	21m	1989	**Belgium Tourists**
	25	20m	1997	**Going the Tonk with Zena**
▲	24	25m	1989	**How Much Can a Koala Bear**

Other classics here:

▲	24	0m	1998	**Zimbabalooba**
▲▲	19	25m	1989, Alien Space Monsters Wall	**Alien Space Monsters**
▲▲	20	9m	Spinning Blades Cave	**Spinning Blades of Steel**
▲▲	18	20m	Gonads Wall	**Depleted Gonad Circumference**
▲▲	24	13m	1995, Moon Wall	**Swallow the Moon**

For those into the big numbers other hardies and classics in the area include:

▲▲	32	9m	1994, P.C. (last move unfinished—go for it!)	**Attack Mode**
▲▲	29	11m	1991, P.C.	**Dude Food**
▲▲	31	20m	1995, South Central	**Dungeon Master**
▲	30	8m	1995, South Central	**Sperm Bitches**
▲▲	31	20m	1994, Rosies	**El Maco**
▲	31	15m	1996, Rosies	**Beefmeister**
▲▲	29	15m	1997, Rosies	**Frosty**
▲▲	30	20m	1994, Cheesedale	**Cheese Monster**

Mt Keira (The Big K)

The mostly small sandstone walls of Mt Keira above the south coast city of Wollongong are cliffs from the past, but they still have some fine routes and are a good local crag for Wollongongites (and on some days can get quite crowded—in areas). There are quite a few nice easy lines here, a good place to learn skills before heading for the steeper Nowra. Nitro Wall at Mt Keira has a number of hard boulder problems by Steve Bullen including *Redline* V11 and *Double Blower* V11.

Geology/type of rock/quality: Sandstone, up to **
Grades: Up to 26.
Height: Up to 50m but generally much, much less.

Number of routes: Many hundred.

Climbing style: Easy sandstone cracks and mostly moderate bolted walls. Popular with beginners.

Brief history: Strangely enough the cliffs of Mt Keira are historically more important than you might think. For some reason this not so mighty cliff rising over the industrial city of Wollongong produced a number of the country's finest climbers during the early '80s. Lumped together as a loose affiliation (the IRA, or Illawarra Rockclimbing Association, with its equally successful alpine wing the ITP—International Turkey Patrol), Wollongong climbers such as Ian 'Ferret' Anger, Russell 'Chunder' Chudleigh, Graeme Hill, Jon Muir and Steve Bullen went on to greater things, often elsewhere. Equally far roaming and successful, were David Bowie aficionado Rod Young and Ant Prehn.

Season: Can be hot in summer and wet in winter.

Location/access: Drive up to the summit of Mt Keira where you will find a car park, café and toilets. To get to the N face walk back down the road to after the bend and then cut E around to the cliff. The W face is the most popular and is accessed from a number of points from a vague track that heads along the cliff top off the summit road (before bend).

Camping and local amenities: All available in Wollongong. The cheapest options are the council run beach camping at Corrimal, Bulli and Windang

Transport: You can catch a train to Wollongong or drive own vehicle. There is a bus (Rutty's) to Mt Keira post office. Hitching up to the cliff is possible.

Guidebooks: *A Rockclimbers Guide to Nowra and Wollongong*, Rod Young, Australian Rockclimber Publications, Wollongong, 1994.

Information: Sydney climbing stores (see Appendix 1); tourist information centre, tel: (02) 4228 0300.

North Face (all sport):

▲	26	12m	**Pakistan**
▲▲	24	15m	**Fizzgig**
▲▲	21	20m	**Wallyard Arête**

West Face

▲	16	8m sport	**Blossom**
▲▲	25	10m sport	**Putain De Pudding**
▲	16	15m	**Corny Hesitation**
▲	18	14m	**Tear along the Dotted Line**
▲▲	21	13m sport	**The Fixer**
▲▲	20	12m	**One Blank Wall and 3 bloody Rooves**
▲	9	10m	**Iria**
▲▲	19	12m sport	**Crawdad**
▲▲	14	12m	**Short Legs**
▲▲	20	10m	**Hernia**
▲▲	11	10m	**Brigetta 6**
▲▲	15	7m sport	**Piece of Piss Direct**
▲▲	17	6m	**Upward Progress**
▲▲	19	9m sport	**Turkey's Take Off**
▲▲	20	7m sport	**Extraterrestrial Turkey**

Point Perpendicular

With a name like this you know what to expect, never mind that it was named 200 years ago by Captain Cook. Point Perp is a series of vertical sandstone cliffs that cap the top of the tall Beecroft Peninsula, the N headland of the S coast of NSW's beautiful Jervis Bay. An atmospheric place to climb if ever there was one, with most of the atmosphere being a mixture of sea-stirred ozone and exposure. The cracks and wall climbs offer a vertical playground almost completely surrounded by azure blue (on a good day)—straining fingers surrounded by sea and sky…

Somewhat bizarrely the peninsula is controlled by the Department of Defence and access is not allowed during bombing practice!

Geology/type of rock/quality: Sandstone **

Grades: Up to 27 but most easy routes (under 15) are not much.

Height: Generally 15–60m but the fact that you are often perched two thirds of the way up the cliff makes it feel higher.

Number of routes: Over 100.

Climbing style: Steep faces, often using horizontal breaks. Most routes require natural gear but there are bolts. Take a rope to access climb bases and ascenders if there is any doubt you'll get up your planned route.

Brief history: In 1984, development was started by Peter Blunt, Ian Brown and others. Towards 1988 Canberra climbers, including Mike Peck, Joe Lynch and Tony Barton, began to visit the area, glad to escape the cold and climb something other than granite. Others busy here include the ubiquitous John Fantini and Andrew Bull.

Season: Generally nice but high wind can be a problem all year round. Of course you can always head back up the road to Nowra.

Location/access: Point Perpendicular is a comfortable drive from both Sydney (3hrs) or Canberra (3.5hrs), and is 35km E of Nowra on the Beecroft Peninsula. Coming from Sydney, cross the Shoalhaven River and turn L at the 3rd set of traffic lights, heading to Currarong (24km). Just before this town, turn R (S) along the Lighthouse Rd (dirt). Another 10km will get you to the lighthouse, where the S cliffs are. The area's finest lines are on Thunderbird Wall but involve an abseil in. The northern areas are accessed from Piscator St in Currarong, near the shops. Mussel Beach is a good area that can be reached on foot.

Camping and local amenities: It is NOT permitted to camp on the peninsula except at the popular Honeymoon Bay, and that is only open on the weekends (6pm Friday to 6am Monday), long weekends and NSW school holidays (book). The Ranger's office can tell you bombing times and take bookings. There is a caravan park in Currarong, or accommodation options in Nowra (see p. 46).

Transport: Own vehicle.

Guidebooks: *Beecroft Peninsula: A Climbing Guide to Point Perpendicular*, compiled by Mike Peck and John Churchill, self-published. A new guide by Robin Cleland is due out soon.

Information: Tel: (02) 4448 3248 (Ranger's office).

Windjammer Wall

▲▲	22	30m	1988	**Turning the Tide**
▲▲	22	30m	1990	**Barracouta**
▲	20	30m		**Windjammer**

▲▲▲	24	30m	1988	**Dirty Dancing**
▲▲▲	26	30m	1989	**Feeding Frenzy**
▲▲	24	30m	1988	**Sail the Nullarbor**
▲▲▲	23	30m	1988	**Walk the Plank**
▲	16	26m		**Man Overboard**
▲▲▲	17	27m		**Grey Mist**

Thunderbird Wall

▲	20	12m	1988	**No Strings Attached**
▲▲▲	21	20m	1988	**Thunderbirds Are Go**
▲	21	20m	1988	**Virgil**
▲	21	20m	1988	**Brain**
▲	21	20m	1988	**Dad**
▲	21	20m	1988	**Aquamarina**
▲	19	40m	1988	**Heavy Weather**
▲▲	24			**Some Weird Sin**

Popeye Wall

▲▲▲	21	25m	1991	**Retro**
▲▲▲	24	25m	1991	**Popeye and Brutus Go Bolting**
▲▲▲	25	20m	1991	**Spinach**
▲▲▲	25	20m	1991	**Eat More Spinach**

Other recommended climbs:

▲▲▲	16	15m	Bayside Lower Cliff	**The Sea, The Sea**
▲▲▲	15	62m	Seaside Lower Cliff	**Dreams and Visions**
▲▲▲	20	35m	1990, Bombora Wall	**From Hoover to Hammer**
▲▲▲	20	35m	1990, Bombora Wall	**The Lost Mariner**
▲	18	30m	1988, Beecroft Head—eves	**Moving Sidewalk**
▲▲▲	23	35m	1991, Chippendale Wall	**Fat Peck and Friends**
▲▲▲	26	30m	1991, Chippendale Wall	**John Smoothy's One Dollar Investment Plan**
▲	17	30m	1988, Chippendale Wall	**Local Anaesthetic**
▲▲	19	30m	1988, Chippendale Wall	**Bodice Ripper**

The Warrumbungles

These grand old monarchs of Australian climbing have lost none of their excitement, even if interest in them has waned. The Warrumbungles National Park, like its neighbour Kaputar, is an island of bush in the middle of cultivated lands, an island dotted with huge volcanic plugs of ancient trachyte. The 'Bungles offer some of the most accessible long routes in Australia, and routes such as those on the 350m Bluff Mountain offer more than enough interest to keep all but the most jaded bolt clipper captivated. These great summits are worth climbing, if only for the rest and view from the top. A magic place, steeped in the history of Australian climbing, of mammoth weekend trips from Victoria to grab new routes, of soul-destroying falls, of a thousand minor epics.

There are five major spires in the park, the remote and lovely Tonduron, the Bread Knife **on which climbing is currently illegal**, Belougery Spire, Crater Bluff and the monstrous Bluff Mountain. Route-finding difficulties, dubious rock at times, difficult protection and the atmosphere all make climbing here a serious if enjoyable undertaking.

Geology/type of rock/quality: Trachyte *

Grades: 4–24 (there are a few aid routes up to 22M3).

Height: 350m.

Number of routes: Tonduron 13, Belougery 12, Bluff Mountain 40+, Crater Bluff 19, plus other smaller areas in the Park.

Climbing style: Traditional face climbing with protection adequate but at times difficult to arrange. Any bolts will be old carrots. Carry hangers/plates. A head torch is a good idea for late descents.

Brief history: The 'Bungles is one of the older areas in Australia, attracting early climbers because of its height and relative closeness to Sydney. Eric Dark (Dr), Eric Lowe, Dot Butler (née English) and Osmar White did some routes here in the '30s including *The Tourist Route* 6 on Belougery and the grade 9 route of the same name on Crater Bluff. In the mid '50s members of the Sydney Rockclimbing Club came to the area. Russ Kippax and Bill Peascod (UK) climbed the *South Arête* 11 on the Breadknife and *Vintage Rib* 15 on Crater Bluff. In the late '50s Ted Batty teamed up with Ron Malor to climb the North Face route on Crater Bluff, possibly Australia's first 17. Funnily enough this reputation was handed undeservedly to a neighbouring route, the incredible *Lieben* 17. This was climbed by Bryden Allen and Batty who also bagged *Cornerstone Rib* 14 and *Out and Beyond* 15. Allen teamed up with a young Chris Regan to do *Heart-Stopper* on the Bread Knife, arguably Australia's first 18. Perhaps Allen's most outstanding climb from this period, however, was the 300m *Elijah* 17 up Bluff Mountain's huge face. Later Allen did *Caucacus Corner* 17 on Belougery, still an intimidating climb.

In 1964 John Ewbank came to the 'Bungles for the first time, and before long he was at home on the area's faces, putting up routes like *Crucifixion* 18 and, with Allen, *Ginsberg* 17M1 and *Stonewall Jackson* 17M4 on Bluff Mountain. In 1969 a number of climbers appeared who would also contribute greatly to the area, especially Keith Bell and Keith Lockwood. Among other climbs, Bell, with Greg Mortimer or Ray Lassman, was to climb *Flight of the Phoenix* 17, *Ulysses* 20, *Icarus* 19 and *Antares* 19 (Tonduron), whilst Lockwood added *Neruda* 18, *London's Dockyard* 19, *Ginsberg* 19 and *A Little Rainbow* 19 (Tonduron). Bell also added the hard *Ultra-violent* 23—all in all Bell's name is on over 21 of the 39 routes on Bluff Mountain!

The '80s new wave did their stint here, and as with other areas it was Kim Carrigan, Mike Law and Mark Moorhead who climbed the hardest with routes like *Aladinsane* 19 (Carrigan), *Stonewall Jackson* FFA 20 (Carrigan), *Cracked Pane* 24 (by Carrigan, Moorhead and Law—the hardest thing here, the first three pitches may have been done by Bell as *Xoanon*), and *For Starters* 23 (with Moorhead). Law and Moorhead bagged *Lusty's* 21, in honour of a fine café in the Blue Mountains.

After this period the cliffs of the 'Bungles lapsed out of favour. In the late '80s Evan Bieske, Lucas Trihey and Roark Muhlen-Schulte all added routes to Bluff Mountain and in the '90s there were a few things done on Belougery.

Season: Like its nearby neighbour Kaputar, and equally because of its altitude, the Warrumbungles can get quite cold (down to 0°C) in winter (July–Sept) and during bad weather. It can also get quite wet.

Summer temperatures can reach the high 30s but it is often cooler up here than on the plains. Carry lots of water and sun protection.

Location/access: The Warrumbungles National Park is 33km W of Coonabarabran on the Newell Highway (39). It can be reached from Bathurst through Dubbo or from Tamworth and the New England Highway (15). From Coonabarabran follow the signs, past the observatory of Siding Springs. From Camp Picham a 3km walk (uphill towards the end) gets you to the Balor Hut on the Grand High Tops. If you stand at the hut and look S the Bread Knife, a thin blade of rock, is close by to your left. Belougery is the spire ENE, Crater Bluff is 1km S, and Bluff Mountain is 1.5km W. Tonduron Spire is accessed from the Gunneemooroo campsite in the S of the park and is reached from the Highway south of Coonabarabran.

Camping and local amenities: It is possible to camp in the park, tel: (02) 6825 4364. Fees apply. The Balor Hut, a 1.5hr walk up into the peaks is an ideal place to camp to prepare for the necessary Warrumbungles early starts. Coonabarabran is a smallish country town with supermarkets, banks, post office, motels, caravan parks and pubs.

Transport: It is possible to get to Coonabarabran by planes, trains and automobiles (buses) but to get to the park you need your own vehicle, or hitch.

Guidebooks: *The Warrumbungles: A Rock Guide*, Colyvan, M., Wild Publications, Melbourne, 1994.

Information: Tel: (02) 6842 0202 for the Ranger.

Belougery Spire
On Belougery recommended routes are:

| ▲ | 10 | 78m | (4) 1961 | **Vertigo** |
| ▲ | 15 | 249m | (9) 1962 | **Out and Beyond** |

Crater Bluff
Crater Bluff offers less serious undertakings than Bluff Mountain, in terms of grades and length only. To get to Crater Bluff take the track from the Grand High Tops through the Dagda saddle to the West Face.

Descent is down the line of *Tourist Route*. Follow the feature known as the Green Glacier, a fern full gully, to where it opens onto the South Face. 50m abseil from here (BR rap station) to terrace. Walk L (FI) over first hump to second hump and 2BR. 50m rap to ramp. Scramble down to ground.

| ▲ | 9 | 63m | (4) 1936 |

Tourist Route — Start: Scramble up series of ramps on N side of W Face, leading R (taking the upper line where there is an alternative). Start beneath small overhang. 1. (15m) Overhang to pillar above. 2. (18m) Chimney to ledge and tree. 3–4. (30m) Walk R to the Green Glacier, then up over muddy rocks. Take care here.

| ▲ | 17 | 260m | (10) 1962 |

Lieben — Australia's hardest climb for many years and a great climb from the past. Start beneath white streak in middle of W Face 1. (25m) Climb buttress on R to tree belay at large ledge. 2. (40m) Up wall, then slightly L to ledge above and R of white streak. 3. (25m) Continue, then L to belay on rib. 4. (25m) Climb rib or corner to L. 5. (25m) Crux corner. 6. (35m) Overhang then wall up to ledge. 7. (35m) Crack heading R, then L. 8–10. (50m) Up. From top head L to descent.

▲	14	190m	(8) 1962

Cornerstone Rib Direct – One of the most popular climbs here. Start at the major rib on the NW corner. 1–3. (90m) Follow the rib until L rib steepens. 4–5. (40m) crux—Cross to L of rib then up steeply to rejoin rib above. 6–8. (60m) Carefully up the loose rib.

Bluff Mountain

An outstanding cliff on which there are many fantastic classics. The seriousness of these climbs is compounded by route-finding difficulties and it is outside the scope of this guide to do this mighty cliff justice. Below are a list of the recommended classics. I suggest finding a guidebook before undertaking any routes on this cliff.

▲	13	240m	(7) 1972	Bastion Buttress
▲	19	300m	(8) 1976	London's Dockyard
▲	18	330m	(8) 1974	Flight of the Phoenix
▲	17	358m	(16) 1964 {later}	Elijah
▲	19	320m	(8) 1974	Aladinsane
▲	19	332m	(11) 1969 {1975}	Ginsberg
▲	18	338m	(11) 1977	Neruda
▲	19	291m	(10) 1972	Icarus
▲	20	240m	(9) 1974	Ulysses
	24	300m	1982	Cracked Pane

Kaputar

The numerous trachyte cliffs of Kaputar in NSW's north, the sleeper of Australian climbing, offer some of the best traditional climbing in the state in a beautiful national park setting, yet they are rarely visited. Though some routes are bolted, most of the really classic lines involve long brain-cramping leads up majestic corners, not quite the current climbing fashion. However, if you are looking for a classic climbing experience, superb surroundings, a bit of loose rock to add spice, and all the intensity you can handle, this is the place for you.

There are a number of very different areas in the park. Euglah Rock, at the end of a 5km walk, is compact, offering excellent two pitch routes, as does the pinnacle of Ninghadun, perched at the top of a steep walk. There are a number of smaller cliffs like the Powerlines and Motor City, and a number of more remote areas. If you are after a full-on adventure outing then one of the horrors on Yulludunida might suit you. But by far the best cliff in the park is The Governor.

Geology/type of rock/quality: Trachyte, grey and volcanic. Can be loose **
Grades: Up to 26 (on Euglah Rock).
Height: Up to 100m on The Governor, 200m on Yulludunida. (The Grade 3 ▲▲▲ *Skyline Traverse of Yulludunida* is 1800m).
Number of routes: Hundreds.

Climbing style: Naturally protected corner climbing and bolted (and natural gear) walls and faces. Take lots of everything.

Brief history: Kaputar was first visited by the Sydney Rockies in 1961 but it was not until 1973 when Joe Friend visited that the areas potential was acknowledged. In the late '70s and early '80s Armidale climbers such as Brian Birchall and Dick Curtis (with Friend) established many of the classics (up to 21). A lightning visit in 1979 by Tobin Sorenson (USA) and John Allen (UK) put up some incredible climbs, one of which, *Aslan*, was one of the state's first 26s and remains the area's hardest climb. In the '80s younger Armidale climbers such as Paul Bayne and Giovanni 'Jack' Lattanzio combined with Narrabri locals Paul and Mark Colyvan, and local Rangers such as Greg Croft and Ian Brown to add some of the better climbs in the area.

Season: Summer (Dec–Feb) can be oppressively hot, but better than down on the plains. Winter (June–Sept) can be cold and wet. Autumn and spring are good but it can rain heavily at these times of year.

Location/access: Kaputar National Park is about 50km E of Narrabri, a town on the Newell Hwy (39). It can be reached from the S from Coonabarabran (or coming down the Newell from Moree) or from the E through Tamworth and the New England Hwy (15). From Narrabri follow the signs out of town. After about 10km the road turns to dirt and winds up steeply into the park. The road passes by the pinnacle of Ningadhun and under the futuristic overhanging wall of the Yulludunida crater. Another 10km or so brings you to the Bark Huts campsite (from where you walk into Euglah) and another 5km brings you to the road end, Dawson's Springs Campground and the Ranger station. About 2km on from the Bark Huts is The Governor car park. A 5–10 min walk takes you down to the cliff. After the first ladder a track leads off to your R down a steep gully. This will take you down to the base of the cliffs. Descent is along the top of the cliff back to this point and down the gully.

Camping and local amenities: The best place to camp is the Bark Huts (toilets, showers, water, fireplaces). There is a fee. Telephone the Ranger for bookings.

Transport: Own transport.

Guidebooks: *Kaputar, A Rock Guide*, Mark Colyvan, Wild Publications, 1993.

Information: Tel: (02) 6792 4724 for the Ranger.

The Governor

Many of these routes are initialled.

▲▲ | 16 | 72m | (2) 1978

Clandestiny — As you come onto The Governor you pass an alcove (*Crystalline Shoeshine* 16) and the first major crack line (▲ *Patient Scruff* 16). 1. (26m) 25m R (Fl) of these start up a slab and head L with thinning pro to crack then zig-zag to ledge. 2. (46m) Bridge up gully and up line.

▲▲ | 19 | 75m | (3) 1973 {1979}

Sago Entrée — Initialled line which splits prow at 40m. 1. (30m) Up 20m to roof then swing up to alcove. 2. (30m) Another overhang then easier. 3. (15m) Up.

▲▲▲ 20 80m (3) 1976 {1981}

Iconoclast – Classic. Initialled line starting up *Sago Entrée*. 1. (30m) Up SE and trav R below overhanging buttress to next line and up to semi-hanging belay. 2. (25m) Up through triangular overhang. Belay below final steep section. 3. (25m) (crux) Up line.

▲ 19 72m 72m (3) 1979

Spook – 1. (12m) Up 5m R of *Iconoclast*, pass overhang on its L side and then move R. 2. (40m) (crux) Up corner from R end of ledge to roof. Trav L to crackline near arête. Up this to stance. 3. (20m) Corner crack.

▲▲ 22 48m 1987

Poltergeist – Initialled. Up corner 2m R of *Spook* to overhang, then 2m R to good hold on wall. Up to BR, through overhang and up seam that leads L into top of *Spook* and ledge. Rap from chains or continue up *Spook*.

▲ 24 77m (2) 1979

White Heat – Initialled 9m R of *Spook*, below L end of main overhangs. 1. (36m) Thin crack splitting middle of roof. Up to stance. 2. (41m) Up line.

▲▲ 23 70m (2) 1979

Double Trouble – 1. (30m) Corner crack below two-tiered roof 5m R of *White Heat*, traversing R at 8m (along horizontal break) into first crack-line that splits side of buttress and to stance. 2. (40m) Line up seams in brown wall near top.

▲▲▲ 21 75m (3) 1979 {1983}

Blood on the Moon – Initialled. 1. (33m) Wall 10m from L end of shattered wall, then through short orange offwidth to rest. Up to next roof (for gear) then step down, go left and up to semi-hanging belay on route to L (▲ *Sky Pilot* 20). 2. (26m) Up crack (as for *Sky Pilot*), up and R, the trav 5m R under overhang to its R end. Up groove for 10m to belay (below corner). 3. (16m) Corner.

▲▲ 23 67m (2) 1979

The Great Barrier Roof – 1. (30m) Up wall to orange cleft as for *Blood on the Moon*. Trav R on lip to arête and up this to horizontal undercling. Trav L, and go up crack splitting top overhangs. 2. (37m) Up line.

▲▲ 23 80m (3) 1987

Live Bait – Marked. 1. (25m) Seam 8m L of *The Millionaire Touch* (below) to small overhang. R and up past BR then up more steeply (BR and fixed wire) to hanging 2BB. 2. (22m) (crux) Step out and up L past BR, trav 3m L (feet just above overhangs) to good crack. Up this until you can move L onto the crack on the arête. Up to semi-hanging belay. 3. (33m) Up line.

▲▲ 24 103m (3) 1982

The Millionaire Touch – Takes smallest part of central roof via a vague line 15m L of *Soul on Ice* (below) just R of a large boulder. 1. (25m) Tend L to shattered pillar and very small stance on top. 2. (33m) R and up onto undercut wall, up and R for 5m then up line to below two lines. 3. (45m) Up and L into undercut corner and up this.

Soul on Ice — Start below R end of main overhangs. 1. (40m) Up orange rock to R of overhanging buttress. Trav L into the dihedral in the middle of the buttress and up to roof with V-crack on L. Over roof to stance. 2. (40m) Up.

Cheek to Cheek — 1. (30m) Through broken bulge with poor pro to R of *Soul on Ice*. and up seam on wall to good ledge (1st belay on *Pomp*—below) 2. (15m) Up crack (as for *Pomp*) for 8m then 2m L and up short corner to small stance on R. 3. (40m) Up, 1m R to twin cracks, and up wall and corner.

Pomp and Circumstance — V-groove R of *Cheek to Cheek*. 1. (30m) Up groove the R round base of square cut pedestal and up to ledge. Up crack on L to top of small pinnacle then down to other side of alcove and ledge. 2. (15m) Up for 7m, R and up and round arête to small grassy ledge. 3. (45m) Up twin cracks to PR and up until angle ceases then up wall.

Sunset Strip — Around to the R of the cliff. Initialled. 1. (45m) Up shallow chimney, turn roof on L, back R then on slopping holds to small bulge. Bridge over and establish semi-hanging belay in crack. 2. (15m) The crack.

Bottled Neat — Initialled. Start just below R gully at R end of main face. 1. (20m) From reddish boulder follow crack to below L-slanting roof. 2. (33m) Pass roof by rib on L. Step R into off-width and up.

The Crescent — The initialled chimney to R. 1. (30m) Line of R wall of gully to short, bottomless chimney. Up this to top of ridge. 2. (15m) Across bridge to main summit.

New England

I must confess to a certain sentimentality for the climbing areas of New England since it is where I first seriously took up climbing. The university town of Armidale in northern NSW is an excellent base for a climber, with a number of different cliffs and rock types within close range. Just outside town to the east, a number of rivers have cut huge gorges down towards the coast, an area now called the Oxley Wild Rivers National Park. The gorges of Wollomombi, Dangars, Ebor, Gara and others all have climbing in them, of varying quality. The most extensive is the long gorge cut by the Gara River down which there are numerous granite buttresses, up to 150m in height. On these are many superb crack, wall and slab routes, with a swag of hard modern sport climbs just out of town at the start of the gorge at the Gara Boulders.

All cliffs located in Gara Gorge can be accessed by a long walk down the gorge (with the exception of Blue Hole/Gara Boulders) or by driving through private property (this involves very difficult navigation and permission is needed) until close behind the cliffs. Therefore, it is advisable just to climb at Blue Hole which has no access restrictions, or to contact local climbers (see below) who over years have developed the art of cocky-sucking (talking to the landowners)

The basalt columns of Ebor (70km E from Armidale) offer good jam cracks only a couple of minutes walk from your car and close to the local pub! Other waterfall faces like Wollomombi/Chandlers and Dangars Gorge have long climbs up rock of an interesting nature—though many can only be climbed in times of drought.

South of Armidale (20km N of Tamworth) are the granite slabs of Moombi (visible from the New England Hwy) which hold some excellent routes but are currently off limits. N towards Qld, and obvious from the town of Tenterfield, is Bluff Rock. Towards Coffs Harbour is the newer sandstone sport area of Fort Knox and the relatively older Wonderland.

Geology/type of rock/quality: Various: granite in Gara ***; basalt at Ebor **; mudstone (greywacke) on the waterfall faces.

Grades: Up to 30/31.

Height: From 10m to 330m (at Wollomombi), but mostly around 10–20m single pitch.

Number of routes: Hundreds.

Climbing style: All styles, often naturally protected cracks, or bolted slabs and faces. Also modern bolted sport routes.

Brief history: Climbing started in the area in the 1960s with the ascent in Dangars of *Action* 15. Throughout the '60s the Delta Club pioneered routes in many of the gorges. In the mid '70s Bob Killip started bagging routes, and was joined by the infamous Prof. Brian Birchall, evergreen local climber Al Stephens, Rob Dixon, Phil Prior and Dick Curtis, as well as the odd traveller. This group claimed many of the classic cracks in Gara and Ebor. This development continued in the strong scene of the early '80s, with some of the older faces being replaced by Giovanni Lattanzio and other youngsters, culminating in ascents by ex-Narrabri climber Mark Colyvan, his superstar brother Paul 'Animal' Colyvan and Paul Bayne, such as *Last Laugh* 26 and *Pin-up* 25. By this time the climbing had moved out onto bolted slabs and faces, for example the 1985 development of the classic slabs at Persian Carpets, now sadly becoming overgrown. The university has continued to pull in a transient and ever-changing climbing population. In the mid '90s Swiss climber Andreas Audetat dragged the area kicking into the limelight with his hard bolted sport routes at the Blue Hole (including *O'Hara* 30/31), the Sea Cliff and The Sphinx in Gara.

Season: All year. Can be hot in summer and cold and wet in winter and it does occasionally snow on the plateau. It is necessary to pick your cliff in both summer and winter.

Location/access: Armidale is the New England tableland (900m above sea level) on the New England Hwy (15), midway between Sydney (600km) and Brisbane (500km). The climbing areas are varying directions and distances from town. To get to the Blue Hole/Gara Gorge drive E for 1km out of town on the Dorrigo Road and turn R (signposted) to Blue Hole (19km). From the Blue Hole head R to boulders and down the gorge.

Camping and local amenities: Bush camping is allowed in most national parks. There are a number of caravan parks and other accommodation options in Armidale, including the Pembroke Caravan Park which is close to the turnoff to Gara (tel: 02 6772 6470). The town has all your other needs, including a good student social scene (of sorts), good pubs and coffee shops.

Transport: Own vehicle. You could ride a pushy (bike) out to the Blue Hole or Dangars and it would be possible to hitch to Ebor.

Guidebooks: There are photocopied copies of *The Upper Gara Gorge, Ebor Falls, Yarrowyk* and *The*

Waterfalls that may be available. The UNE web page (see Appendix 3) has a few online guides.

Information: The university (try the UNE Mountaineering Club) generally has a small but committed group of climbers who are willing to bag you onto their latest projects (see Appendix 2). The local Mountain Designs climbing store (see Appendix 1) can help you with information and guides. The National Parks office is in Armidale, tel: (02) 6776 4260.

Bouldering: There is lots of bouldering at Blue Hole (Gara Gorge) and Mt Yarrowyck to the W of Armidale. In a recent (2000) visit, Swiss boulderer Fred Nicole established three V12s *Nanjanuka*, *Il Globo* (The Globe) and *Vampire Dagger*.

Gara

▲▲▲	22		Yellow Wall	**Teddy Bear's Picnic**
▲	23		Yellow Wall	**Magnifascent**
▲▲	25	30m	1976 {1983} Yellow Wall	**Pin-up**
▲	17	28m	1975, Yellow Wall	**Dynamic Beaurocrat**
▲▲	18	36m	1981, Dome Wall	**Working Class Heroes**
▲▲▲	21		Dome Wall	**Post Modern**
▲▲	23		Dome Wall	**Down for the Count**
▲▲	19		Dome Wall	**Jackhammer Blues**
▲▲▲	23		Dome Wall	**Sweet Dreams**
▲▲	19		Dome Wall	**Overkill**
▲	16	10m	1981 Dome Wall	**Petit Fleur**
▲▲▲	15		Dome Wall	**La Cucaracha**
▲▲▲	20	25m	1981 {FFA later} Dome Wall	**Autumnal Beauty**
▲▲▲	21		Dome Wall	**Curtain Call**

▲	17		Persian Carpets	**Country Member**
▲	20		Persian Carpets	**Salad Days**
▲	19		Persian Carpets	**Flesh Dance**
▲	20		Persian Carpets	**Xenophon**
▲▲	16		Persian Carpets	**Stop In The Name of Love**
▲▲▲	22		Persian Carpets	**Wolf Tracks**
▲▲▲	26		Persian Carpets	**Last Laugh**
▲▲▲	24		Reality Wall	**Rant and Rave**

▲	24		Blue Hole	**Sweet Surrender**
▲	25		Blue Hole	**Paper, Scissors, Rock**
▲	26		Blue Hole	**Rodney's Garibaldi Metwurst**
▲▲	16	25m	1975, Blue Hole	**Hope**
▲▲	22	15m	1980, Blue Hole	**Savage Amusement**
▲	13	20m	1976, Blue Hole	**Illusion**
▲▲	23		Blue Hole	**Psychomatic**
▲	29		Blue Hole	**Hitman**

▲	26		The Sea Cliff	Se A Cabo/Happy Birthday Francis
▲	29		The Sea Cliff	Ravage
▲	23		The Bastille	Deep Thought
▲	29		The Bastille	No Frills
▲	15	150m	1966, Dangars Falls	Action

Ebor

▲▲	20	1980	Anyone for Tennis
▲▲▲	19	1976	Rooflet
▲	20	1977	Backdoor Man
▲	22		It's My Party
▲	24		New Blue Dress
▲	26		The Proverbial
▲	17		The Joker
▲	19	1976	Narcissus
▲	22	1975 {FFA Later}	Supermouse
▲	15	1980	Hitman
▲	13		International Woman's Year Cracks
▲▲	16	1976	Twist
▲	19	1977	Sleight of Hand
▲▲▲	18	1976	Jugular

THE AUSTRALIAN CAPITAL TERRITORY

Despite being the seat of government, Canberra is really just a large country town with pretensions of being a sophisticated, worldly city. It is, however, a clean, pretty place with some excellent cultural activities such as the National Gallery and Questacon (the science museum). The best thing about the city, though, is the amount of bushland that surrounds it. This means that if you are into outdoor pursuits there is lots of bushwalking, mountain bike riding, skiing and of course rock climbing to be had in the vicinity. (Be careful, though, local climbers seem to turn into lawyers almost overnight, as if bitten by vampires.)

In the past Canberra climbing had a reputation for long, scary slabs routes and although these are still probably among the area's classic climbs there has been a shift to shorter, harder bolted face routes. The mighty cliffs of Booroomba have been eschewed for shorter cliffs like Gibralter Peak with easier access. Also, the relative closeness of areas like Nerriga, Bungonia, and the sunshine drenched Point Perpendicular (all in NSW) has drawn climbers away from ACT rock.

There are a number of other Canberra areas, of varying quality and with access of varying degrees of difficulty. Most, but not all, are granite. There are climbs in the Orroral Valley (past the ridge), at Pierce's Creek, Mt Scabby (a large slab in the south of the Territory) and White Horse Rocks. There are also cliffs at Mt Coree, Kambah Rocks, and Ginninderra Falls. Kambah Rocks, about 15min up river from Kambah Pool (W of the suburb of Kambah), is a great place to boulder, top-rope, and swim.

There are a variety of bouldering and buildering areas around Canberra including on the west slopes of Black Mountain and the Torrens Shops.

Booroomba

From its thin cicatrize cracks to the huge buckling planes of granite, Booroomba has long been the premier climbing area of the ACT, and the ancestral home of Canberra climbers. Booroomba Rocks is a number of large buttresses (up to 180m) sitting on a crisp tree-covered hillside looking down at the nation's capital far below, and that is just the way things should be. In winter you can climb here in full (though cool) sun while the city is covered by fog all day. The cliff's finest routes are mostly long multi-pitch slab extravaganzas, with just enough gear (perhaps). The perfect place to while away a sunny autumn day.

Geology/type of rock/quality: Granite ***
Grades: Up to 28.
Height: Up to 180m on the North Buttress.
Number of routes: Over 300
Climbing style: There are a lot of traditional routes here. The slabs often have bolts and bolt-plates should be carried on the older routes. Most of the newer bolted routes have FH but even they may need some natural gear.
Brief history: Real climbing started here in the years following 1966 with Peter Aitchison's ascents (often with Tony Wood) of routes like *Aitchison's Needle* 13, *Sunstoke* 9, *Hermes* 16, *Determinant* 15, *Fiasco* 18, *Jetts Set* 18 and *Indecision* 18. In June 1969 he turned his attention to the blanker slabs,

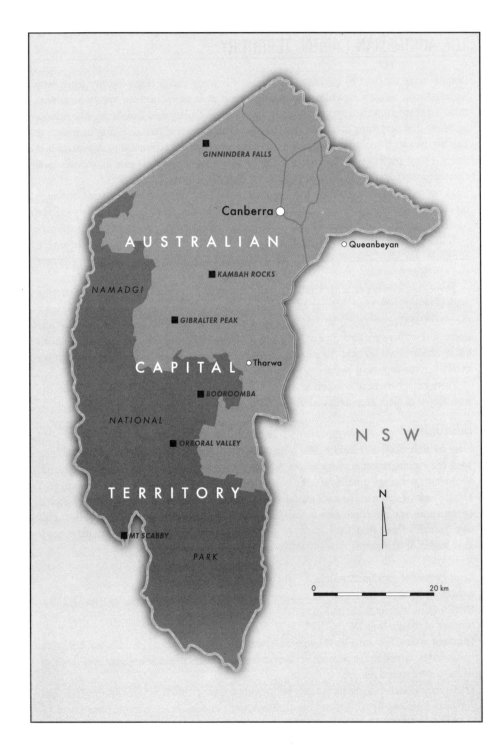

producing the classic bold *Equilibrium* 17 and *Outer Limits* 18. He finished up with the ascent of one of Australia's great lines, *Integral Crack* 19. Though there were visits by Bryden Allen, John Fantini, Joe Friend, Keith Bell and a young Mike Law, and keen locals like Chris Larque, Norm Booth and Ray Lassman, Aitchison's ascents were not to be bettered really until Henry Barber dropped by in 1975 and freed *Soolaimon* 22 (Trojan Wall, Orroral Ridge). For a while ACT climbers got more hung up on ethics than climbing but in the late '70s John Smart began to prove his exceptional ability. Smart climbed long, hard and free slabs like *Only the Good Die Young* 22 as well as short, hard face and crack routes like *Hotwired* 25, *Moral Turpitude* 23, and *The Promised Land* 24. In the '80s climbers like Roark Muhlen (*Steele Beeze* 20, *Rock Lobster* 22, *Rocketman* 24, *Powder Finger Finish* 23 and the excellent *Immaculate Deception* 24), Paul Daniels (*Astrodyne* 20), Joe Lynch (*Smash Palace* 23 and *Space Wasted* 23 FFA) and the pocket Hercules Mike 'Crushed' Law-Smith continued to put up superb granite slab routes. Law-Smith in particular matured to become one of the ACT's most able climbers, as ascents like *Extreme Youth* 24, *Anything So Nothing* 23, *Technocrat* 27 (at Legoland), *French Connections* 26 (Gibralter Peak) and *Rat Bat Blue* 26 show. In the late '80s climbers such as Tony Barten, Mike Peck and Richard Watts established some hard climbs at Booroomba before the focus shifted away. Most recently, Jamie Valdivia has added *Truth* 28 to Snickers Wall (not on topo).

Season: Booroomba is at 1300m and it snows up here in winter. Often, however, in winter the day can be fine, though cool and clear and it is possible (and often beautiful) to climb. Route names like *Sunstroke* tell you what to expect on hot summer days on the slabs. Spring (Mar–May) and autumn (Sept–Dec) are best. The cliffs generally face W but it is possible to find walls or gullies that point in any direction.

Location/access: (See maps, pp. 64 and 68.) Booroomba Rocks is in Namadgi National Park, S of Canberra. Find your way to Tharwa, 30km S of the GPO then follow the Naas road for 10km S. Turn R onto Apollo Road and wind up the hill. After 5km, and about 400m before the deserted Honeysuckle Creek Tracking Station, turn R (dirt). Follow this for about 2.5km to its end at an obvious parking and camping area. Find and follow the well-worn walking path up the hill to a fireplace/campsite. On your L is a stretcher and water etc. in case of an emergency situation.

If you walk to the cliff top you are now above Middle Rocks. To your R (FO) are the Northern Slabs. The S buttresses are not visible from here. The descent for the Northern and Central slabs is to your L. Follow the cliff line until a track takes you down into a gully. Scramble down this to the bottom. Head around (R–FO) until you get to the beginning of the Northern Slabs. Head on up to the cliff. To get to the S end of the South Buttress follow the vague track (W), then down a wide gully with chossy boulders at the top.

Camping and local amenities: It is traditional to camp at the car park (see above) or, if you're feeling fit, to carry all your gear up to the top camp. There are three designated national park campsites within Namadgi: Orroral Valley, Honeysuckle Creek and Mt Clear. All have only basic facilities including pit toilets, picnic tables and fireplaces. Water must be boiled before consumption. Bush camping is allowed anywhere within the park away from roads.

Transport: Own vehicle.

Guidebooks: *ACT Granite*, ed. John Churchill and Mike Peck, ANU Mountaineering Club, 1998.

Information: ACT climbing stores (see Appendix 1); National Parks and Wildlife Service, tel: (02) 6297 6144; the Rangers, tel: (02) 6247 8153 or (02) 6247 8146.

South Buttress

As you walk around the south end of the South Buttress you will shortly come to an obvious thin crack splitting a 50m wall/slab. This is *Integral Crack*.

| ▲ | 23 | 23m | 1982 |

A Little Dab'll Do Ya — Slab climbing past thin cracks for gear and a BR 3m R of *Integral*. Up trending L then R to belay on small ledge to L of arête.

| ▲▲▲ | 19 | 48m | 1969 |

Integral Crack — Don't get lost. Enjoy. They don't get much better.

| ▲ | 23 | 45m | 1981 |

No Beans for Bonzo — A bold route up the water run 3m L of *Integral*, with side runners in that route.

| ▲ | 14 | 50m | 1966 |

Roy's Crack — The deep crack 8m L of *Integral*. An old style classic.

| ▲▲ | 24 | 35m | 1986 |

Ruffles — Start as for *Moral*, go up to overlap, and pull through into the crack. Trav R and up to BR, past this and 2BR. Finish up corner on *Moral*.

| ▲▲ | 23 | 45m | 1979 |

Moral Turpitude The thin crack 2m L of *Roy's Crack*. 1. (30m) Up to roof, then L to break just before arête. Over bulge, and up wall past 2FH (small krabs needed) to another bolt. R to belay below corner. 2. (15m) Up corner crack.

Middle Rocks

A broken area of walls and buttresses with quite a few classics sprinkled through the area, and some of Booroomba's harder and more sporty climbs. To get to Hurricane Cracks Wall follow the track from the campsite that heads along the ridge past the turn-off down to the North Buttress and rap in, or scramble down loose gully to R (FO) to large sloping ledge at base of wall. To get to the base of *Hurricane Cracks* follow the North Buttress track down and after the gully turn L (FO) and follow around the base of the buttress. Around the corner is a slab on which is the first pitch of *Hurricane Cracks*. Climbs are described L>R.

| ▲ | 14 | 55m | (2) 1968 |

Hurricane Cracks — The second pitch is excellent. Can rap in. To do the 1st pitch start at the slab below a fine steep wall. 1. (38m) Up slab and corner to ledge. Then up dirty wall and ramp to the large bushy ledge. 2. (20m) Up flaky crack in centre of fine wall.

| ▲▲ | 20 | 25m | 1979 |

Morning Thunder — The obvious crack/groove to the R. Up crack, then R into thin V alcove. Up groove/crack above.

Two Minute Hate — 7m R of *Morning Thunder*. Climb up to BR then R and up to short crack. Up wall moving L at top to belay as for *Morning Thunder*.

▲▲   25   35m   1984

Beau Temps — 3m R of *Two Minute Hate* past 3BR to a horizontal break. R and up to BR, then thin crack (crux) through overlap and up.

▲▲   24   22m   1986

Diva — 1m R of *Beau Temps*, clipping the first BR on that route. Up and R across flake to a stance on the arête. Up arête past 2BR and PR.

North Buttress

To get to North Buttress follow the track down through Middle Rocks, heading for the bottom of the obvious tall buttress (Big Boris). *Hermes* is the manifest roof, high up to the R. It is best to rack up at the top camp and then walk back along the top of North Buttress rather than leave gear at the base.

▲   12   50m   1968

Little Hermes — Start in the small recess on the R of the pillar below the *Hermes* roof. 1. (32m) Up slabs and ledges to tree, up crack and wall to good ledge, then use the L-wards slanting crack to climb slab to grassy ledge and tree belay (as for *Hermes*). 2. (18m) Walk 15m R and belay at big blocks before climbing short wall, hanging flakes and corner. Up rib on left of gully.

▲▲   16   50m   (2) 1968

Hermes — One of the cliff's most popular routes. Start at L side of pillar below roof. 1. (24m) Up chimney and crack, step R at top and climb short wall to ledge. Up thin crack on slab to belay. 2. (26m) Up the corner crack and out R under roof.

▲▲   19   90m   (3) 1978

Incisor — Starts below fang on the L wall of the chimney 10m L of *Hermes*. 1. (20m) Up the crumbly wall to fang, undercling L then follow crack up to belay 2m R of corner (*Indecision* 17). 2. (35m) Up crack through overlap, and R at horizontal to the arête. Up knobs on the L to large ledge then up and back R to arête and up short V-groove. Go R at top into short corner (pitch 2 of *Big Boris* 17). Up to belay. 3. (35m) (as for *Big Boris*) Climb to top of large leaning flake then step onto face and up scoops to the huge *Fearon* block.

▲   15   144m   (6) 1968

Determinant — 1. (20m) Start 25m L and down from *Hermes* at the biggest tree. Climb the easy slab, keeping to R, to a large bushy ledge. (Can walk up manky ramp to R) 2. (30m) From L of ledge move L across slab (crux) then up and L to short corner crack up to 'The Prow' (an obvious feature). 3. (20m) Climb the R-hand side of the block on the L side of The Prow, then trav R along break and up slab to belay. 4. (26m) Up easy slab to base of corner crack. This is the start of the *Terminant Corner Finish* 15. 5. (25m) Up corner. 6. (10m) Move L and then exit R (loose).

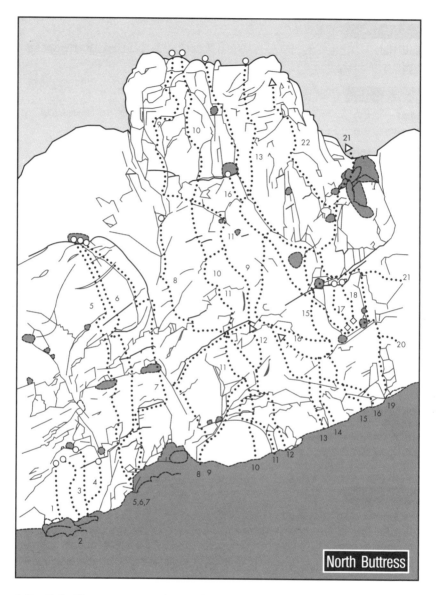

North Buttress

1. *Frog Tactics* 25
2. *Snickers* 25
3. *Designer Drugs* 25
4. *Boy's Brigade* 25
5. *Only the Good Die Young* 22
6. *Smash Palace* 23
7. *Powderfinger Finish* 23
8. *Jubilate* 18

9. *Outer Limits* 18
10. *Space Wasted* 23
11. *Crimble Cromble* 20
12. *Further Out* 19
13. *Extreme Youth* 24
14. *Chanel 19* 23
15. *Anything So Nothing* 23
16. *Rubbishman* 19

17. *Madrigal* 19
18. *Rocketman* 24
19. *Jetts Sett* 18
20. *Fiasco* 18
21. *Determinant* 15
22. *Yellow Brick Road* 19

The following routes are on the topo (opposite).

▲	24	25m	1980	**Rocketman**
▲▲	19	25m	1978	**Madrigal**
▲	19	75m	1979	**Rubbishman**
▲▲	23	110m	1982	**Anything So Nothing**
▲▲	23	65m	1982	**Chanel 19**
▲▲	24	135m	1982	**Extreme Youth**
▲	19	60m	1972 {1974}	**Further Out**
▲	20	98m	1977	**Crimble Cromble**
▲▲	23	155m	1984 {1984}	**Space Wasted**
▲▲	18	179m	1969	**Outer Limits**
▲	18	100m	1971	**Jubilate**
▲	17	61m		**Jubilate/Outer Limits Combination**
▲▲	18	105m		**Outer Limits/Jubilate Combination**
▲▲	23	100m	1980	**Powderfinger Finish**
▲▲▲	23	90m	1985	**Smash Palace**
▲▲▲	22	100m	1982	**Only the Good Die Young**
▲	25	18m	1987 {1989}	**Boy's Brigade**
▲▲	25	22m	1986 {1989}	**Designer Drugs**
▲▲	25	25m	1985 {1986}	**Snickers**
▲	25	22m	1987	**Frog Tactics**

To the left end of the Northern Slabs there are a number of good, easy routes, including the classic *Equilibrium* (marked).

▲	17	140m	1969

Equilibrium – Starts at the initialled shallow groove on the L of the Northern slabs. 1. (40m) Up groove for 20m, then R to ledge. Up on R to another ledge and BB. 2. (30m) L along fading ledge then up for 5m to BR. Straight up past BR (R of vertical break). 3. (40m) Diagonally R to ledge, up to L of bushes and crack through overlap. Trav R to belay in corner. 4. (30m) Up slab to R of bushes for 6m then trav R and up slab.

▲▲	9	120m	1986

Sunstroke – An easy classic. Starts at slanting (R-wards) crack 8m L of *Equilibrium*. 1. (40m) R-wards up crack, then follow groove L to a sloping ledge. Belay at wedged blocks. 2. (20m) L up groove to tree belay in corner. 3. (25m) Up wall on R, the L and up steepening groove. Up to tree and ledge on R. 4. (35m) The twin grooves to large terrace.

The Orroral Ridge

The Orroral Ridge is a group of boulders and small buttresses that offer a good, shaded option in summer to the more exposed Booroomba.

Geology/type of rock/quality: Granite ***
Grades: Up to 27.

Height: Up to 90m at Honeysuckle Crag but mostly smaller (around 20m).

Number of routes: Many hundred.

Climbing style: Granite slabs, cracks and crimpy walls.

Brief history: See Booroomba history, p. 63.

Season: As for Booroomba, however it is more sheltered here on the ridge, both in winter and summer.

Location/access: Continue up Apollo Road all the way to the Honeysuckle Creek tracking station. A dirt road starts from a gate to the right. Follow this, taking R fork 150m along. The road winds (passing Honeysuckle Crag) up to the tower. Park here and walk L or SE to get to The Belfry and The Cloisters. Tower Rocks is only 100m SW along the ridge. Legoland is about 600m NW. Other areas such as Mushroom Rock, Trojan Wall, The Halfway Hotel and Sentinel Rocks are further out.

Camping and local amenities: Bush camp at cliffs, at Booroomba or stay in luxury in Canberra. All supplies are available in Canberra. The local store at Tharwa has the closest ice-creams and petrol.

Transport: Own vehicle.

Guidebooks: ACT *Granite*, ed. John Churchill and Mike Peck, ANU Mountaineering Club, 1998.

Information: As for Booroomba.

Classic on the Ridge include:

▲▲	16	90m	Honeysuckle Crag	**Deep Space/Sickle Connection**
▲▲	19	60m	1982, Honeysuckle Crag	**In City Dreams**
▲▲	24	30m	1988, The Belfry	**Tracey Anne**
▲	18	15m	1978, The Cloisters	**Sasha Cracker**
▲	9	15m	1978, The Cloisters	**Breakaway**
▲	14	20m	1978, The Cloisters	**High Diddle**
▲	18	15m	1978, The Cloisters	**Rocketman**
▲▲	22	20m	1978, The Cloisters	**Julius Caesar**
▲▲	24	18m	1986, The Cloisters	**Zoo Fear**
▲▲	24	25m	1984, The Cloisters	**Corvus**
▲	22	20m	1978, Legoland	**Easy Wind**
▲	27	20m	1998, Legoland	**Technocrat**
▲▲▲	22	70m	1974 {1975}, Trojan Wall	**Soolaimon**

Gibraltar Peak

Gibraltar Peak gained a certain fashionable chic in the late '80s because it was closer to Canberra, closer to the pub, lower in altitude and warmer. It still offers good granite climbing, often quite hard (up to 35m and grade 26), but does not have the grandeur of Booroomba. Climbs here are bolted (may need plates) and naturally protected.

Geology/type of rock/quality: Granite ***

Grades: Up to 26.

Height: Up to 35m.

Number of routes: Over 100.

Climbing style: Granite slabs, cracks and thin faces.

Brief history: See Booroomba history, p. 63.

Season: As for Booroomba. Gibraltar is much lower than Booroomba, and collects a lot of sun (on the N side of the hill) which makes it a better option in winter or on wet and colder days.

Location/access: To get to Gibralter Peak you need a 4WD or a car with high clearance, or face a long walk. Take the Corin Dam Road from the south of Canberra and 1.5km from Paddy's River Road there is a pine plantation on your R. A number of dirt roads cut up through this forest to the ridge and crags, however some are extremely steep and rough. The best option is the fourth turn-off then L,R,R (follow most obvious way) till you come to locked gates. Walk in along the track, turning L to find the grassy saddle and the back of Gibraltar Peak. The Jism and Fortress are back to the R (E).

Camping and local amenities: Camping is not allowed but there are a lot of other options in and around Canberra. The nearby Cotter Tavern is an excellent place to imbibe refreshments by a large open fire.

Transport: Own vehicle.

Guidebooks: *ACT Granite*, ed. John Churchill and Mike Peck, ANU Mountaineering Club, 1998.

Information: As for Booroomba.

Recommended routes:

▲▲	24	28m	1986	**Skylark**
▲	15	30m	1987	**Juveniles and Geriatrics**
▲▲	25	20m	1987	**Antipodean Atrocities**
	26	13m	1987	**French Connections**
▲▲	21	18m	1978	**Overnight Sensation**
▲▲	19	35m	1978	**Scarborough Fair**
▲	18	25m	1987	**No Glove to Love**

VICTORIA

There is a lot of good rock in Victoria. To the north of Melbourne is the great granite area of Mt Buffalo with its long gorge routes and fine slabs. To the far west of the state (three to four hours from Melbourne) is the extensive sandstone area of the Grampians with its long classics and modern sport climbs, and further west is Arapiles, the grand old cliff of Australia, hard quartzite steeped in history, legend and myth. Within an hour (or a little more) of Melbourne there are also a number of cliffs including slabby Ben Cairn and Black Hill, and the steep Camel's Hump. To the south-west is the You Yangs, an extensive area of granite boulders on which the climbs seem to get shorter every year. To the west is the shattered rock of Werribee Gorge with a handful of good climbs and to the north-west is the famous Hanging Rock, where climbing is currently banned. To the east there are a number of cliffs, including some good climbing at the Jawbones and Cathedrals.

Elsewhere there is climbing around Bendigo (Mt Alexander and Melville's Caves), Ballarat (Mt Beckworth) and in the superb setting of Wilson's Promontory.

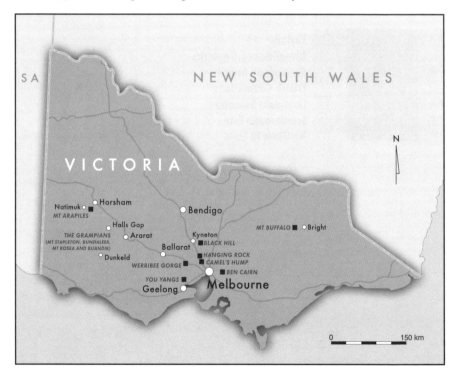

Melbourne local

There are many things that Melbourne has going for it as a city. A view is not one of them, nor are good local crags. Melbourne is rather drab and flat and as a result all the action occurs mostly inside—it has some of the best restaurants in the world. The cosmopolitan smorgasbord available in these places is a stark contrast to the bland offerings of the local cliffs. In my opinion the best of the crags are the strangely popular Camel's Hump, the good granite area of Black Hill, and to the east the unique and exquisite Ben Cairn—the best cliff around Melbourne.

There are far less bouldering options in Melbourne than Sydney, with Burnley perhaps being the best. Under the freeway in Burnley is a glue-up project that is excellent (Melway's p. 58, J1). There is another, east along the river, under the McRobertson Bridge. Richmond Bridge (Melway's p.44, K11) is a bluestone wall under the railway bridge over the boulevard in Burnley. Less popular now is Merri Creek, a bluestone wall in Clifton Hill/Northcote (see Appendix 3).

Ben Cairn

Geology/type of rock/quality: A smooth, granite like rock ****

Grades: Up to 26.

Height: Up to 30m.

Number of routes: Over 30.

Climbing style: Weird, frictiony, slabby stuff and a few cracks. Natural gear and carrots, plus one huge bolt on *Skating Away* (need wire to clip). Most of the weirder pieces here, bashies and such, have been replaced.

Brief history: After a brief foray in 1977 when they discovered the cliff covered in snow, Steven Griffin and Glenn Tempest returned when it was warmer to start claiming first ascents. Tempest and Jerry Maddox did quite a few of the early routes including the classic *Skating Away*. Kevin Lindorff chipped in with the extreme *Protagonist* 23 in 1979. In the early '80s it became Mike Law's favourite local crag and he, with various others, ticked most of the remaining classics (often with extremely weird protection), including the desperate *Fiction* 26 and *Rentadoddle* 26.

Season: It sometimes snows up here in winter but can be nice if it's fine. At least when it's cold the friction is good, unless the cliff is damp (which it often is—it dries slowly). This is a great place on a summer's day. Being high up it is often quite pleasant here when Melbourne is oppressive. The cliff faces SE and is in a cool forest.

Location/access: Take the Maroondah Hwy out of Melbourne (E) through Healesville, and turn R into Don Rd (after the bridge on the E of town). Drive up this towards Mt Donna Buang, and at the Launching Place intersection (10km) take the L branch. 5km on (turns to dirt) there is a small parking area and a sign to Ben Cairn 1043m (altitude not distance). There is a path on the uphill side of the road and 5–10 min walk will bring you to the top of the crag. The descent (down a slab) is to your R (FO) which brings you out above the lower cliff. Walk L (FO) or N for a few metres and then cut back S to access these climbs, or continue N along the base of the cliff.

Camping and local amenities: No camping. There are caravan parks and other accommodation options in the area though, including Healesville. There is fuel and food there as well. There is no shortage of cafés in the area to hit for coffee and cakes after a hard day's slabbing.

Transport: Own vehicle essential.

Guidebooks: *Eastern District Guide*, Glenn Tempest and Richard Smith, Victorian Climbing Club, 1988; *Melbourne's Best: Selected Climbing In and Around Melbourne*, Mike Hampton, Wild Publications, Melbourne, 1995; *A Rock Guide to Three Crags Near Melbourne*, Wild Publications, Melbourne, 1991; *Black Hill*, Michael Hampton; *Camel's Hump and Hanging Rock*, Chris Baxter. A new guide by Simon Mentz and Glenn Tempest is also due to be released this year.

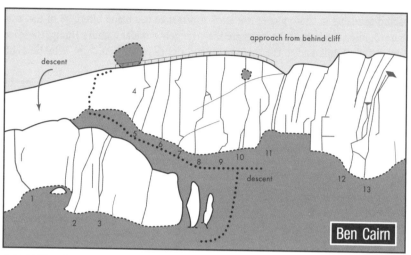

1. *My Brilliant Career* 19
2. *Frankenstein and the Wereturkeys* 19
3. *Flapjack* 18
4. *Raspberry Ripple* 12
5. *Plumb Jamb* 12
6. *The Protagonist* 23
7. *Pie in the Sky* 15
8. *Gnippils* 22
9. *Fiction* 26
10. *Rentadoddle* 26
11. *Skating Away* 20
12. *Pancake Flake* 18
13. *Digit Dancer* 20

▲ 19 12m

My Brilliant Career – Walk to the L of cliff on a ledge and climb middle of slab past BRs.

▲ 19 12m

Frankenstein and the Wereturkeys – R of *My Brilliant Career* is a gully. Start about 4m R and climb to jug and up.

▲ 18 12m

Flapjack – Corner to R.

▲ 12 12m

Raspberry Ripple – The first crack you come to walking along R (Fl) from the base of the descent slab.

▲ 12 12m

Plumb Jamb – The crack 3m R.

▲ 23 12m

The Protagonist – The funky groove 3m R with FHs.

▲ 15 14m

Pie in the Sky – 3m R of *The Protagonist*. Onto block and up crack.

▲ **26** 20m

Fiction — Starts 2m L of the following climb (*Rentadoddle*), gaining crack from L and climbing slab to shallow crack past BRs.

▲ **26** 20m

Rentadoddle — About 10m further R is a deep groove. Hard.

▲▲ **20** 22m

Skating Away — The classic of the cliff. Start 4m R of *Rentadoddle* at fading crack. Up this and on to slab past huge BR (clip with wire) and up. *Musk, Hashish* and *Blood* 21 goes L from the big BR and then up past another BR.

▲▲ **18** 30m

Pancake Flake — Follow the cliff R round to its most protruding point. You'll see a flake on the wall. Up to flake (BR) then up its L to tree, finishing up corner through overlap.

▲▲ **20** 28m

Digit Dancer — A nice slab. From the BR on *Pancake Flake* go directly up past 2 BRs to ledge. Up slab, and through small overlap.

Camel's Hump

The Camel's Hump is a lump of rock of indeterminate quality high on Mt Macedon, NW of Melbourne (1hr). It is unusual for a local Melbourne crag in that it offers steep almost modern face climbing, at reasonably hard grades, as well as a few easy classics. The climbs here need a selection of natural gear and bolt plates.

Geology/type of rock/quality: Volcanic and dubious.

Grades: Up to 29.

Height: Up to 129m but mostly 30m or lower.

Number of routes: Fifty plus.

Climbing style: Easy, long rambles or more modern face climbing.

Brief history: Climbing started here in the late '50s and '60s. Climbing legends like Peter Jackson, John Fahey and Steve Craddock added some climbs including *Oxbow* and *Witch*, Victoria's first 17. Andrew Thompson and local Nic Taylor added some climbs in the '70s including *Bloodline* 22 and *Warlock* 20 but it remained to Mike Law in his systematic exploration of Melbourne crags in the early '80s, and Melbourne boy Mark Moorhead, to fully develop the Omega Block. They added, amongst others, *Bop till You Drop* 25 (Moorhead) and *Methotrexate* 25. More recently, Melbournian Mathew Brooks has climbed here, adding *Satanic Verses* 26 and *Hollow Screams* 29.

Season: A pleasant enough place most of the time, even in summer (Dec–Feb) except on the hottest days. In winter (Jun–Sept) it can be very wet and miserable.

Location/access: Take the Tullamarine Fwy (43) to the Calder Hwy (79) and turn off this 5km after passing the town of Gisborne (which the highway bypasses now). Drive through the hamlet of Mt Macedon and up the mountain for 3km. Turn L to the Memorial Cross Lookout but park about 500m past the turn-off (on L) and take sign-posted path opposite. Take this path for about 450m and where it swings R take the L fork, up to and over a saddle to some boulders from where you can see the back of the Omega Block and the crack of *Witch*. Walk down to your L (FO).

Camping and local amenities: Generally people day trip from Melbourne. There is a caravan park and hotels in nearby Woodend, plus a number of more expensive accommodation options in the area. Towns like Woodend and Gisborne have necessary supplies.

Transport: Own vehicle, or train to Woodend and hitch.

Guidebooks: *Northwest Victoria: A Rockclimber's Guide*, Chris Watson, Bill Andrews and Michael Hampton, Victorian Climbing Club, Melbourne, 2000; *Melbourne's Best: Selected Climbing In and Around Melbourne*, Mike Hampton, Wild Publications, Melbourne, 1995; *A Rock Guide to Three Crags Near Melbourne*, Wild Publications, Melbourne, 1991; *Black Hill*, Michael Hampton; *Camel's Hump and Hanging Rock*, Chris Baxter.

Information: Melbourne climbing shops (see Appendix 1); MUMC and VCC web sites (see Appendix 3).

On the lower part of the main Omega Block (down to the L) are two old classics:

▲▲   6   129m   (4) 1962

Oxbow — The chimney to large ledge. Wall. Arête. Trav L round two ribs to a cave, back 4m and up wall and groove.

▲▲   17   30m   early 80s

Poxbow — Crack 4m L of *Oxbow*. R to arête at 10m, and up face to bulge, up R and off.

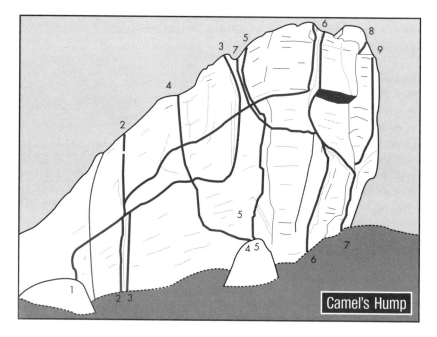

1. *Powder Hound* 21
2. *Bloodline* 22
3. *Methrotexate* 25
4. *Bop till you Drop* 25
5. *The Broomstick* 23
6. *Boogie till you Puke* 21
7. *Warlock* 21
8. *Witch* 17
9. *Wishful Thinking* 16

	Grade	Height	Year	Route
	20	12m	1990	**Evil Brew** (not marked on topo)
▲▲	21	30m	1983	**Powder Hound**
▲	22	20m	1978	**Bloodline**
▲▲	25	25m	early 80s	**Methotrexate**
▲	26	25m	1994	**Satanic Verses** (not marked on topo)
▲▲	25	22m	1982	**Bop Till You Drop**
▲	23	21m	1966 {1982}	**The Broomstick**
▲	23	32m		**Boogie Till You Puke Variant**
	29		1999	**Hollow Screams** (not marked on topo)
▲▲	21	30m		**Boogie Till You Puke**
▲	21	30m	1977	**Warlock**
▲▲	17	21m	1964	**Witch**
▲	16	21m	early 80s	**Wishful Thinking**

Black Hill

An area of fine granite slabs, some hard faces and other playthings, in a nice rural setting not far to the NW of Melbourne. *Ugly Voyage* is a composite route of 'two existing but damaged routes', Ferret's *Pumping Ugly Muscle* 25 1988 and *Bon Voyage* 23 1988.

Geology/type of rock/quality: Granite **
Grades: Up to 26.
Height: Up to 30m.
Number of routes: Over 70.
Climbing style: Granite slabs and walls mostly.

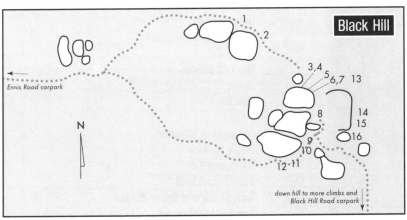

1. *Ugly Voyage* 25
2. *Barefoot and Pregnant* 19
3. *Acid Rain* 25
4. *The Cult Master* 24
5. *Havoc* 24
6. *Thin Ice* 18
7. *Miliwa* 17
8. *Frog's Hollow* 14
9. *Touch and Go* 17
10. *Scratch and Sniff* 20
11. *Toxic Shock and Razor Blades* 26
12. *Gumboot Diplomacy* 23
13. *Squeal Like a Pig* 21
14. *Maid to Undress in the Wilderness* 21
15. *Work the Meat* 20
16. *Fear of a Black Planet* 20

Brief history: The area was briefly visited in 1980 by Iain Sedgeman and Dave Lia. Mick Hampton started climbing here in 1983, bringing along James Falla and Andrew Corlass (*Milawa* 17). At the same time, the area was independently found by Angel Black who dragged Ian 'Ferret' Anger (*Pumping Ugly Muscle* 25, *Scratch and Sniff* 20, and *Gumboot Diplomacy* 23) and Simon Vallings (NZ) along. Later, Jeff Shrimpton and Mike Law also added a few hard routes. Other developers included Paul Vlahovic (*Squeal Like a Pig* 21), Andrew Cannon (*Bon Voyage* 23), Andrew Stevens (*Dicky Knee Dihedral* 21) and Peter Campbell (*Touch and Go* 17) with later development by Kevin Lindorff, Glenn Tempest (*Toxic Shock* and *Razor Blades* 26) and Peter Stebbins (*Ultra Violet* 23).

Season: A pleasant enough place most of the time, but in summer (Dec–Feb) it can be hot and airless. In winter, Black Hill can be a better option than many other Melbourne crags.

Location/access: Take the Calder Hwy (79) past Gisborne (see Camel's Hump) and on to Kyneton. The highway now bypasses Kyneton but it may be best to take the first exit into the town. Just as you enter the town turn R on the Edgecombe–Eppalock Rd. Follow this for about 7km (you should pass the main highway) and turn R into Ennis Rd, following this until it too swings 90° R. Park here (big gum) and enter the bush via a stile. Turn L and follow an old track for about 500m and then head up ENE (past an old sand pit) to a saddle. There are some boulders to your L (Virgin Tor) but ignore them and head down to the good stuff (for topo, see map).

Camping and local amenities: Generally climbers day trip from Melbourne. There is a caravan park and hotels in nearby Kyneton, plus a number of more expensive accommodation options in the area. Towns like Woodend and Kyneton have necessary supplies.

Transport: Own vehicle.

Guidebooks: See p. 76.

Information: Melbourne climbing shops (see Appendix 1); MUMC and VCC web sites (see Appendix 3).

▲	25	32m		Ugly Voyage
	19	23m	1986	Barefoot and Pregnant
	25	26m	1992	Acid Rain
	24	25m	1992	The Cult Master
	24	23m	1992	Havoc
	18	25m	1992	Thin Ice
▲	17	23m	1986	Miliwa
▲	22	12m	1997	Greenpiece (not on topo)
▲	14	25m	1987	Frog's Hollow
▲	17	20m	1988	Touch and Go
▲	20	22m	1985	Scratch and Sniff
▲	26	22m	1993	Toxic Shock and Razor Blades
▲	23	30m	1988	Gumboot Diplomacy
▲	21	26m	1986	Squeal Like a Pig
▲	21	23m	1986	Maid to Undress in the Wilderness
▲	20	22m	1985	Work the Meat
	20	20m	1992	Fear of a Black Planet

Mt Buffalo

Buffalo changes its face like a person in sleep. Soft and inviting, seductive, hard and aggressive. It is a plateau of dreams. There are such good climbs here they have to be done to be believed.

The Mt Buffalo plateau is a raised alpine plateau that is covered in granite tors, boulders and bluffs. One of the creeks that come off the plateau has cut a large (300m) gorge leaving one large steep wall, the North Wall. There are hard free routes and overnight aid climbs on the wall and the plateau is home to many fierce cracks and excellent slabs, as good as any in Australia.

Geology/type of rock/quality: Granite *** Protect ropes when rapping or jugging as Buffalo granite is very abrasive.

Grades: Up to 30. There are few good, easy (under 18) climbs here, and they tend to be spread out.

Height: From 10m on the tors to 270m on the North Wall.

Number of routes: Over 800.

Climbing style: The climbing here is mainly granite slab or crack climbing. The modern slabs tend to be well bolted and though they are often ring bolts (or FH) there are a lot of carrots so carry some brackets just in case. You might find the sharp cracks more pleasant if you tape-up. Purchase the tape before you go there. (Note: Dates at Buffalo are often listed as, for example, 1981/2. This does not mean that the route took two years to do but that it was done over the summer period of late 1981 and early 1982.)

Brief history: Climbers came to the gorge in the '30s doing routes on the Cathedral and Wall of China and the Melbourne University Mountaineering Club picked their way up Sewer Wall in the '50s. The ubiquitous John Ewbank started the modern ball rolling with his ascent of *Maharajah* (with aid) in 1964. Throughout the '60s Victorian climbers like Reg Williams, Mike Stone, Ted Batty and Ian Speedie came to the gorge to bash their way up routes on the North Wall culminating in the incredible ascent of *Ozymandias* by Chris Baxter and Chris Dewhirst. Ewbank had tried this route with Baxter and failed, having to be happy with an ascent of *Sultan* and freeing his route *Maharajah*. Other teams busy in the gorge included the Gleddies, Geoff and Alan Gledhill, John Moore, Phil Secombe, Peter McKeand, Andrew Thompson and Ian Guild.

Free climbing came to Buffalo in the '70s, starting with the clean aid ascents (without hammer) of *Ozymandias* and other routes by Queenslander Rick White. Attention turned to free rock climbing, and during this decade climbers started to explore the plateau's potential, including Keith Lockwood (*Winnie the Pooh* 19, *Angels*), Ian Lewis (*Black Road* 22), Andrew Thompson (*Winnie the Pooh*), Joe Friend and Kim Carrigan (*Führer Eliminate* with five aids). The late '70s, however, brought climbers such as Glenn Tempest, Kevin Lindorff and Nic Taylor to the plateau. Lindorff was to have a lasting effect on the climbs up here, putting up quality routes (though often scary, and often with Jeremy Boreham) into the '90s (including *Woodpecker Wall* 22 and the beautiful *Peroxide Blonde* 21). Nic Taylor made his mark with the ascent (with some aid) of *Hard Rain* 22M1, and the 1975 ascent of *Country Road*, Australia's first 24.

The awesome triumvirate of Mike Law, Kim Carrigan and Greg Child were busy adding routes like *Glace* 22, *Superfine* 22, *Needling Doubt* 22, and the ominously named *Death and Disfiguration* 22. The free highpoint of this period was Carrigan's ascent of *Flair* 27, whilst in the gorge Tony Dignan and Geoff Little produced *Clouded Queen* M9 and Colin Reece went for a solo ramble to produce *Holden Caulfield* M6.

The '80s though saw a change in mentality with Ian 'Ferret' Anger pioneering some of the most superb slab routes in Australia, as well as developing the fun park Dreamworld. Routes like *Substance Abuse* 23, *The Dreaming* 23, *Glossop Skins Direct* 24, *Heaven on a Stick* 26, *Edge of Pleasure* 21 and

Chronic 26 are evidence of his skill and creativity. Anger also conceived the Dreamworld hardie that was stolen by German Gerhard Horhager to give *Gondwanaland* 29.

Development flourished all over the plateau at this time with good routes being put up at areas on Le Soeuf plateau, the Backwall, Dreamworld, Viewpoint and Buckland slabs, among other areas. Bob Cowan has been active with good routes all over the plateau.

In the late '80s granite super climber Malcolm Matheson began to pick off plumb lines at Buffalo: *Rough Justice* 28, *The Great Shark Hunt* 30, *Mussolini* 28, *Lebensraum* 25 (*Copperhead Rd* A4) and many others are testament to his strength and ability. He has been matched by UK expat Steve Monks who grabbed the coveted first free ascent of *Ozymandias*, backing it up with the FFA of *Ozy Direct*. Though five grades off the cutting edge of Australian grading, neither route has been repeated. Instead of resting on his laurels, Monks has been working on freeing *Lord Gumtree*.

Season: Unless you are planning winter ascents of the North Wall classics, winter is not a good time to visit Buffalo—the plateau is generally covered in snow. The good news is that in summer (Dec–April) the area can be up to 5°C cooler than the hot lowlands. The sun burns here even if you feel cool so use sunscreen. The weather here can change rapidly and extreme drops in temperature are not unknown.

Location/access: The Mount Buffalo National Park is about 320 km NE (4hrs) of Melbourne via the Hume Fwy and Great Alpine Road—look for the turn-off after the big petrol station/junk food circus 6km after Glenrowan. After Porepunkah (before Bright) look for signs to the park. The last 25km is up a windy, sealed road. There is a park entrance fee. When you crest the hill you come to a turn-off to the L which takes you to the Chalet, lookouts and gorge (2km). Continuing straight ahead for another 2km brings you to the Lake Catani campsite. The Galleries are near here. It is another 9km to the Horn (the last 3km unsealed), the end of the road. On the way you pass the large Cathedral. The Hump is just next to this, facing away from the road.

Camping and local amenities: There is camping at Lake Catani available Nov–April. Bookings are needed in busy periods. Bush camping is not allowed. Guest house style accommodation is available at the chalet; motel and lodge style at Mt Buffalo Lodge. There is a wide range of accommodation off the plateau.

With the exceptions of drinks and fast food at the chalet there is not much in the way of supplies on the plateau. These are all available from Bright (30km). Petrol is not available on the plateau.

At the camp the cold waters of Lake Catani are ideal after a hot day on the rock. Another excellent way to cool down is the underground river, down from the lake. It involves crawling through smooth, polished chambers full of icy water, sometimes swimming, and sometimes climbing up small waterfalls.

Transport: Unless you come up on a tour you must either bring your own car, or hitch up the hill (which is not too difficult).

Guidebooks: *Mt Buffalo*, Jeremy Boreham and David Brereton, Victorian Climbing Club, 1996; *Victoria: A Guide to Selected Rockclimbs at Mt Arapiles, The Grampians and Mt Buffalo*, Chris Baxter with Glenn Tempest, Wild Publications, Melbourne, 1994.

Information: Park information, tel: 13 19 63; Bright Tourist Info tel: (03) 5755 2275.

Bouldering: There is lots of potential here but little has been recorded or worked.

Eurobin Falls

Eurobin Falls are below the plateau (at about 600m) and the water-washed slabs offer a smoother style of climbing than up on the rougher granite. On the road below the plateau, approximately 75m up the road from where it crosses the Eurobin Creek, is a small parking area.

There is a signposted track to the foot of the falls, a 10 minute walk. Descent: From the longer routes, step over creek and descend on the upstream side of the cliff.

| ▲ | 14 | 185m | (5) 1976 |

Mother of Pearl — Starts at the square corner 100m. L of the main waterfall. 1. (20m) Take the corner 2. (45m) Up the corner 5m to a tree, then out R and up slabs to belay in corner. 3. (30m) Up to the halfway ledge. 4. (45m) R then up any of the cracks. 5. (45m) The slab or the corner.

| ▲ | 23 | 45m | 1991 |

Tiger Angel — Run out. 30m R of *Mother of Pearl* follow 4BRs up through bulge. Up and L for 10m. R to *Under Glass* rap station.

| ▲▲ | 23 | 45m | 1983 |

Muscle Beach 2 — Start at R-hand white streak 5m R of *Tiger Angel*. R into short flake corner and up past 6BRs to 2BB. R to *Under Glass* rap station.

| ▲ | 24 | 45m | 1991 |

Zero Rose — Sustained and run-out. 4m R of *Muscle Beach* on R of white streak take line with 5BRs to *Under Glass* rap station.

| ▲ | 22 | 45m | 1991 |

Under Glass — 18m L of waterfall (6m R of *Zero Rose*) follow a faint run-out rib. 5BRs to rap station.

| ▲▲ | 21 | 190m | (5) 1976 |

No Holds Barred — 4m R of *Under Glass*. 1. (35m) Up to the L end of the overlap at 10m to BR then R along lip of the overlap to some flakes. Up past little smooth section (PR) to BB. 2. (35m) Up R to a flake, then up to belay on a square flake. 3. (45m) L to groove, then up via porthole to big ledges. 4. (30m) Diagonally L to a ledge and crack. 5. (45m) The slab above.

| | 15 | 80m | 1988 |

In for a Swim — 1. (30m) Black forbidding crack 10 R of falls to bushy ledge then cross the waterfall and belay poolside. 2. (50m) Up twin cracks, L to ledge to finish up 3rd of *No Holds Barred*. *Up the Creek* 18 18m can be done 6m to the L past 3BR to give a direct start (and avoid crack).

Angels Buttress

Where Angels Fear to Tread is one of the most coveted and climbed routes at Buffalo. It is a long series of cracks that run up Angels Buttress, an obvious buttress that is the centrepiece of the S side of the gorge. Angels Buttress is situated below Burston's Crevasse into which it finishes.

Getting to the bottom can be difficult the first time. You can orientate yourself by looking across from Wilkinson's Lookout atop the North Wall. Find your way E of the chalet, following the signs to Mushroom Rock. From here drop down then contour L and drop through a cleft. Devilled Cream Buttress is across L (FO) from here (where the ▲▲ *Commander Cody* 21 flake is). From here a cairned track leads across below Isotope Wall, then drops into a gully which runs out of the side gorge below Bent's Lookout. Go down the gully to cross a little creek then around to the foot of the buttress.

▲▲　17　228m　　(9) 1970–71

Where Angels Fear to Tread/Direct Finish — The dominant crack in the nose of the buttress. 1. (23m) Up to belay on a large bush. 2. (29m) The crack, then swap to R-hand crack and up to a ledge. 3 (14m) Up to a small stance on the R. 4. (27m) Up and slab L to a good crack then up this to belay. 5. (27m) Up and over the bulge. Step R to the crack and up to a small tree. 6. (30m) Up the crack to the gully then up the chimney to the foot of the pinnacle. 7. (27m) Chimney to the top of the pinnacle then take the wide crack to a large ledge. 8. (21m) Down R then up into scrubby crack and up to exit up L to a ledge below a short wall. 9. (30m) From L of ledge, up jugs to vertical wall, then L and across into Burston's Crevasse.

▲▲　23　110m　　(3) [23,20,22,-] 1992

Pearly Gates ('While You're Down there Squeak') — From the top of the second pitch of *Angels* (or rap in) this line takes the L arête of the buttress. 1. (40m) From *Where Angels Fear to Tread* 2nd belay, move up and step L. Up flake and out to arête past BR. 3BR to a BB. 2. (35m) Up short crack, then past 3BR to 2BB at base of pillar. 3. (20m) Up arête past 5BR to pillar's top. (Lasso pillar and BR for belay) 4. (15m) As for *Where Angels Fear to Tread*.

Bent's Lookout

Bent's Lookout is the main lookout in front of the chalet. To reach the routes below abseil down from the lookout, down *Establishment* (L side FO—find BR on finish to last pitch) or *Status Quo* (large gum over fence on the far R of lookout). It is usual to rap 2x50m ropes with a knot change.

▲▲　21　117m　　(3) 1970 {1976}

The Status Quo — 1. (34m) The overhanging crack in the R of the main wall. At about 21m, move wide L into the main corner to a small stance. 1b. (34m) Alternatively move L and up into the corner proper. Up to small stance. 2. (40m) Up the corner, past the steepening to a double BB on the R wall. 3. (43m) The crack. Hope it's clean.

▲▲　27　50m　　(2) [20,27] 1984

Flair — 1. (20m) Start as for *Status Quo* until it moves L. Instead continue up flake to 2BB on R. 2. (30m) Up shallow corner then change to L crack. Up past 2BR then join *Hard Rain* to 2nd belay.

▲▲▲　22M1　125m　　(4) 1976 {1976}

Hard Rain — One of Australia's top ten climbs! 1. (40m) The line R of *Status Quo* takes a pure crack which curves R to a HBB. 2. (30m) Tension R to the flake. Up to a small stance. 3. (30m) The superb flake until it thins. Slab L past a BR then diagonally L to belay. 4 (18m) Up the last part of *Status Quo*.

The *Establishment* is the corner line R of *Hard Rain*, up the obvious dyke line. The dyke/arête to the L of the corner is the excellent:

▲▲　23　38m　　1994　　**Hurricane**

There is a number of different variants on *Establishment*, at various grades. If you follow the dyke all the way from its start in the corner you have done:

| ▲▲ | 22 | 40m | 1980 | **Established Anarchy** |

| | 21 | 110m | (3) 1970 {1977} |

Establishment — To do *Establishment* proper rap to the base of the wall then climb up the chimney R of *Hard Rain*
1. (43m) Up the diagonal line to a prominent corner and up to HBB. 2. (27m). Continue up corner and past a bolt to a small stance. 3. (40m) To the top.

| ▲▲ | 23 or 18M1 | 21m | 1974 {1977/78} |

Dyke Finish — Cuts off from the stance at the end of the 2nd pitch, then climbs up the line and travs R to the dyke which is climbed to the top. The trav R is done normally with tension making the grade 18 — it is possible to pendulum across on your rap ropes.

| ▲▲ | 19M1 | 66m | (3) [16,19,18M1] |

The Establishment Composite Variant — 1. (30m) Passes the original 1st belay to a 2BB just below the overhang. 2. (15m) Step L and up to crack. Past BR to small ledge and BB (original 2nd). 3. (21m) *The Dyke Finish* as above.

| ▲ | 21 | 20m | 1980 |

Backless — Looking out from Bent's Lookout (as the name would suggest) there is an obvious rock down to the L. This is traditionally called the 'climbers' look-out' and is a good place to check out Bent's wall before taking the plunge. If you scramble down and around L (looking out) from that 'lookout' you can then abseil down a corner above what is called Burston's Crevasse (a very narrow gully running parallel to the main gorge. In the top of the crevasse is a large gum with a name plate on it). In the corner there is a H2BB. *Backless* climbs the corner.

| ▲▲ | 20 | 30m | 1984 |

Coming Up for Air — From the HBB on *Backless* head out and down L to ledges then up past BR to arête over the sickening void. Up arête past BR and PR to ledge on R. Then back L to arête to finish.

| ▲▲▲ | 26 | 60m | (2) [26,25] 1990/91 |

Breathless — Directly below the arête of *Coming Up for Air* is the immaculate route *Breathless* which starts from the end of Burston's Crevasse 60m below. You can either do the wide crack start of *Monarch* to reach it or simply rap in and do 1 or 2 pitches. 1. (30m) Follow the arête past 6-7 FH and natural gear to semi-HBB 2. (30m) Up past FH to arête, slab moves past more FH to join *Coming Up for Air*.

The North Wall

The North Wall of the gorge is the premier granite face in Australia, with routes up to 270m. It was the traditional aiding cliff in Oz and retains this crown, one of the few areas where this style of climbing is still enjoyed. In the last 20 years a number of excellent hard free routes have been added or created by freeing old aid climbs and there remain many aid lines to free if you are interested. Winter aid ascents here are possible but cold and difficult. I have only included a few of the (almost) 50 aid and free routes on the wall.

To access routes on the top part of the wall such as *Defender* and *El Supremo* you can rap in. There is a 2BR rap point on a rock slab (leave gorge rim track 20–30m before the fork to Reed's Lookout, head SE for about 50m). Access to the rest of the wall is via Comet Ramp, which is the obvious diagonal ramp that starts between Pulpit Rock and the L end of the North Wall and heads down L (FO). Remember to protect ropes when rapping The descent involves a number of abseils and scrambling. Start from tea-tree down L (FO) from the lookout. From here the first rap is 55m—hard pull so leave fixed —and then 2 more 50m raps get you to the base. You are on a large ledge (The *Führer* ledge) half way down Comet Ramp, at the base of *Defender* and *Rough Justice*. In the middle of the ledge there is a smaller chimney that leads up into the big chimney line, *Emperor*. R of this is another obvious line—*Führer Direct*, and R of this a large tree. At the extreme R of the ledge is another obvious reference line, *Tyrant*. Note that routes on the North Wall are often done with different belays than in the descriptions here, and pitch lengths should only be taken as a rough guide.

▲▲   23   185m   (5) [23,22,22,21,-] 1970 {1991}

Defender Of The Faith – 1.(45m) Up the small chimney to exit L and up the ramp. Then into the corner. When this thins look for a PR 0.5m to the L. Climb 1.5m further up corner then make your way L to flakes and into next crack, then up to HBB. 2. (37m) Up and around overhang. Follow the crack to a small stance with BB. 3. (50m) Up to, and L around, the overhang. Up the crack system to exit R around the arête onto a ledge. BB. 4&5. (55m) Up to and up pinnacle then up thin seam to ramp which is followed across L. Then up easy corner. These last two pitches are normally not done, especially if wet, instead most parties take:

▲   20   80m   (2) [15,20] 1995

Defender Of The Faith Variant Finish – 4. (30m) Up to short wide corner, up 3m then L. Across ledges R to R-facing corner. 5. (50m) Clip BR and go L around arête. Up past BR to cracks which are followed to break. Go L past PR then up easy R-facing corner. Step R and up short crack to finish. From the break you can go up past FH and ring-BR at 24.

▲▲▲   25   105m   (3) 1982 {1982}

El Supremo – It is possible to rap down this route or a great way to do it is to do the first two pitches of *Il Duce*. 1. (45m) Move R a few moves and up finger flake past PR to end. R, past BR and up, tending R the whole time, past 2BRs to the big ledge that comes out of *Führer* (see below). 2. (25m) From the L of the ledge, up the corner line till it ends, then follow the seam that tends R into *Führer*. 3. (35m) Best to step R and do last pitch of *Lebensraum* 25 which goes up arête past 7BR.

▲   21   150m   (4) 1974 {1977}

Führer Eliminate – *Führer Eliminate* is the easiest of all free routes on the North Wall, although the climbing is a bit archaic (read wide). *Führer Direct* is the straight line that runs almost all the way up this section of the wall, starting at the R of the *Führer* ledge. *Führer* itself climbs up to the R again, up a large corner system just L of the large tree. The *Eliminate* starts to the L of the *Direct*, in the small chimney that is *Emperor* 1. (34m) Up *Emperor* to ledge. Go R and up flake to small stance below end of flake 2. (42m) Up flake then go R and climb the diagonal line to the sentry box (which is on *Führer*). 3. (40) The line to BB. 4. (34m) The line to top, past sickle on L.

In the same area are the excellent:

▲▲	25	140m	1991	**Mein Kampf**
▲▲▲	25	55m	1992	**Lebensraum**
▲	25	139m	1971 {1991}	**Lord of the Flies**
▲▲	28	170m	(5) [24,25,28,-,-] 1992	**Rough Justice** (above *Defender*)

R and down from the end of the *Führer* ledge (27m R and down from *Tyrant*) the line of *She* 21M6 200m heads out R for a pitch of grade 21 free climbing. The ▲ *She-Ozymandias Eliminate* 22M1 257m 1978 also starts here before joining *Ozymandias* higher up. From this extreme R of the *Führer* ledge another 46m abseil puts you at the base of *Knocking on Heaven's Door* which starts in a shallow corner with a grassy ledge and tree at 12m.

▲▲	M8	250m	(7) 1981

Clouded Queen — One of hardest aid routes in Australia starts 6m R again.

▲▲	28 or 18M4 (A2)	260m	(9 or10) [22,28,26,24,22,21,20,18,-] 1969 {1988/9}

Ozymandias — If you look over onto the North Wall you can't miss the long line of *Ozymandias* (Ozy), a series of corners running up the tallest section of the cliff, one of the finest climbs in Australia, especially free. It starts 250m below Wilkinson's Lookout, and another abseil down from *Knocking On Heavens Door* gets you to the base. Most people take 2 days to do the route, if only for the joy of bivouacing on Big Grassy. 1. (24m) Past 2 bolts, then up and into corner, BB on small ledge. 2. (34m) The corner. HBB. 3. (40m) Up corner, move L and up to small ledge on the L. 4. (6m) Up to bivvy ledge —Big Grassy. Can run 1&2, 3&4 together to make here in 2 pitches. 5. (34m) The corner and around yellow roof. Up corner/ramp to HBB on the L. 6. (25m) The corner, then trav L and up the ramp to belay on the arête. 7. (35m) Up into peapod and over bulge. Up corner, over roof and up line to belay on small ledge. 8. (10m) The obvious trav line to the foot of the big chimney. 9. (29m) Up to belay above the huge jammed blocks. 10. (23m) The line.

▲▲▲	28M4 (A2) or 18 M4	135m	1972

Ozymandias Direct Finish — 5. (35m) Climb *Ozy* to the yellow roof. Instead of the large corner ramp above which tends L, take the smaller one directly above to a HBB. 6. (20m) The corner, then follow bolts to a HBB on the arête. 7. (25m) Follow bolts to the roof, around and up corner to HBB (bivvy site) or better still, to avoid drag, head R and up crack 5m (joining *Lord Gumtree*) to alcove (PR and good cams). 8,9. (55m) Either continue as for *Lord Gumtree* or swing R and do two pitches of *Holden Caulfield* (the rivet ladder—now free at 27,24) before rejoining *Gumtree* for the last pitch.

▲▲▲	28	55m	(2 separate) [25,28] 1996

Ozymandias Direct Finish Free Eliminant — An outstanding climb. 6. (10m) Trav R from corner on original to the HBB on *Ozy Direct*. 7.(45m) Up to and through roof. Up corner until a few metres below bivvy bolts. Move out past BR to belay in niche of *Lord Gumtree*.

▲	18 M6	246m	(8) 1971 {mostly free 28 above pitch 4}

Lord Gumtree — 1. (24m) As for *Ozy*. 2. (27m) Move R and up small corner to HBB on R wall. (Can run 1&2 together.) 3. (40m) The corner and wall to the sloping grass ledge and HBB (ledge leads up to Big Grassy). 4. (40m) Up the corner a little way and onto wall following twin thin cracks to a hanging belay (BR and nut). 5. (35m) Up L on the small ramp, 2BR, then main crack to belay (bivvy site). 6. (25m) Up line through roof, past BR and up to the alcove and belay. 7. (25m) Follow crackline L through 2 roofs to a HBB (can belay here) and up to a ledge. (BR—can belay here.) 8. (30m) Up chimney to belay ledge below summit block. Up the crack to the L of the corner to top. Or do *Holden Caulfield*'s rivet ladder to R to avoid 7 & 8.

Chalwell Galleries

The Galleries are an excellent place to hone your slabbing skills before heading out on the bigger climbs. It is close to camp and relatively user friendly. Approach from the sign-posted walking track leading south from the entrance to the Catani camp ground (5–10 mins). Before the track hits the Galleries proper, a granite outcrop can be seen down L. Here you will find:

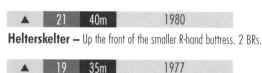

Helterskelter – Up the front of the smaller R-hand buttress. 2 BRs.

▲ 19 35m   1977

Untouched by Human Hands – On the R of the main buttress is a L-slanted crack, then finish up slab.

▲ 22 35m   1977

Glace – On the L is a prominent flake crack. This climb takes R side. Up the short crack, then the slab past 4 BRs.

▲ 23 35m   1977

Superfine – The L of the flake, then the slab past 4 BRs to the top.

From just before reaching the boulders of the Galleries proper, head up R along the boulders and follow them around to the L to an obvious slab face. On this are:

Son of Epic – The R arête past 2 BRs.

▲ 19 18m   1978

Join the Dots – In the centre of the face, up the crack then slab past 2BRs.

   21 18m   1980/81

Shady Tactics – Starts L of the centre of the face. Climb the line to the ledge, then slab past BRs to the top.

▲ 19 18m   1971 {1974}

Epic – A few metres L, towards the L-hand edge of face. Up the crack to break then up the slab past BRs.

The Cathedral

You can't miss the Cathedral as you drive out along the plateau: a large collection of boulders close to the R of the road. From the car park a walking track leads up to the Cathedral (and onwards to the Hump). Descent is via a tourist route on the W side of the Cathedral.

As you approach the Cathedral, a large corner capped by a roof is obvious on the R, on a separate very large pinnacle (leave track about 50m prior to saddle—lesser track leads up to chasm behind the pinnacle). The obvious corner leading around R to the L side of the prominent flakes is *Sultan*.

▲▲　20　65m　　(4) 1968 {1974}

Sultan – 1. (20m) The corner to the large sloping ledge. 2. (15m) Up and R around nose, continuing R to BB. 3. (21m) Up to stance just below summit. 4. (9m) To summit. BB. Descent is an abseil down the back.

▲▲　17　42m　　1964 {1968}

Maharajah – Starts at the wide crack on the north side of the pinnacle. You can get to it by going through behind the pinnacle. It is best done with the ▲ Flake *Start* 17 10m up the thin L-facing flake to the L. 1. (9m) The flake. 2. (15m) Move L and up to the crack. Up this, then stretch L and up. 3. (9m) Up the corner crack. 4. (9m) To summit. BB.

To get to the longer routes on the Cathedral it is best to rap in from the summit (though you can scramble down R, looking out, from base of *Maharajah*). Take the tourist track to the summit which goes around to the west side then up a large chimney formed by a large boulder. There are chipped handholds at one point. The best routes are on the North face with an abseil descent. You need to scout around a bit to find the rap bolts.

▲▲▲　23　90m　　(2) [21,23] 1990

The Dreaming – Immaculate. The L arête of the face, L of *Woodpecker Wall* (see below). 1. (40m) Up vague ramp to BR then up until you can head R to dyke line. Follow this L then up to belay on ledge. 2. (50m) Up.

▲▲　22　90m　　1982

Woodpecker Wall – Starts at the crack splitting the main northern buttress, a couple of metres L of R arête. 1. (40m) The crack to BB. 2. (50m) Past BR-ladder, tend slightly R into shallow scoop. L past BR and around the nose, up past another BR to top.

▲▲▲　23　55m　　(2) [22,23] 1991/2

Substance Abuse – Equally superb. Takes thin cracks 2-3m R of *Woodpecker Wall*, then up edge of wall past BRs to BB. The 2nd continues past BRs to end at chain.

R again, up the R wall/arête of a large rounded corner (*Calliope* 14) is the well named:

▲▲　21　90m　　(2) 1991/2

Edge of Pleasure – Lots of BRs. The top pitch alone is worth rapping in to do.

The Hump

Follow the footpath up past the Cathedral to the open saddle. Where the track heads L, leave it and head across the slabs and scrub to the large boulders on the R. When you can, cut down through these onto a terrace that runs above the main Hump cliffs. Follow this around L (looking out W) to the highest point and hunt around for rap station. This is the top of *Glossop Skins*. 2 x 50m abseils get you to the ground.

▲▲　24　90m　　(2) [24,20] 1990

They Might Be Giants – Start at the L edge of the large main (*Glossop Skins*) buttress. 1. (50m) Up the L tending crack to a ledge and FH. Up into the easy crack for 3m then back R onto the arête. Straight up the arête past

8 FH tending L at the top to double BB at the chicken head. 2. (40m) Up past FH onto the crack and up as for the original third pitch of *Glossop Skins*.

▲ **25** **90m** (3) [25,23,20] 1982

Glossop Skins — Starts 15m R of *TMBG* at the groove/crack. 1.(20m) Up this then past BR to dyke. Trav R then up to 2BB. 2. (30m) R and up past 2BRs to R end of ramp. L across this to BR and up to next ramp. L and up past BR to belay from chains. 3. (40m) Up slightly L past 2BRs, then L to line. Follow this to finish then back R and up.

▲▲ **23** **90m** (2) [23,21] 1989

Glossop Skins Direct — Can just rap in and do the 2nd pitch which is ▲▲▲ superb. Start halfway between the original first pitch and *The Initiation*, 5m R of groove on GS. 1. (50m) Up into the groove past a BR and into the next crack. Clip the first BR on the original 2nd pitch and follow that to the belay. 2. (40m) Follow the original 3rd pitch to the 2nd BR then head up R past 3 FH.

▲▲▲ **18** **97m** (4) 1970 {1976}

The Initiation — One of the best easier multi-pitch climbs at Buffalo. It is the obvious flake crack on the R side of the main buttress. 1. (14m) The flake. 2. (26m) R then up to a small ledge. 3. (27m) Up the line and around the nose. To the top of the flake and a BR. Down R past two more BRs to a crack. Down and across then up to belay below chimney. 4. (30m) The crack to the R wall, then around and up the flake crack.

▲▲ **23** **25m** 1990

Redbacks — The well protected wall with 6 BRs about 100m R of *The Initiation*, on a separate buttress and clearly visible from the top of the cliff. You'll want a #3 1/2 Friend for a pocket between 2nd and 3rd BRs. Double BB at top.

Dreamworld

This is a collection of user friendly boulders below the road about 100m before the Horn car park. The main face faces W, on your L as you approach. On the L arête of the main face is:

▲▲ **22** **15m** **Injustice**

The L side of the dyke just R of the L arête is:

▲▲ **19** **15m** **This Is Not Our Land**

On the face inside the boulder (facing the same way as the main face) is some juggy fun protected with slings:

12 **15m**

Beware the Strathbogie — Throw rope end down and get second to tie it off for belay and escape.

The Horn

Follow the track from the car park to the lookout. Looking back towards the Cathedral (NE) from there, the following takes the sharp bolted arête down to your R (rap in off lookout):

Peroxide Blonde

If you continue down another 25m you are at the base of:

Big Fun
They Dance Alone – On the steep slab R of *Big Fun*.

Another 20m below and 12m L is the start of:

The Pintle – Takes the L of the two parallel cracks. 2nd pitch goes up onto the ledge on the L, then steps R into the break in the roof. Onto the ramp and up. The easy 3rd pitch takes the corners R of *Peroxide Blonde*.

The Pintle L-hand Variant – Takes the line immediately L of the original second pitch then up via the thinning flake to the top.

Hoi Polloi – Around to R of the base of *Big Fun*.

Glitterati – Above *Hoi Polloi*, the centre of the block down and L (looking down) from the summit block. 2nd pitch of *Hoi Polloi* takes the L arête of this block.

The Grampians

Like the Blue Mountains outside Sydney, the Grampians (Gariwerd) 2.5hrs west of Melbourne is a large area of bushland and escarpments that has so many individual cliffs of differing nature that it is next to impossible to generalise about them. Like the Blueys the area is all sandstone but unlike them it is all national park. Fortunately, at the moment the only access restrictions are to do with endangered animals. Also unlike the Blueys, there are no towns, railways and highways just up the track.

Not only is the Grampians the historical (as well as practical) home of Victorian sport climbing with the incredible Taipan Wall, one of the finest cliffs in the world (and the compact Buandik), it is the location of the user-friendly Staplyton and the historically important and classic studded Bundaleer and Mt Rosea.

If you have time, invest in one of the many guidebooks to the area and investigate such wondrous places as Mt Difficult, The Fortress (home of the much photographed *Passport to Insanity*), the sport crags of Van Dieman's Land or Millenium Caves, the alpine experience of Mt Abrupt, the remote Green Gap Pinnacle, the fine walls of Eureka Wall, Slander Gully, Tortoise Wall, The Red Cave (with Malcolm Matheson's outrageous 50m naturally protected roof, *Welcome to Barbados* 30), and so much more. Halfway between the Grampians and Arapiles is the quiet Black Range cliffs and the little funopolis of Black Ian's Rocks.

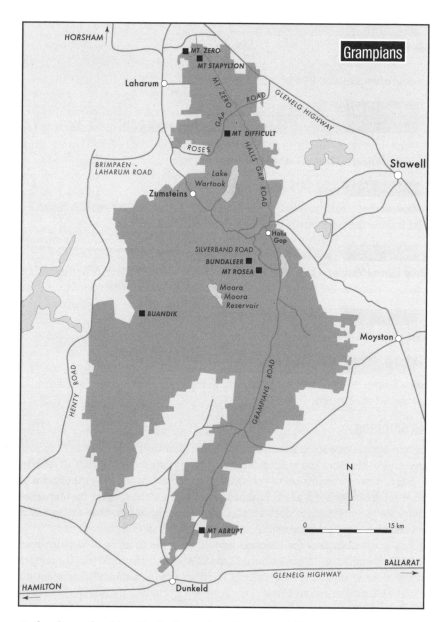

Geology/type of rock/quality: Sandstone. Generally very good. ***

Grades: Up to 32.

Height: Up to 175m (Mt Abrupt) but cliffs vary greatly in height.

Number of routes: 1000s.

Climbing style: Various. Lower Taipan, Buandik, Van Dieman's Land and Millenium are sport. Most other cliffs naturally protected, or carrots.

Brief history: In the '50s Eric Webb did some climbing on the Chimney Pots. This was followed by ascents there in the early '60s by members of the Victorian Climbing Club. In 1961 George Glover and Greg Lovejoy put up *Mixed Climb* at Rosea, and Lovejoy returned in 1963 to aid the *Tourist Buttress* (with German Herbert Schlipper). In 1964 Peter Jackson and Bob Bull put up the first routes at Bundaleer and a year later the Melbourne Uni Climbers put up the first routes at Stapylton. During the '60s the activists of Victorian climbing (Mike Stone, Ian Guild and others) put up climbs at Rosea (*RIP Corner, Debutante* and *Speculation*) and breached the incredible Taipan Wall (*The Seventh Pillar*). In 1969, Bruno Zielke and John Ewbank established *Blimp* (with three points of aid—it was freed in 1974 by Joe Friend and Ian Lewis). Grampians climbing had come of age, growing up even more when Roland Pauligk freed the first pitch of his route *The Liquidator* on Redman's Bluff, creating Victoria's first 20.

Henry Barber dropped by in 1975 and attempted to free *Manic Depressive*, a feat accomplished not much later at 25 by Greg Child in 1978. By this time Chris Peisker had established Australia's first 25 with the FFA of *Ostler* though he graded it only 24. For much of the '70s the real pace of development was elsewhere, Arapiles mostly. In 1982 Kim Carrigan freed the incredible trench of *Ogive* 28 at Bundaleer and around the same time Mike Law shonked his way up *Dive, Dive, Dive* 25+.

In the '80s climber's eyes and dreams began to turn again to the Grampians. Stapylton was awakened by a number of climbers, including Kevin Lindorff (*Sandanista* 23, *Powder Monkey* 23). Swiss climber Martin Scheel showed what was possible with routes like *Milupa* 28 and later *Daniel Or-Tiger* 30. They were lessons that had already be learned by a young Malcolm 'HB' Matheson who found the steep, pumpy unclimbed walls of the Grampians suited his style. Over the last 20 years he has put up many excellent routes in the Grampians (including *Serpentine, Contra Arms Pump* 30, *Journey to Nicaragua* 30 and the amazing roof of *Welcome to Barbados* 30). In 1986 diminutive Nyrie Dodd freed the mighty roof *Passport to Insanity* 27 (that had been aided in 1974), a route that has had far more posters printed than ascents.

In the '90s development has continued. In 1991, another Grampianophile, Steve Monks, put up the immaculate routes on Eureka Wall (*Pythagoras Theorem* 26 and *Archimedes Principle* 26). In 1991 Glenn Tempest and others discovered the Gallery at Buandik and ushered in the age of sport climbing. Matheson attacked the steep walls here with fervour, putting up the classic *Monkey Puzzle* 28 in 1992, a good day's pump. In 1996 wunderkind Garth Miller added *Nicotine* 32 to this wall and climbed the project of Gordon Poultney on Spurt Wall to produce *Who's a Naughty Boy* (now *The Tyranny of Distance* 31). More recent routes in these upper grades on Spurt (and Afterglow) Wall include Dave Jones' *Academia* 31 and Julian Saunders' *Bossanova* 31. On the Sandanista cliff Jones also added *Samosa* 32. The other trend in the '90s has been the development of Taipan Wall (see separate history).

Season: The Grampians can be cold and wet in winter (July–Sept), prompting a move to steeper areas, and if the cliff faces W (like Taipan) the area can be very hot in summer (Dec–Feb). There are good shaded cliffs for all but the hottest summer day. Spring and autumn are generally ideal.

Location/access: (See map, opposite.) The Grampians covers a large area and is divided into North, Central and Southern. Coming from Melbourne (235km) you can enter it through Dunkeld, Halls Gap or Roses Gap. Many of the popular crags are on the northern tip and are easily accessed from the main Melbourne–Adelaide Hwy (8). The area can be accessed from the W through Horsham, or by cutting across from Mt Arapiles/Natimuk. See individual cliff sections for access.

Camping and local amenities: There are a variety of great camping spots throughout the Grampians. National park sites (fees apply, roughly $10 per site per night) have pit toilets and barbecues. It is possible to 'bush camp' throughout the Grampians and there are often good camping caves (though some such as

Bundaleer are becoming increasingly popular). See individual cliffs (below) for nearest official campsite. Water is not always readily available (summer and autumn especially) so it is best to carry your own.

There are lots of other accommodation options in towns like Halls Gap, Horsham and Stawell. There are cabins and a tavern (the Trooper's Arms) just down from Mt Difficult on the Roses Gap Road. With the exception of Hall's Gap (and Wartok on the W side) there is no petrol in the Grampians.

Transport: Own vehicle or hitch. From Hall's Gap you can walk to a number of cliffs.

Guidebooks: *Grampians Selected Climbs*, Simon Mentz and Glenn Tempest, Open Spaces Publishing, Melbourne 1988; *Victoria: A Guide to Selected Rockclimbs at Mt Arapiles, The Grampians and Mt Buffalo*, Chris Baxter with Glenn Tempest, Wild Publications, Melbourne, 1994; *Rock Climbs of Hall's Gap and the Wonderland Range*, Bill Andrews, Victorian Climbing Club, 1987; *A Rockclimber's Guide to the Northern Grampians*, Bill Andrews, Victorian Climbing Club, 1987; *The North Grampians Update*, Bill Andrews, Victorian Climbing Club, 1995; *The Black Guide (Black Range)*, Bill Andrews, Victorian Climbing Club, 1987; *Wonderland Supplement*, Bill Andrews, Victorian Climbing Club, 1992; *The Victoria Range*, Kieran Loughran, Victorian Climbing Club, 1989; *Mount Stapylton Amphitheatre*, Kieran Loughran, 1997; *South-east Grampians*, Chris Baxter, Victorian Climbing Club, 1991; *New Climbs in the South-Eastern Grampians*, Chris Baxter, Wild Publications, 1993; *South Western Grampians Interim Climbing Guide*, Gordon Talbett, James MacIntosh, Victorian Climbing Club, 1987; *Black Ian's Rocks and Central Grampians Update*, Rock Guides, Glenn Tempest and Chris Baxter, Wild Publications, 1989; *A Grampians Rock Climbing Guide: The Mount Difficult Range*, James Macintosh & Bill Andrews, Victorian Climbing Club, 1999; *A Grampians Rock Climbing Guide to the Asses Ears*, Glen Donohue, Victorian Climbing Club, Melbourne, 2000.

Information: Rangers station in Halls Gap, tel: (03) 5356 4381

Bouldering: The Grampians have shaped up to be one of the top bouldering destinations in the world. Currently the hardest problems in Australia all reside here. This includes *Eve Rêve*, Hollow Mtn cave, V14, by Swiss Boulderer Fred Nicole, *Cave Rave*, Hollow Mtn cave, V13/14, by Austrian Klem Loskot, *Ammagamma*, Citadel, V13 by Loskot, *Sleepy Hollow*, Hollow Mtn cave, V12/13, Nicole and a host of other V12s by Nicole on his 2000 visit. For more information visit the Boulder Lounge web site (see Appendix 3).

Mt Staplyton (Northern Grampians)

Includes the areas of the Summerday Valley, Wall of Fools, Stapylton Amphitheatre, Hollow Mountain, Taipan Wall, Spurt Crag and Lower Taipan.

Geology/type of rock/quality: Sandstone ***

Grades: Up to 32.

Height: Up to 100m.

Number of routes: Several hundred.

Climbing style: Stapylton offers a good range of sandstone climbing. There are the old style classic lines of the Main Wall and the consumer beginner classics of Summerday Valley. Opposite this the Wall of Fools offers excellent, if hard, routes on a steep wall. In the Amphitheatre there are long traditional routes and on Taipan Wall immaculate, steep, pumpy, modern routes—sometimes sporty. At the base of Taipan Wall, Spurt Wall offers modern sport routes on steep, orange rock.

Season: As for Grampians.

Location/access: Coming up the Western Hwy (8) from Melbourne, turn L into Wonwondah Rd (the sign is to Laharum/Wartok/Mt Zero and Halls Gap), 11km past Dadswell Bridge and the Giant Koala. Turn L off this sealed road (2.9km) onto the Flat Rock Road (dirt) then R at first intersection (Halls Gap/Mt Zero Rd—dirt). The Hollow Mountain Campground, an old quarry, soon appears on your L. Summerday Valley is accessed from here. Continue along this road to the Mt Zero picnic ground for Taipan Wall.

Camping and local amenities: You can camp at the Hollow Mountain campsite (fees apply) but it does get quite crowded. There is a new Mt Stapylton campground 6km further along this road (curve around S) at the end of Plantation Rd (fees). It has toilets etc. and is a nice spot.

Transport: Own vehicle or arrange a lift over from Natimuk/Arapiles.

Guidebooks: *Grampians Selected Climbs*, Simon Mentz and Glenn Tempest, Open Spaces Publishing, Melbourne, 1988; *Victoria: A Guide to Selected Rockclimbs at Mt Arapiles, The Grampians and Mt Buffalo*, Chris Baxter with Glenn Tempest, Wild Publications, Melbourne, 1994; *A Rockclimber's Guide to the Northern Grampians*, Bill Andrews, Victorian Climbing Club, 1987; *The North Grampians Update*, Bill Andrews, Victorian Climbing Club, 1995; *Mount Stapylton Amphitheatre*, Kieran Loughran, 1997.

Information: Rangers station in Hall's Gap, tel: (03) 5356 4381.

Summerday Valley

Take the track that starts on the W side of the quarry car park. A track junction is soon reached with the R-hand branch leading up to the old campsite and the other to the W valley. **The Wall of Fools** is R—the big orange wall with a huge arch in the middle, and black streaks on the L end. On the L side the wall is called the **Back Wall**. It has some of the best easy climbs in the Gramps. The descent is a scramble down on the long south end of the buttress, into a slot. The climbs L>R are:

▲	13	20m		1979

Regatta — The good looking line at L on wall.

▲	12	20m		1979

De Blanc — The companion route up the attractive corner to R.

▲	10	20m		1984

An-tics — Thin crack on face 1m R.

▲	22	20m		1984

Tootsie Direct — Juggy crack to R. Step L and up to slot then R and up black streak to top. *Tootsie* 19 20m 1983 finishes L from slot.

▲	17	23m		1983

Overkill — 3m R of *Tootsie* (marked with a square). Up seam and steep pocketed wall.

▲	7	22m		1985

Eat More Parsley — Corner 4m R of *Overkill*, in front of 2 blocks. Up line on L wall, then finish up jugs on R.

▲	9	26m		(2) 1984

Hard Drain — To R are two initialled lines, *Drooby* 10 and *Odlid Baggins* 9. 1. (15m) Starting between these climb up line to ledge. 2. (11m) Up crack on R.

On the **Wall of Fools** the L most of the three prominent cracks on the L is:

▲▲	21	30m	1983	**Soweto**
▲▲	25	25m	1985	**Diazepam** – Takes the middle streak. Pro is thin.
▲	29	25m	1986	**Innocent Fool** – R streak. 3 bolts.

▲	28	25m	1990

Zero Blunder – Wall and seam 10m R of *Innocent Fool*. 5 BRs.

▲▲	28	25m	1989

Milupa – Takes the L side of the arch. 4BR and a fixed wire to top.

▲	24	34m	(2)[24,24]1985

Idiot Wind – 1. (17m) Start directly below arch and climb up to high FH (scary clip). Up and R to hanging belay. 2. (17m) Up and L around arch. Hard past poor BR leads to a limited rest then up short steep crack.

▲	21	33m	2)[21,20] 1985+

Lofty Odours – R of *Idiot Wind* is a closed seam. 1. (17m) Up seam to ledge on L. 2. (16m) Step off L of ledge and pull onto overhanging wall. Up and R to finish up arête.

▲	15	25m	1985

Flake of Fear – The black streak and flake to the L.

The **Main Wall** is the wall that faces the same direction as the Wall of Fools, but is behind the Back Wall (descent is the same). It can be reached by walking L (S) around the Back Wall, L of *Regatta* (or through slot around R). There is a number of good old style routes here including (R>L):

	16	30m	1979

Underneath the Arches – Initialled R-hand line.

▲	20	30m	1980

Wasp – Bulging jam crack 1m to L.

▲	19	30m	1979

Master Kate – Initialled weakness 2m L.

▲▲	18	40m	1980

Walking on the Moon – Starts as for *Frogs Hollow* 15 (initialled) going up corner using flake on L wall, then stepping L and following the roof line diagonally up L to finish as for *21st CSM* (below).

▲	21	35m	1980

21st Century Schizoid Man – Initialled crack 5m L.

| ▲ | 23 | 35m | 1984 |

Sixty Second Sixpence Man – Move L from 21st CSM at 6m (where obvious) and up line.

| ▲ | 18 | 25m | 1979 |

Halfway Hotel – Initialled line 8m L, finishing up L-hand corner (or R).

| ▲▲ | 17 | 25m | 1980 |

Texas Radio and the Big Beat – A gem. Initialled pocketed crack 5m L, stepping L to follow corner to top.

| ▲ | 16 | 20m | 1979 |

Rat's Tail – Faintly initialled crack 4m L.

| | 16 | 25m | 1981 |

The Changeling – Initialled line up face, trav L for 2m and up.

| ▲▲ | 11 | 25m | 1979 |

Waxman – Start R of descent gully (initialled) and climb R—leading flake into obvious line.

| ▲ | 24 | 25m | 1984 |

Fritz and Cyclops – 30m L of descent gully is a steep line with an undercut start.

Up the hill towards Hollow Mountain is **Gun Buttress** with the classic:

| ▲▲ | 23 | 20m | 1983 | **Powder Monkey** |

And above this (on Hollow Mountain walking track) the ferociously leaning **Sandanista Cliff** which has the hard routes (L>R):

▲	30	20m	1989	**Contra Arms Pump**
▲▲	30	22m	1989 (sport)	**Daniel Or-Tiger**
▲▲	32	22m	1988/9	**Samosa**
▲▲	23	35m	1982	**Sandanista**

The obvious diagonal (L>R) line:

| ▲ | 26 | 30m | 1992 | **Sandanista Direct** |
| ▲ | 30 | 20m | 1987 | **Journey Through Nicaragua** |

From Sandanista a walk L brings you to **Cut Lunch Wall** with some excellent routes, and past this is the sport area **Van Diemen's Land** with many good routes including the classic:

| ▲▲ | 24 | 25m | 1992 | **Body Count** |

Stapylton Amphitheatre

The Mt Stapylton Amphitheatre, or the Horseshoe, is a grand area with long, moderate-graded routes. It may be approached by either slithering down the descent gully (carefully—it is most dangerous at the bottom or when wet) which is situated at the end of the Red Wall (at the end of Hollow Mountain) or bashing in from Clicke Wall. It is more common to come by following the walking track in over Flat Rock (from the Mount Zero picnic area car park). It is also possible to come via a 4.4km walk from the new Stapylton campsite.

If approaching via Flat Rock follow the track down into the bottom of the Amphitheatre and follow the lesser track on the L which heads up toward the bottom of the obvious corner of *Simpleton* on Central Buttress. To the L (N) the Northern Walls are divided from the Central by the descent gully. To descend it is best to abseil from various points, though the dangerous gully (above) is an option.

Northern Buttress

▲▲▲   14   40m   (2)[14,14] 1965

Trident – A newly recognised old classic. Start about 60m L of descent gully at a flaring groove (initialled). 1. (21m) Up the R wall of groove to ledge. Trav 3m L then up another groove to small stance. 2. (19m) Trav 3m R and up steep crack. Exit L or R (loose blocks). To descend scramble 20m R (exposed) to tree (40m rap) or carefully to top of cliff.

Central Buttress

This is the area that runs to the R from the descent gully as far as the Grey and Green Walls and is readily identified by the striking corner line of *Simpleton*. Descent is by chains 5m below finish (easy scramble) of *Simpleton* (50m rap). The climbs L–R are:

▲▲   18   78m   (3) 1966 {1975}

Simpleton – A superb route. 1. (27m) Bash up the corner line until it is possible to step into a cave (or come in from R). 2. (30m) Move up past BR and continue up the corner for 15m then step R to shallow corner which is followed to a small ledge (dodgy BR). 3. (21m) Continue up the corner to below the roof. Hand trav L to finish (or trav L 4m below roof).

▲▲▲   23   70m   (3)[22,23,23] 1988

Missing – A superb sustained route. Starts 15m R of *Simpleton* at trees on ledge, and 3m R of crack system that is *Technical Ecstasy*. 1. (15m) Pull onto the wall and climb up R past BR to a fixed RP, and up to a flake (on R) and up to belay. 2. (35m) Step L to the line and follow the thin crack up the wall, over the bulge and up a hard slab to a second bulge. Trav L past BR, make a long reach past the bulge and move back R to the line. Up the line to an easy trav line taking this L to belay in the corner. 3. (20m) Move back R to the line and go up to the roof and out the flake system.

▲▲   19   90m   (30)[16,19,-] 1977

Technical Ecstasy – Starts 3m R of *Missing* at attractive crack system. 1. (35m) Up through the bushes to bottom of a crack. Up the thin crack continuing in the line to belay on 2nd ledge to R. 2. (30m) Up a short deep groove to an overhang, passing on L. Continue up to an overlap, move L to a thin crack and up to next main overlap. Trav L and up crack through bulge. L again to belay in *Simpleton*'s corner 3. 30m Up corner to roof and hand trav L to finish.

Mania (Direct Finish) – Start and 1. (35m) as for *Technical Ecstasy*. 2. (30m) Move R to groove on far R of wall. Up this to belay 10m below capping overhang. 3. (20m) Climb the slab just L of the arête to the overhang and through (!)

The Grey and Green Walls are the huge slabby cliffs to the R (S) of the Central Buttress. To get there walk along from Central Buttress until you reach the twin cracks on the L side. You are heading up towards the centre of the diagonal roofs above.

▲▲ 21 105m (5)[19,21,21,15,19] 1990–95
The Navigator – Start just R of the twin cracks. 1. (20m) Up face for 3m, R and up past BR to ledge. Up easy slab (no pro) to tree. Bring up seconds then move the belay 10m R to boulders below short overhanging wall. 2. (40m) Up wall to BR then L a little and up to large horizontal break. Up wall to R-hand end of long bushy ledge then trav R to line of flakes up centre of face (BR). Up flakes, then slabs to BB. 3. (20m) Up slabs past BRs to diagonal crack leading to roofs. Hand trav L, along flake, the hand trav R to rest. Wide step R to semi-hanging belay (cams). 4. (15m) Diagonally R up face to ledge and R across this to belay in next line. 5. (25m) Up line through overhang. There is a rap chain on a bushy ledge to the S (R-Fl), down a short chimney gully (2 x 40m). Second chain at L end of large terrace. Or walk off S.

Taipan Wall

The premier cliff in the Grampians: 70m of overhung sandstone that catches the afternoon sun and sends an orange beacon across the plains, calling climbers in. This cliff has some of the finest lines in the country. There is nothing easy on this cliff so if you are looking for something to amble up this afternoon you had better skip this section.

The routes on Taipan are a mixture of naturally protected and bolted. Virtually all the climbs are done as sport climbs, in that they are pre-equipped from rap and rehearsed. Even so, these routes are sustained and intimidating and patience is needed by both leader and belayer.

It wasn't until the '60s when the first route was completed, with the team of Ian Guild and Mike Stone bolting and bivvying their way up the wall to produce *The Seventh Pillar* (16A4). This was an impressive effort in its day and while mostly free now (28 via variants) it can still be done with a bit of aid at 18 M2 to give middle-grade climbers the chance to experience this excellent route. Kim Carrigan came and went in the early '80s and dabbled around at the L-hand end of the cliff, putting up some good routes (including *The Great Divide* 27), but he failed to develop the main wall's free climbing potential. In 1988 Steve Monks freed the old aid route *Seventh Banana* at 27 and soon after HB (Malcolm Matheson) climbed the outstanding *Serpentine* 29 (31 in its original style). The next few years saw more excellent routes put up by Andy Pollitt (*Rage*, *Black Adder*, and *World Party*), Jared McCulloch (*Mr Joshua*), the UK's Pete Cresswell (on *Black Adder*, and *World Party*), Simon Mentz (*Father Oblivion*) as well as HB (*Mirage*, *Sirocco*, and *Annaconda*) and Steve Monks (*Venom* and *Kaa*). More recently Stuart Wyithe (*Cardigan St*), Gordon Poultney (*Invisible Fist*, *Medusa*) and the UK's Richard Heap (*Groovy*) have chipped in, as has Dave Jones (*Tourniquet*, *Daedelus*)

To get to Taipan (25min) walk up and over Flat Rock (from Mt Zero picnic ground) and into the Amphitheatre. After crossing a clearing you'll see a track marked (arrow on boulder) leading R. Follow old track for 50m turning L and heading up to wall at distinctive 8m high pinnacle. Cliff faces W. See map on p. 98 for topo.

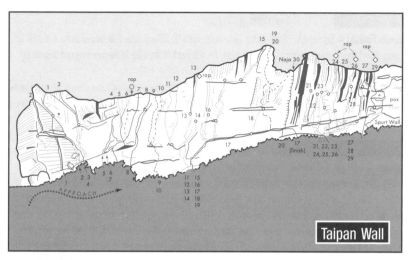

Taipan Wall

1. *Atomic Tadpole* 20	11. *Sirocco* 26	20. *Serpentine* 29
2. *Tokyo Connection* 18	12. *Father Oblivion* 26	21. *Groovy* 28
3. *Sordid Orchids* 26 M1	13. *Cardigan Street* 31	22. *Snake Flake* 26
4. *Black Adder* 29	14. *Mirage* 27	23. *The Invisible Fist* 26
5. *Dinosaurs Don't Dyno* 26	15. *The Seventh Pillar* 28 or 18 M2	24. *World Party* 27
6. *Clean Sweep* 24 M1	or LHV 23	25. *Anaconda* 28
7. *Dance of Life* 24 M1	16. *Medusa* 25	26. *Mr Joshua* 26
8. *The Great Divide* 27	17. *Lawrence of Arabia* 21	27. *Venom* 28
9. *Daedelus* 28	18. *Scud Buster* 24	28. *Tourniquet* 30
10. *The Seventh Banana* 28	19. *Rage* 29	29. *Kaa* 24

	18	45m	(2) [18,18] late 80s	**Tokyo Connection**
▲	20	45m	(2) 1977	**Atomic Tadpole**
▲	26 M1	40m	(2) [25,26M1] late 80s–1990	**Sordid Orchids**

▲	29	40m	(2) [25,29] 1990

Black Adder – Trav R , then up past roof. Many BR. Pumpy.

▲	26	35m	1984

Dinosaurs Don't Dyno – A nice route leading up to an intermittent flake system.

▲	24 M1	35m	1985

Clean Sweep – Sustained and a little bit bold.

▲	24 M1	35m	1984	**Dance of Life**

▲▲	27	50m	(2)[27,24] 1984

The Great Divide — This climb takes the elegant arête which divides the L side and the main wall.

▲▲	28	52m	(2)[21,26] 1989	**Daedelus**

▲▲	28	65m	1975 {1988}

The Seventh Banana — Crux pitch offers some thin wall moves near belay and a pumpy run-out finish.

▲▲	26	60m	(2)[23,27] 1975 {1988}

Sirocco — Another classic tackling a seemingly blank wall. The first pitch is becoming very popular as a climb in itself (21). Rap off. The 2nd pitch has a very hard move past the first BR before blasting up the brilliant wall above.

▲▲	26	52m	(2)[21,26] 1991	**Father Oblivion**
▲▲	31		(2) 1995–1999	**Cardigan Street**

▲▲▲	27	35m	1990

Mirage — How do you grade a 6'6" dyno? An amazing move at the end of another great pitch.

▲▲▲	28 (by variants) or 18 M2	115m	(4) 1966 {1997}

The Seventh Pillar — More of an adventure route than anything else. If you do the original 1st pitch, the old rusty bolt ladder provides some fun. The variant 1st pitch offers a real pump at the grade, and a scary but safe, run-out trav. The 3rd pitch is a novelty crawl along a ledge, while the last pitch is relatively easy (17) but very exposed as it takes you to the top of the turret.

▲▲▲	23	43m	1980	**The Seventh Pillar L Hand Variant**
▲▲▲	25	45m	1995 (unfinished)	**Medusa**

	21	100m	1991

Lawrence of Arabia — A novel trav that starts at *Seventh Pillar* and ends on the ground!

▲	24	75m	(2)[21,24] 1992	**Scud Buster**
▲▲	28	68m	1998	**Feather Boa**
▲▲	29		1992	**Rage**

▲▲▲	29	75m	(2) 1988

Serpentine — Arguably the premier route in Australia. The 2nd pitch offers 40 metres of ultra sustained cranking and is protected by 8 BR as well as natural protection (which was placed on the lead for the first ascent to give it a grade of 31).

▲▲	27	30m	2000

Sidewinder — at 4th bolt on 2nd pitch of *Serpentine* hear R and up past 4BR to 2BB.

▲▲	30	55m	(2) 1998

Naja — An old Steve Monks project finally succumbed.

▲▲	28	30m	1997	Groovy
▲	26	25m	1990	Snake Flake
▲▲	26	26m	1996	The Invisible Fist (of Professor Hidditch Smidditch)
▲▲	27	54m	(3)[21, 27,24] 1990	World Party
▲▲	28	55m	(2)[22,28] 1993	Anaconda

▲▲▲	26	50m	50m (2)[25,26] 1989

Mr Joshua – A classic and justifiably one of the most popular routes on the wall.

▲▲	28	60m	(3)[23,28,25] 1995	Venom
▲	30		(2) [30,27] 1997–98	Tourniquet

▲	24	80m	(4)[23,24,24,23] 1992

Kaa – A wandering route that looks for the line of least resistance and consequently is the easiest free route on Taipan proper.

At the base of the manky R-hand end of Taipan is the popular and sporty **Spurt Wall** and R again the newly named **Afterglow Wall**.

Routes L>R:

	28	1996 (not sport)	Naughty Tickle Town
▲	31	1997/98	Academia
▲▲	31	1998/2000	The Tyranny of Distance
▲▲	31		Lifestyling
	27	1994	Not too Bad
▲▲	24	1994	Menstrual as Anything
▲	24	1995	Dial-A-Lama
▲	27	(3)[21,27,24] 1990	Fabio's route
▲	28	1998	Spurt Girl (aka Wide World of Spurts)
▲	26	1994	This Sporting Life
▲	22	1994	Spurting Mildly

There are a few more uninspiring routes here before reaching Afterglow:

▲	31	18m	2001	Bossanova
▲	29	20m	2000	Chicane
▲	25	18m	2000	Romancing the Tango

Bundaleer

An older, traditional cliff with classic cracks and modern steep face routes. Access is a 10 minute walk, there's a great camping cave and the cliff faces east—a shadier, cooler option in summer.

Geology/type of rock/quality: Sandstone **
Grades: Up to 28.
Height: Up to 50m.

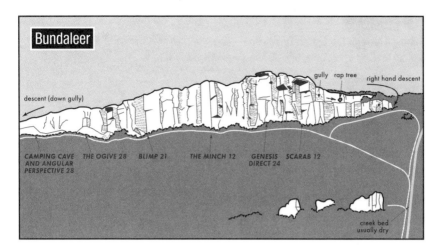

Number of routes: Over 130.

Climbing style: The older, easier routes are traditional sandstone crack lines but some of the more modern, harder routes are very steep, pumpy excursions through steep territory.

Brief history: See Grampians history and refer to guidebooks for more detail.

Season: As for Grampians. Bundaleer gets morning sun and can be good in the afternoon on a hot day.

Location/access: The cliff is not far from Halls Gap. Drive W (at the Mt Rosea Turntable camp site and start of the walking track to Mt Rosea) on the Stony Creek Road (dirt) from the Silverband Road (which can be reached either on the Zumsteins or Dunkeld roads out of Halls Gap). After 2km take first L (the Mt Rosea track). Less than 1km along this is a parking area on the L. A well-formed walking track heads up to the cliff opposite, following a creek bed at first. After a few 100 metres it involves a short, rocky scramble. Immediately above, it forks; the L main branch arrives at the R end of the main cliff near Abseil Crack, and the R one towards the R end of the R-hand section of the cliff. Descent from both the L cliff and the L half of the main cliff is by the major gully just L of the cave, separating the L and main cliffs. Abseil crack divides the main and R cliffs and is commonly abseiled, but there are descent gullies R of this.

Camping and local amenities: The camping cave is at the L end of the main cliff.

Transport: Own vehicle or hitch up from Hall's Gap.

Guidebooks: *Grampians Selected Climbs*, Simon Mentz and Glenn Tempest, Open Spaces Publishing, Melbourne, 1988; *Victoria: A Guide to Selected Rockclimbs at Mt Arapiles, The Grampians and Mt Buffalo*, Chris Baxter & Glenn Tempest, Wild Publications, Melbourne, 1994; *South-east Grampians*, Chris Baxter, Victorian Climbing Club, 1991; *New Climbs in the South-eastern Grampians*, Chris Baxter, Wild Publications, 1993.

Information: Ranger's station in Hall's Gap, tel: (03) 5356 4381.

▲   26   15m   1994

Skulthuggery – Sport route with 6BR and chain on L of camping cave, starting above two blocks on ground.

▲▲▲   28   35m   1983–1995

Angular Perspective – Pump-packed. Sport route 8m R of *Skulthuggery* at finger pockets. Follow line of bolts up wall (27 to chain) and through ceiling.

△ 28 10m 1990

Free Snaking Through the Eighth Dimension – More sport. Start a few metres R of *Angular* and climb line (3BRs) that heads out R, then curves back L to join *Angular Perspective* at chain.

△△ 28 36m 1964 {1982}

Ogive – The roof crack (read horror trench) in the Throne Room (160m R of camping cave).

△△ 23 30m 1983

Dark Passage – Arête R of *Ogive*, starting off the huge block. Step L into shallow line and continue up to a BR. Past this and a PR. R to finish up arête.

△ 24 30m 1982

Front Line – The sabre slashed wall R of the 'dank old-fashioned line' (*Pumpernickel* 17). Up the wall on edges to the crack. Across blankness to an exit into the corner crack line (*Kasolve*).

26 20m 1989

Gotham City – On to wall as for *Front Line*. Up (2BRs) to BB under roof. Lower off to belay.

△ 23 25m 1982

Tough Tips – Dimpled wall R of *Front Line*. Step onto rib and up to useless BR. Continue up *Kasolve* above.

19 48m 1969

Kasolve – Old style struggle. The corner crack, L groove and exit R. Up gully to finish.

△ 25 20m 1989

Berlin Wall – From block R of *Kasolve*, climb wall and seam to BR. Finger pockets to break then quickly to 2BB. Lower off to belay.

△△ 22 25m 1966 {1978}

Dagon's Temple – The two-tiered wall just R of *Berlin Wall* is split by a prominent crack (initialled). An exposed step L to finish.

△ 29 20m 1991

Castlereagh Line – Sport. Seam (3BR) 2m R of arête (*Morepox* 23—initialled). Lower off from chain.

17 30m (2) 1966 {FFA later}

Narcotic – The undercut and overhanging off-width 4m R of *Castlereagh Line* (initialled) 1. (18m) The line, mainly on R wall. 2. (12m) Trav R and down to ledge on nose. Steep wall above.

△△ 25 45m 45m 1971 {1978}

Manic Depressive – Sport route up overhanging arête between *Narcotic* and *Blimp* starting off cairn and following BRs to BB.

Blimp – Classic in all senses of the word! Corner 8m R of *Manic Depressive* (PR, BR). L under roof and step up to ledge. (BBs—most people abseil from here). Step R, climb bulge then on up.

▲▲ 28 46m 46m (2) [28,26] 1989

Touchstone Pictures – Done in one pitch originally. This route eclipsed ▲▲ *Dive, Dive, Dive* 25+ which traversed in from *Blimp* using chipped holds and finished early. Start 3m R of *Blimp*. 1. (26m) Up to the 'brains'. Up and R to corner. Up to 'tatty lower off'. 2. (20m) Thin wall (PR), then up L to cracked overhang. Over this to hanging corner (2BRs). Finish past old PR on R.

▲▲ 25 50m (3) [25,21,21] 1966 {1978}

Ostler – 1. (19m) Thin crack R (initialled) of *Touchstone Pictures* to BB. 2. (13m) Corner crack on L. L to ledge and L on this to BB. 3. (18m) Up to overhang and up crack. L and up corner.

▲ 26 25m 1994

The Beckoning – Up arête above where *Ostler* eases (4BR to rap).

▲ 25 20m early 80s

Bliss – Delicate groove then wall, 3m R of *Ostler* past 3 BR to old PR belay. Finish as for *Ostler*.

20 28m 1989

Blankety Blank – Climb the juggy groove 3m R of chimney (*Infidel* 14). Step up and R, then veer L to easier ground. Finish up *Infidel* or preferably trav R and finish up *Pathos*.

▲▲ 21 54m (2) [21,21] 1969 {1977+}

Pathos – 1. (29m) (crux) Follow the thin cracks (initialled) 2m R of *Blankety Blank*. Many abseil from tree at 25m. 2. (25m) Bridge chimney on L to an airy trav L on horizontal crack. Up vertical crack, wall and short cracks above.

▲▲ 12 40m (2) 1965

The Minch – Big crack 25m R of *Pathos* (L of huge jutting prow).

▲▲ 21 50m 1991

The Flying Circus – The most exposed route on the cliff. Trav R (sparse pro) from *The Minch* above the lip of the ceiling to 'the prow of the battleship'. This is split by a hidden thin crack, which accepts wires. Straight up and finish direct over roof.

▲▲ 16 46m (3) 1965

Gerontian – 1. (15m) Climb small corner (initialled) above step in track 30m L of *The Minch*. Step R at 3m and climb poorly protected wall (original) or step directly to arête (better) and up and L into crack. 2. (17m) (crux) Corner (PR). 3. (14m) Step up from ledge and trav L in hand crack under overhang to enter vertical crack. Up. (Or climb hand crack above belay at 15.)

▲ 23 35m 1969 {early 80s}

Genesis – Up to and up incipient corner 8m R of *Gerontian* (in middle of impressive wall), starting from block on R.

At top get into horizontal trav (*Odysseus* 17) and follow it R (below line of old BR) to good ledge. Can do *Stone Ocean* from here.

▲▲　24　50m　　　1983

Genesis Direct – Follow the corner as for *Genesis* and continue directly up the wall past two BRs. Pull through the overhang to a ledge —walk off to the L.

▲　22　35m　　　1982

Stone Ocean – Scary. Up *Moloch Variant* or *Genesis* to ledge. The arête is followed to a niche on R. Out L up and across past 'bizarre washbasin' feature, then up to prominent roof on arête. L to a hanging ledge. Up wall above to belay below overhang. Walk off L.

▲　18　46m　　　(2) 1967

Moloch – Crack struggle (finish on R) behind conifer 10m R of *Genesis*.

▲　22　27m　　　1996

Moloch Variant – The unlikely looking seam R of *Genesis*. From block, up 5m, trav R and then up *Moloch*.

▲▲　16　46m　　　(3) 1965

The Frog – 1. (12m) Start (initialled) 5m R of *Moloch* and go straight up to corner on R at 6m. Up this (PR) and exit L. BB. 2. (15m) (16) Corner (PR). Exit L below ceiling. 3. (19m) As for *Moloch*.

▲▲　16　64m　　　(4) 1965 {FFA later}

Basilisk – 1. (15m) Climb initialled line 1m R of *The Frog* until level with roof on R. 2. (16m) Continue up line (old BR on L) to stance. 3. (9m) Trav R (PR), easing. Dramatic! 4. (24m) R and up wall under 'horns'. Chimney. ▲ *The Direct Finish* (original) goes through roof instead of going R. ▲ *Basilisk Variant* 14 20m (2a) travs R above the lip of the big roof, then diagonally up and around arête to prominent corner, then up easily to ledge and finishes up *Basilisk*.

▲▲　12　62m　　　(3) 1964

Scarab – Faintly initialled line below huge roof and near where walking track reaches cliff. 1. (28m) Climb crack switching to L crack at 17m (BR), then to R crack. Up this to BB on R. 2. (10m) Trav L. 3. (24m) As for *Basilisk* pitch 4.

▲▲　23　27m　　　1970 {early '80s)

Scarab Direct – The mighty capping roof starting from *Scarab* and up open book corner. Go around R and straight up.

Mt Rosea

The grand old cliff of the Grampians, where reputations have been made and lost, along with lunches. Still one of the best places in Victoria to go out for a big adventure on moderate multi-pitch routes. The climbs are described here L>R starting at the Giant Staircase and old walking track. The cliff faces NE. There are some large dangerous blocks on a few routes here. Take care—wear a helmet.

Geology/type of rock/quality: Sandstone * to ***
Grades: Up to 26.

Height: Up to 140m.

Number of routes: Over 150.

Climbing style: Traditional sandstone lines with some harder lines on arêtes and seams.

Brief history: See under Grampians and refer to guidebooks for more detail.

Season: As for Grampians. Gets sun in the morning.

Location/access: A walking track (20min) leaves the W side of the junction of the Silverband (off either Dunkeld or Zumsteins roads from Halls Gap) and Stony Creek roads. You can camp here (fees apply). After about 5–10 minutes a junction is reached. The old track heads off left (signposted climbers only) and meets the cliff at the foot of the Giant's Staircase (the most convenient descent for almost

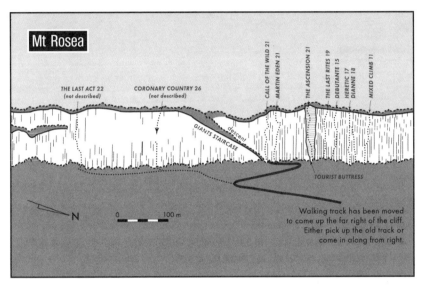

all climbs) and then continues up this mighty ramp, then S along the cliff top to the summit. The new track for walkers swings to the R and up and back L along the cliff meeting up with the old one. You can take this track and come in along the cliff from the R.

Camping and local amenities: There is a national park camp site (fees apply) at the car park at the start of the walk in.

Transport: Own vehicle or hitch up from Hall's Gap.

Guidebooks: As for Bundaleer, p. 101.

Information: Ranger's station in Hall's Gap, tel: (03) 5356 4381.

▲▲   21   126m   (5) [18,-,21,17,-] 1976

Call of the Wild — Start at indistinct crack 50m R of olf Giant Staircase track, L of substantial tree. 1. (48m) Crack for 17m, L and up grey crack to slabby area. 2. (25m) Jog up to ledge R of big corner (*Bus Stop* 17). 3. (23m) Climb up towards off-width roof (loose block) and at 3m go L and into corner above. After a couple of moves trav back R, and up to tree. 4. (9m) Hand trav R to an exposed belay. 5. (21m) Up wall R of arête.

▲▲▲ 19 112m   (3) 1976

Martin Eden – One of Rosea's best. 1. (25m) Climb the difficult, poorly protected grey wall 10m R of *Call of the Wild* (just R of tree) then head up easily towards orange corners and ledge on the R. 2. (43m) (crux) Up to and up the short corner above, then into orange V-groove on R. 3. (44m) Follow the line from the middle of the ledge. Trav L under ceiling and pull into the final hanging V-groove.

▲▲ 22 82m   (3) [22,19,21] 1983–89

Crank Hard, Crank Fast – Cruising – 1. (25m) Veer up L from start of *Tourist Buttress* (see below) to arête. Up 2. (25m) Up and R, around arête and into 2nd pitch of *Fringe Dweller*. Up this to ledge. 3. (32m) From ledge move L and make some committing moves to BR. Continue up wall and through cracked roof to reach big ledge. Either finish up *Scarface* or rap 2 x 50m from big tree on L.

▲ 21 38m   1991

Scarface – The *only* way to finish *Tourist Buttress* or *The Ascension*. Next to the large tree (2BB) at the foot of the final pitch of *Tourist Buttress* then climb the shallow corner and arête on the R.

▲▲ 23 116m   (5) [23,18,19,14, -] 1963 {1974–78}

Tourist Buttress – The tourist buttress is the obvious large proud buttress that dominates the cliff. 1. (24m) (crux – can be aided at 19M1) Climb the broken, initialled crack on the front of the buttress. The thin crack (either direct or by 23 variant to L) above bristles with old PRs from the first ascent. Step L at top. 2. (20m) Step up R and climb the wall. Step R to arête. Then either go up for 10m to a ledge or step L and follow a groove to the same ledge. 3. (24m) Climb the thin groove above to make a tricky move on to the L wall. Climb the beautiful wall bristling with more PRs. Step L to next line (more old PRs). Finish up the groove above. 4. (15m) Trav 3m R ad go up to a ledge just R of large tree (landmark). 5. (33m) Chimney or finish up *Scarface*.

▲▲▲ 21 117m   (4) [21,-,21,-] 1969 {mid '70s–1977}

The Ascension – Classic. 1. (33m) Climb up into the corner 3m R of *Tourist Buttress* and ascend it with increasing difficulty. R round overhang and up (crux) to next corner, which is climbed to where it steepens. Step L and climb the arête for 12m to ledge. 2. (9m) Diagonally up and L around arête to second stance on *Tourist Buttress*. 3. (40m) Step R and climb the face with twin, thin cracks. 4. (35m) Easily up L hand line or *Scarface*—or rap off from big tree (2x50m)

▲▲ 21 130m   (5) [21,19,-,20,-] 1976

Fringe-dweller – 1. (27m) Climb *The Ascension*, finishing up the corner direct. 2. (24m) Step L, then up by way of an overhang and flaring crack to a ledge at the foot of a prominent R-facing corner. Pro poor. 3. (27m) Trav 3m R on the ledge to a second smaller R facing corner. Climb it until a few m above two BRs. Trav L to the R-facing corner and climb it steeply for 6m to stance on L. 4. (12m) Go up and R to 1.5m R of triangular overhang. Enter the shallow, R-facing corner above. 5. (35m) Up, or *Scarface*, or rap. ▲ *Fringe-dweller Direct* 23 18m takes the thin corner above 2nd belay. The ▲▲ *Skywalker Finish* 22 70m (2) [22,18] 1981 is also good. 4a. (45m) Move R into the crack and up steep exposed old aid line (*The Prescription* 22). Up to overhang and up corner above. Step R and climb line to ledge. 5a. (25m) Trav L under prow, finishing up deep line above.

▲▲ **22** **18m (1st pitch only)**

The Prescription – 1. (18m) Climb the clean initialled corner R of *The Ascension*. Rap off.

▲ **18** **30m (1st pitch only)** 1966 {FFA Later}

Rip Corner – A good test of skill. Distinctive clean flake (initialled) 3m R of *The Prescription*. Rap off.

▲▲▲ **19** **124m** (4)[18,18,19,17] 1968/9 {1976}

Requiem—The Last Rites – 1. (33m) Climb the faintly initialled crack 10m R of *RIP Corner*. From ledge (PR) at 12m, move R and climb up to the overhang and through and up to a small stance on the R. Take care with anchors! 2. (24m) Step L and climb corner, exiting to small stance. 3. (26m) Trav L to daunting corner above. Climb it past PR and exit L above a small overhang; climb juggy wall to ledge below overhang. PR. 4. (41m) Up L-facing corner to foot of crack (can belay here) and up.

▲▲ **15** **117m** (5)[12,15,13,14,11] 1966

Debutante – Sustained and popular, however there is loose rock on this climb (especially on 2nd pitch) 1. (24m) Climb wall (3m R of *Requiem–Last Rites* at rippled wall) and trav R to corner at 12m. Climb the corner to a block and trav R to a ledge. Chain. 2. (36m) The magnificent and sustained corner above. 3. (15m) Up to ledge then trav L to base of a major corner which leads up to a sheltered nook below a corner-crack. 4. (27m) Climb the corner, 'which gets harder, until you find yourself astride the enormous loose block, contemplating the intimidating trav R to a small stance on the arête in a position of considerable exposure'. 5. (15m) Step R and go up for 5m. Trav L and finish up L groove.

▲ **20** **24m** 1970 {70s}

Debutante Direct Start – A classic crack, usually done as a climb in its own right. Start at the obvious crack on the wall just R of *Debutante*. Surmount the overhang and climb the classic crack to the first stance of *Debutante*. Abseil from chain.

▲ **26** **60m** (3)[26,18,26] 1983—1st pitch not yet lead.

Angry Young Men – A lonely lead up a blank arête. 1. (25m) Blank arête just R of *Debutante DS* past 2BR to *Debutante* chain. 2. (20m) R to arête. Up to belay on *The Jesus Factor*. 3. (15m) L on to rib and up past BR. Finish on R.

▲▲ **23** **60m** (2)[23,23] 1983

The Jesus Factor – 1. 20m R of *Debutante DS*. Climb up L to crack. Step L at cracked bulge and climb it. Trav L at horizontals. Up prow. Single BB. 2. (30m) R arête, with hard moves past BR (back it up with a nut!) R and up to big ledge. Rap off slings.

▲▲ **17** **117m** (5)[15,17,17,17,16] 1969

Heretic – Watch out for loose blocks. Start at the line leading to a conspicuous L-facing corner, 4m L of large tree and 27m R of *Debutante* (4m R of *The Jesus Factor*)—faintly initialled S (*Speculation* 15). 1. (24m) Up line, through steepness and up to ledge on L (pro to L). 2. Step R and climb corner to sloping ledge. 3. (24m) Move L for 3m and climb diagonal flake leading back to corner. Up corner (loose) to ledge on L. 4. (23m) From top of detached block pull onto juggy wall and up to thin crack. Veer R and up to small bottomless L-facing corner. Up this (loose) then L and up to ledge. 5. (23m) Up, then L to L-facing corner and to top.

▲▲▲ | **18** | **120m** | (4)[18,17,17,16] 1968-1970

Dianne – Starts 8m R of *Heretic* and 4m R of big tree. 1. (32m) Up easy crack, then step up and R and follow groove through overhang. Up, then L more easily to ledge below corner. (*Direct Start* 19 starts behind tree and climbs weakness there). 2. (40m) Up corner until it becomes broken (24m) then step R, up a few metres, and back L. Up to exit on to good ledge to L. 3. (25m) Up flaw through overhangs. Veer L-wards up easy (poor pro) rock to L end of overlap (*Heretic*). Up small L-facing corner to stance. 4. (16m) Up, then slightly L to L-facing corner and top.

▲▲ | **19** | **146m** | (5)1975-77

Hard Times – 1. (38m) Up V-groove just R of *Dianne*. Just above the level of the first belay of *Mixed Climb* (tree to R), move R below a bulge (you can go straight up twin-cracks here to 2nd belay – 20 50m) and climb the crack above the tree to a second (smaller) tree in corner. 2. (20m) Corner crack. 3. (38m) Trav L to tree at base of two grooves. The R one of the two grooves gives superb climbing to a ledge below an overhang. Trav L over blocks. 4. (25m) Go back R from the blocks and enter a groove above. Committing climbing leads diagonally R up the wall to a pedestal below the final crackless corner. 5. (25m) (crux) Trav L to a crack on the L wall and climb it and above.

▲▲▲ | **11** | **120m** | (5) 1961

Mixed Climb – Start at faint initials 6m R of *Dianne* and 1m R of *Hard Times*. 1. (24m) Climb up to the foot of the deceptively steep corner. 2. (24m) Up this leading to a small stance, and PR at the foot of a chimney. Up this for 2m, then trav 5m R. Now up (PR) to comforting ledge. 3. (20m) Line to ledge at 15m. Step R to foot of corner. 4. (21m) Go 3m R and climb a scrubby gully to a ledge in the corner. Corner to a ledge on R. 5. (31m) Up for 5m, then R to distinct crack which veers up R to an old tree.

Buandik (The Gallery)

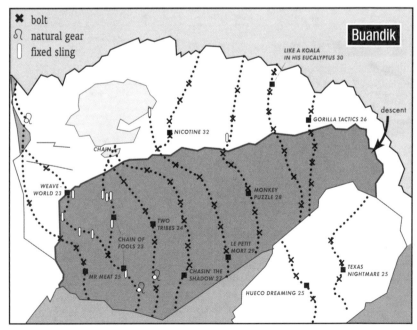

The Grampians first sport cliff (pity about the walk) and a lovely piece of rock on which to burn your muscles to ash. Don't bother making the walk if you want anything under 23. The cliff is shady virtually all day (although it faces W) and stays fairly dry. It is cold up here in winter. Most routes are completely bolt protected (with some weird in situ tat threads) but a couple require a piece or two.

Geology/type of rock/quality: Sandstone ***
Grades: Up to 32.
Height: Up to 23m.
Number of routes: Over 15.
Climbing style: Steep, pumpy sandstone sport routes.
Brief history: A brief foray by 'The Wasters' was followed in 1991 by Glenn Tempest, which started the development of the Grampians first sport crag. Tempest added four routes including *Chasin the Train* 27. In 1992, Malcolm Matheson attacked the steep walls here with fervour, the best of his routes being *Monkey Puzzle* 28. Other hard additions have been Helmut Nesadba's 1992 *Le Petit Mort* 29, Jean-Minh Trinh-Thieu's 1994 *Like a Koala* 30 and the 1996 ascent of *Nicotine* 32 by Garth Miller.
Season: As for Grampians. Buandik is in shade most of the day and stays pretty dry because it so steep. It can be bitterly cold here in winter though.
Location/access: The Buandik area of cliffs (of which the Gallery is one) is on the W side of the southern Grampians. Coming from Melbourne you can wind through the Grampians from Halls Gap or come from the S, along the Glenelg Hwy (112) from Ballarrat to Dunkeld, up the Dunkeld–Cavendish Rd to Cavendish, and turning N towards Horsham on the Henty Hwy (107).

 The walk is 30min uphill. Follow the track L towards Billimina Shelter from Buandik picnic area (not R to the falls). Before reaching the shelter there is another fork (takes the L uphill). Continue on the track which becomes progressively fainter, curving slightly R. Near the top of the hill the track fades out and ends at a chimney cleft. Descend this, and go straight out from the cliff for 20–30m. To your R (FO from the cleft) is a wall covered in chalk.
Camping and local amenities: Camping is at the Buandik campground (fees apply) accessed via Billywing Rd from the Henty Highway. Coming from Arapiles and Natimuk, turn off SE at E edge of Natimuk then R at T-intersection and silo), go S through Noradjuha and turn L (E) into Jallumba Rd (turns into Mockinya Rd). This will bring you out on the Henty Hwy. Turn S and (after about 30km) watch for L turn to Buandik campground.
Transport: Own vehicle or arrange a lift over from Natimuk/Arapiles.
Guidebooks: *Grampians Selected Climbs*, Simon Mentz and Glenn Tempest, Open Spaces Publishing, Melbourne, 1988. For other cliffs in the area: *The Victoria Range*, Kieran Loughran, Victorian Climbing Club, 1989; *South Western Grampians Interim Climbing Guide*, Gordon Talbett & James MacIntosh, Victorian Climbing Club, 1987.
Information: Ranger's station at Hall's Gap, tel: (03) 5356 4381.

The climbs (L>R) are (see topo, opposite):

	25	24m	1991	**Mr Meat**
▲▲	23	25m	1991	**Weaveworld**

▲	23	15m	1992	**Chain of Fools**
▲	24	15m	1991	**Two Tribes**
▲	27	15m	1992	**Chasin' the Shadow**
▲	29	20m	1992	**Le Petit Mort**
▲	32	23m	1996	**Nicotine**
▲▲▲	28	22m	1992	**Monkey Puzzle**
▲	30	20m	1994	**Like a Koala in His Eucalyptus**
▲	26	15m	1992	**Gorilla Tactics**
	25	9m	1992	**Hueco Dreaming**
▲	25	12m	1992	**Texas Nightmare**

Arapiles

Mount Arapiles is a rugged scarp that sticks up surprisingly out of the dusty plains 350km west of Melbourne. It is one of the finest climbing areas in the world and for any aspiring Australian climber it is an essential inclusion in their future plans.

From a distance, its finely detailed surface appears as if it is made of millions of orange, yellow and grey Lego blocks. Many climbers, on first sight, have expressed grave doubts as to its quality. It is, admittedly, an unlikely looking super cliff. But anyone put off by its original appearance soon realises that this ungainly looking crag is absolutely wonderful to climb on. The fact that good climbs at ALL grades exist here makes Arapiles quite unique as cliffs go—very rarely are areas good for easy rambling climbs as well as short, hard desperates.

Added to this, Arapiles has one of the most popular camping areas in Australian rock climbing circles, with climbers from all over camped together in the dust. It is the perfect place to find partners, socialise with climbers from all over the world and pick up information on Australian climbing.

Geology/type of rock/quality: Hard quartzite, a hard metamorphosed sandstone. Extremely strong and with good natural gear placement—very secure (if placed properly). ***
Grades: 1–32.
Height: From 10m up to 170m.
Number of routes: Close to 3000.
Climbing style: Arapiles has faces, slabs, cracks and all sorts of weird combinations. It is one of the most staunchly traditional of Australian climbing areas for a number of reasons. The gear is usually good and even the harder climbs have natural gear. RPs (small brass wedges invented for here) are a necessary addition to your leading rack on harder climbs. Many of the bolts at the Mount are of a carrot type.

The abundance of protection and lack of bolts means Arapiles is definitely not a sport crag. It is a cliff where the older traditions of climbing survive; those of doing climbs from the ground up, placing protection as you go and possibly getting scared. It is a good idea for climbers not used to placing natural protection to try a few easier routes until they get the hang of it.

There are a few areas, such as Doggers Gully and Flight Wall, where a profusion of bolts has meant sport climbers could climb in their fashion, however most serious practitioners travel over to the nearby Grampians where bolted sport crags have been developed.

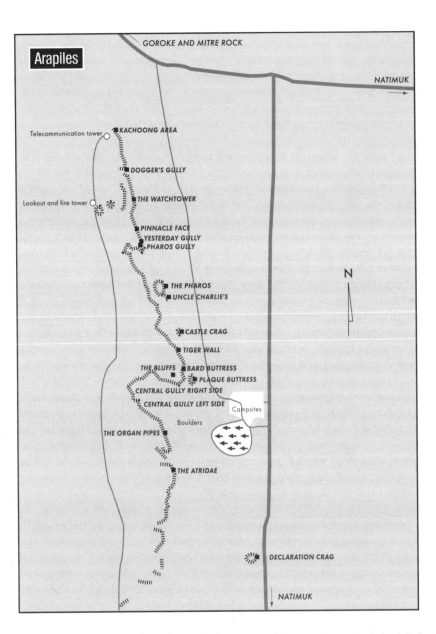

Arapiles

GOROKE AND MITRE ROCK

NATIMUK

Telecommunication tower ○ ◗ **KACHOONG AREA**

◗ **DOGGER'S GULLY**

Lookout and fire tower ○ ✳ ◗ **THE WATCHTOWER**

◗ **PINNACLE FACE**
YESTERDAY GULLY
◗ **PHAROS GULLY**

✳◗ **THE PHAROS**
◗ **UNCLE CHARLIE'S**

✳◗ **CASTLE CRAG**

◗ **TIGER WALL**

THE BLUFFS ◗ **BARD BUTTRESS**
◗ **PLAQUE BUTTRESS**
◗ **CENTRAL GULLY RIGHT SIDE**
◗ **CENTRAL GULLY LEFT SIDE**

Campsites

Boulders

THE ORGAN PIPES ◗

◗ **THE ATRIDAE**

✳◗ **DECLARATION CRAG**

NATIMUK

N

Brief history: Louise Shepherd's *Guide to Arapiles* has a very good history section written by local climber Keith 'Noddy' Lockwood and there is a pamphlet available on the Aboriginal heritage of Djurite (Mt Arapiles).

There are rumours that three people climbed at Arapiles in the '50s and the three involved were subsequently killed in NZ. More verifiable is the 1963 visit by father and son Bob and Steve Craddock who had seen a photo of the lesser Mitre Rock in a RACV pamphlet and found the hulking scarp on the other side of the road. Their visit unleashed a torrent of development on the mountain and many of Arapiles' best climbs were done in 1963 and '64. Development continued in the late '60s with climbers like Bob Bull, Ted Batty, Reg Williams, John Fahey, Chris Baxter and Peter Jackson ticking many of the obvious lines, including *The Watchtower Crack* 16 and *Fang* 18. Youngsters John Moore and Chris Dewhirst got in on the act, climbing (with some aid) *Skink* and *Kingdom Come*, and Ian 'the Beast' Guild climbed *Scorpion* with one aid. Roland Pauligk (*Electra*) and Phillip Stranger (with Dewhirst freed *Werewolf* 19) contributed. During this period a lot of the bigger lines were aided, as was the fashion.

In the early '70s climbers like Mike Stone and Ian Ross (*Kingdom Come*) came into their own, and a swag of climbers including Natimukian Keith 'Noddy' Lockwood (who started here in the late '60s), schoolboy Mike Law, an equally young Glenn Tempest, Joe Friend and Ian Lewis all began to establish climbs, including ascents of *Little Thor* 20 and *Christian Crack* 20. American Henry Barber turned the cliff on its end, doing his usual incredible amount of routes, freeing many aid routes including *Kama Sutra* 23, *Squeakeasy* 22 and *Kachoong RHV* 21. His visit inspired the young locals, and Law and Tempest (*Atlantis* 23) were joined by others. Andrew Thompson (*Hellspite* 23), Greg Child (*Starless* and *Bible Black* 22), Coral Bowman (*Snow Blind* 23), Chris Peisker (*Horrorscope* 24) and Kevin Lindorff (*Birdman of Alcatraz* 23) quickly showed that they too had learned the lessons of Barber's tour.

In the late '70s these climbers were joined by Kim Carrigan and Mark Moorhead who were to push the boundaries of the possible. Law and Child established the *Undertaker* 25, a grade they had been beaten to (in hindsight, by Peisker with *Ostler* in the Grampians). During this period Carrigan launched an unparalleled assault on the mountain, climbing hundreds of climbs, and introducing the grades 26 (*Procul Harem*) and 27 (*Fox on a Hot Thin Roof*) to Arapiles and Australia. Mark Moorhead, though prone to undergrading, launched a similar offensive, doing many hard classics before tragically dying on Makalu in the Himalayas in 1983. His route *Cobwebs* is recognised as the first 28 in the country. At the same time, another notorious undergrader, Law, established a triptych of hard climbs, *Sustained Metaphor* 26, *Slope'n'Sleazin* 28 and *Slime Time* 28. Not to be outdone, Carrigan introduced the grade 29 with *India* (subsequently down to 28), *Masada* and possibly 30 with his ascent of *Ethiopia*. Geoff 'Ralph' Weigand, a NSW climber who went on to live in the US, stopped off occasionally to add such climbs as *You're Terminated* 29.

Other visitors besides Barber had an affect on the mountain. In 1980 American Mike Graham gave us the fine *Ride Like the Wind* 25, and Tobin Sorenson and John Allen stopped by in their tour in 1979, producing the excellent *Tjuriga Wall* 25. However, it was a trio of Europeans that were to have the most effect. Swiss climber Martin Scheel did more new routes in the Grampians but his lasting legacy was the bolting (and chipping) of a wall on Uncle Charlie's pinnacle. He was unable to do it, however, and it remained for German superstar Wolfgang Gullich in 1985 to climb what was one of the hardest climbs in the world, *Punks in the Gym*. It was originally graded 32, but subsequent hold enhancement and retrobolting have seen it drop a grade. Another German ace, Stephan Glowacz, dropped by not long after and claimed the second ascent of *Punks* and as a consolation prize did the first 31 with his ascent of an outstanding Carrigan project, *Lord of the Rings*.

Stuart Wyithe grabbed the first Australian ascent of *Punks* in 1994 and added *Pretty in Punk*, and in keeping with the tradition Dave Jones also climbed *Punks*, adding *Punks Addiction* 32 to the wall. By now, however, the fire-front of development had moved away from Arapiles to the Grampians,

Nowra and the Blue Mountains and the mountain settled down to be merely a popular haunt for climbers of all grades.

Season: The climate is almost perfect for climbing all year round, with only the hottest days of summer or the coldest and wettest days of winter too unpleasant. In summer (Dec–Feb) the cliff is hot and dry. The wise climber needs to climb in the early morning or evening, or stick to the darker gullies like King Rat, Intrepid and PB. Areas like Central Gully Right Side, the back of the Pharos and Bushrangers can all be in the shade when you need it.

Spring (Sept–Dec) can be tempestuous with wind and not infrequent wet days. It is generally a good time to climb although occasionally it is best to hide in a gully or put up with a rest day. Winter (June–Sept) can be cold and wet but is also often mild and nice enough to climb in the sun. Areas like the Watchtower faces or Central Gully Left Side act as good sun traps. The boulders are always a nice option in either winter sun or in rain (provided you pick the right boulders).

Autumn (March–May) is the season where Arapiles is perfect. Long stable periods of 18–25°C temperatures make perfect climbing weather. On top of this, the light in the Wimmera is particularly nice at this time of year, and the sunsets simply amazing.

Location/access: Mt Arapiles is 320km NW of Melbourne, 30km from the large town of Horsham on the main highway (8) from Melbourne to Adelaide and 8km W of the small town of Natimuk. The road from Horsham through Natimuk forks just out of the latter town, the L road going to Edenhope and into South Australia and the other to Goroke and then also into South Australia. These roads pass either side of the mountain and can both be used to access the camping ground, which is signposted on both roads.

If you approach the campsite from the S you will pass a small lump of rock on your L. There is a car park here and usually a bunch of people standing around watching someone top-rope a small orange corner (*Little Thor*). This is Declaration Crag.

If you walk up to the top of the campsite and stand there gazing on the acres of quartzite there are several key features from which to orient yourself. To your R, the highest part of the cliff is capped by the two huge blocks of 'the Bluffs'. The skyline arête heading up to these is Bard Buttress. L of the Bluffs there is a gully (Major Mitchell) and then another large buttress, Dunes. The large gully between the rock on the R and the rock in front of you is Central Gully and the cliffs leading down the L side of this gully are imaginatively called Central Gully Left Side.

In front of you is a fluted area reminiscent of a microscopic enlargement of some brown corduroy from a '70s pair of flares, the Organ Pipes. L of these, past another gully, is the Atridae. The central feature of the Atridae is a large red corner, the L wall polka dotted with chalk: the Flight Deck.

If you walk along the base of the cliff (N) from camp you pass a little buttress with a plaque on its L-hand side, Plaque Buttress. Continue walking past the majestic Bard Buttress and along the base of the tall Tiger Wall. After this you will come to a 15m, free standing pinnacle, Castle Crag. Further on there is a larger pinnacle, with some walls in front of it and to the L. This pinnacle is the Pharos and the wall just in front is Uncle Charlie's. L again is Death Row Pinnacle.

Continuing N you pass the large Pharos Gully (Yesterday Gully runs off this to the R looking up) and then the broken Pinnacle Faces with the obvious leaning pinnacle of Tiptoe Ridge. Past this is the smooth Watchtower faces, L and R, divided by the Watchtower Buttress (under the fire tower and lookout). Up to the R of the R face is a shaded gully facing S (Henry Bolte or Doggers Gully), best accessed from the lookout car park on top of the cliff (turn off Edenhope Rd S of campsite). N of here is the Northern Group (below the telecommunications tower) with its obvious roofs up high

(*Kachoong* etc.), again usually accessed from above. To the N, and separate, can be seen the low Mitre Rock—the turn off to this is on the Goroke Rd (N of the campsite).

Camping and local amenities: There is camping available at the mountain but only in the camp sites. It is in the State Park and therefore restrictions apply: no pets, firearms or fires except in fireplaces. There are toilets, water (not the most palatable—perhaps collect some in Natimuk), rubbish collection and fireplaces. There is also a telephone.

There is a camping fee of $2 per person per night. Firewood is pretty scarce around camp and should not be collected in the park anyway. As with all national parks a stove is a good option: by the time this guide goes to print fires may have been banned altogether. On total fire ban days in summer no fires can be lit, including stoves, and there are strict penalties for breaking this rule. (The ultimate penalty could be the destruction of all your fellow campers and the cliff environment.) In summer the area is extremely dry; be extremely careful. This includes disposing of cigarettes and matches carefully. The park is within the North-West Fire Ban District.

There are three campsites at the mountain, all adjacent: the 'Pines' (good for summer); the Gums (better for spring and winter); and the new North Campground. The latter has no fireplaces and can be quieter than the others.

Natimuk and the surrounding area have plenty of accommodation options. There is also the Natimuk Caravan Park at Natimuk Lake. This has good showers and is the better option if you have a vehicle. When the lake is not dry you can swim here. There are backpackers' hostels and a hotel in Natimuk and other accommodation options in Horsham. Natimuk has a climbing shop, newsagent, a milk bar, the National Hotel (pub), a garage (closed Sunday afternoons), a chemist and post office, as well as a number of guiding companies. Horsham has three supermarkets and numerous other shops. Organic vegetables are available from O'Connors near the turn-off to the camp site from the Edenhope road (S), a quick walk down from the camp site.

Transport: If you are coming by public transport the bus/train travels daily from Melbourne's Spencer Street Station to Horsham. The bus arrives at the new bus station in Roberts Street. From here you can take a small local bus to Natimuk and the Mount. You can either catch it from the bus station or opposite Coles supermarket. This bus leaves at 2pm and the fare to Natimuk is $4.60. From Horsham to Arapiles the fare is $5.50 (some concessions apply). It is also fairly easy to hitch from Horsham to Arapiles and from Natimuk to Arapiles, with most locals trusting climbers.

Guidebooks: *Arapiles, Selected Climbs*, Simon Mentz and Glenn Tempest, Open Spaces, Melbourne, 1999; *A Rockclimbers' Guide to Arapiles/Djurite*, Louise Shepherd, Victorian Climbing Club, Melbourne, 1994; *Mt Arapiles 300 of the Best*, Gordon Poultney and Donna Bridge, Mr Chicken Productions, Natimuk, 1998; *Victoria: Mainly Bolts*, Gordon Poultney, Mr Chicken Productions, Natimuk, 1997; *The Weird Guide to Arapiles*, Hero Fukutu, T.O.P, Natimuk, 1997; *The Big Book of Problems* (bouldering guide), Hero Fukutu and Innigo Montoya, T.O.P, Natimuk, 1996. (There is some bouldering information in the back of the Mentz/Tempest guide.)

Bouldering: There is also some bouldering at Araps, but more are found over in the Grampians. Nevertheless, it is a good place to develop bouldering and, by extension, climbing skills. The main areas are the boulders in Central Gully, and along the base of Tiger Wall and in front of the Pharos. There are also good problems below the northern group cliffs. See guidebooks above. Here are some of the more famous problems:

V0+		Golden Streak (or Slime)
V1		Animal Acts
V4		Gonzo Gladiator
V4		Heartstopper
V4		L, S, or D
V6		Attack a Helpless Chicken
V9		Slea Stacks
V10		Between Fear and Desire

Declaration Crag

About the most public place to climb at Arapiles. This detached pinnacle is situated next to the sealed road—it even has its own parking area—and is 600m S of the main entrance to the Pines camp ground. The roadside has a deep crack on the L, a low ramp and a gully.

▲ **2** 12m early 60s

Sunny Gully — The L leading easy ramp.

▲ **7** 12m 1975

Marshmallow Sea — The sparsely protected smooth wall to with a small overlap up high. Start from L-hand side of gully (FI). The direct approach is more like 14!

▲ **3** 13m 1964

Hammer — Around to the R (N-face) is another deep cleft (*Sickle* 8). Start in this and climb out onto L wall and up, then back R at top.

▲ **16** 12m 1966

Marmot's Mall — Climb middle of glossy wall just L of the corner (*Little Thor*).

▲▲▲ **20** 12m 1965 {1974}

Little Thor — Take care with your gear on this one. The corner, R then back L to finish.

▲▲ **29** 18m 1984

Steps Ahead — The thin wall to the R of *Little Thor*, past 4BR.

▲▲ **26** 18m {1984}

Wild Drugs and Crazy Sex (aka Hit the Deck) — Start 8m R of *Steps Ahead* at short weakness. Up this to BR, then L and up wall past 4BR.

▲ **24** 15m 1979

Look Sharp — Start as for WDaCS. Up to BR, then R to BR and up past PR, finishing R.

22 15m 1982

A New Toy — 2m R of *Look Sharp*. Up crack to bulge and BR.

| 22 | 10m | 1979 |

Problematic – The thin bulging seam 2m R of *A New Toy*.

| ▲ | 24 | 20m | 1982 |

Remembrance Day – Start at finish of *Problematic*, level with small roof. Trav L below roof for 12m (at BR) then up and continuing trav L with feet on the lip of the roof.

Behind (W) Dec Crag, up on the slopes of Arapiles is a series of buttress, one of which (**Colosseum Wall**) has a large S facing square corner. On the E facing wall of this corner are two cracks (descent is by the corner crack—*Spasticus* 5). From L>R:

| ▲▲ | 20 | 13m | 1966 {1974} | **Christian Crack** |
| ▲▲ | 18 | 13m | 1968 | **The Rack** |

The crack in the S facing wall is:

| ▲ | 14 | 13m | 1966 | **Nero** |

The Atridae
L of the Atridae, around the blunt arête of Cassandra Wall is a smooth wall:

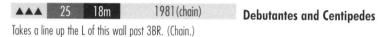

| ▲▲▲ | 25 | 18m | 1981(chain) | **Debutantes and Centipedes** |

Takes a line up the L of this wall past 3BR. (Chain.)

| ▲ | 18 | 20m | 1975 | **Cassandra** |

The line of old bolts up the white slab (capped by large roof). (2BR rap.)

| ▲ | 22 | 23m |

Cassandra Direct – Continues up to roof before going R.

| ▲ | 23 | 15m | 1978 |

Pain Street – Tackles the roof.

R of this is another large square corner, The Flight Deck. Other routes are:

| ▲ | 29 | 25m | 1990 |

Jet Lag – Start in middle of L wall, climbing up to middle of wall past BRs. (L to rap)

| ▲▲ | 24 | 25m | 1982 |

It'll Never Fly – Start to R. Up (slightly L) crossing *Jet Lag* at half height and heading L to arête and up (rap).

| ▲▲ | 25 | 20m | 1982 |

Have a Good Flight – In flight entertainment. A direct finish to *It'll Never Fly* to R (L of Jet Lag). (rap)

▲▲▲ 24 40m (2) [24,19] 1966 {1979}

Orestes – 1. (20m) The corner, and R along lip to ledge (can rap from here) 2. (20m) Back L and up corner.

▲ 22 15m 1968 {1978}

Plimsoll Line – The groove to R of corner.

▲▲▲ 13 42m (2) [13,12] 1965

Muldoon – R of the Flight Deck is a broken wall and this climb takes this face, L of the R arête. Start around the arête on the N facing wall, at the base of a short crack (behind native pine). 1. (20m) Up crack to ledge at 9m then step L and up through bulge (old PR) and up to good ledge. 2. (22m) Through bulge, step R and up to small, square flat overhang. Another step R, up weakness and back L to finish up arête and jugs.

▲▲▲ 10 40m (2) [6,10] 1964

Agamemnon – One of the best and most exciting climbs for the grade in Victoria. R of *Muldoon* are a couple of gullies leading to chimneys (the R-most is *Clytemnaestra* 12) and R again is a deep, dark chimney. Start at the base of this. 1. (18m) Up chimney L wall (FI), climbing back in to the depth to belay. 2 (22m) Climb crack on R wall (FI) and then follow series of flakes and cracks out towards the plains, either chimneying or face climbing (further out) the thrilling finish. Walk off to gully to N.

The flared crack on the S wall opposite *Agamemnon* is:

▲▲ 20 40m 1975   **Wizard of Ice**

The large crack to the R of the start of *Agamemnon*'s chimney is:

▲ 19 45m 1966 {1973}   **Electra**

The Organ Pipes

▲▲▲ 14 35m (2) [10,14] 1964/5

D Minor – The crack up the front of the L most pinnacle in the Organ Pipes (take care with gear). Rap chains at back (W) on pinnacle.

▲▲ 11 35m 1965

Piccolo – The line through smooth bulge up the face of the thin pinnacle R of *D Minor* pinnacle. Scramble down back.

To descend the following routes walk back into gully (small climb down) or find rap chains to south (into Organ Pipes gully).

▲▲ 9 50m (2) [9,9]

D Major – The deep crack on the R wall on the next (broad) pinnacle R of *Piccolo*. 1. (25m) Up crack and either under or around (to L) of huge chockstone boulder. 2. (25m) Step off the top of chockstone to R (FI) and then trend R and into crack that leads to top.

▲▲ | 16 | 50m | (2)[14,16] 1968

Libretto – The line to the R, stepping back L at ledge to slick little corner and up to join *D Major*.

▲ | 15 | 50m | (2)[14,15] 1967

Ejaculation – The curving finger crack on wall opposite *Libretto*, finishing up cleft.

▲▲ | 7 | 55m | (3)[6,4,7] 1963

Diapason – An easy and popular classic. Up line on front of next pinnacle R (from *D Major*), R of *Ejaculation*. From plaque swing up R and twist around to R side of pinnacle before stepping back L to rib and large ledge. Take one of the possible exits to L (FI).

▲▲ | 9 | 75m | (2)[9,6] 1964

Conifer Crack – A line up the front of next pinnacle R (on L). 1. (35m) Start below groove in slab (1m R of big dead gum) climbing this to ledge and through bulge (on large dubious looking blocks) then up to top. 2. (40m) Up flute behind. Scramble back into gully.

▲▲▲ | 13 | 33m | 1976

Horn Piece – The excellent line up the front of the next pinnacle to R (*Didgeridoo* pinnacle). There are chains at top to rap or finish up *Conifer*. **▲▲** *Didgeridoo* 11 35m 1965 starts to the R and crosses to exit at L.

▲ | 19 | 50m | 1976

Wyrd – On the Red Wall above *Horn Piece* (can be reached by scrambling up gravelly gully to R). *Wyrd* climbs the L of the wall, starting to L of grey pedestal. Up this, up shallow corner to roof. Trav L and up undercling until break leads back R. Finish up L leading ramps. **▲** *Wyrd Direct* 21 steps R at roof and up a shallow corner to join original. Chains.

▲▲▲ | 19 | 40m | 1976

Tannin – The chalk on the line to the R betrays it popularity. Up crack on R of pedestal, R 2m below roof, up, and then back L up weakness. Chains. **▲▲** *Tannin Direct* 20 1985 pulls through roof L of centre.

▲▲ | 21 | 35m | 1976

The Wraith – The weakness R of *Tannin*, finishing up line R of *Tannin's* roof.

▲ | 14 | 50m | (2)[14,13] 1965

Toccata – At the far R of the Organ Pipes is a slick looking L-facing corner crack. 1. (27m) Up to ledge. 2. (23m). Up. To descend scramble up and L (S) until you come into the upper reaches of Organ Pipes Gully.

The Plaque Buttress

An over-popular spot for groups to practice their abseiling. The pale, low buttress to the NW of the campsites, it has two cracks in the centre (the R one more of a corner) and a large roof at the R.

▲ | 14 | 12m | 1965

Minimus – The L crack (R of plaque).

▲ 10 13m 1965

Camelot — The corner/crack to R.

▲ 17 13m 1976

Maximus — The line up the wall 2m R.

▲ 24 15m 1978-90

Cumelittle (Direct) — Climb up past the 2BR to R.

▲ 21 15m 1964 {1975}

Dramp — Up the slick crack to roof and out L.

▲ 25 12m 1981

Sonic Boom — The roof R of *Dramp*. BR to seam and up and R.

The Bard Buttress

This is the square-faced orange tower that juts out between Fang Buttress and Tiger Wall. It runs up to the Bluffs and its base has a distinctive, gleaming apron slab. The broad ledge at the top of *Bard*'s 4th pitch is labelled the Bard Terrace. Escape is possible off this, by traversing carefully L, across a gully, then up and L until you can down-climb to the top of *Ali*'s, a grade 3 descent route (some parties will want to rope up for this). If you continue to the top of the buttress you will need to sidle around the R side towards the Bluffs and follow a ramp down (L–FI or S) into the (*Ali Baba*'s) cave, and step UP taking a narrow tunnel through to the other side. Walk down to your L (FO) and either scramble or abseil down chains/line in corner (Ali's) or look for links to rap off on top of the buttress to S.

▲▲ 19 90m (2)[19, 17] 1967–1982

The Desired — On the face overlooking the camp are two obvious intersecting diagonal lines. The L-wards one is *Orpheus* and the R-ward *Eurydice*. This climb starts below the 'bottomless corner' of *Orpheus*. 1. (50m) Climb straight into the corner then follow the crack directly over a series of bulges to a small ledge. 2. (40m) Directly up to *Bard* ledge. Walk off L, or continue up any of the finishes above.

▲▲▲ 18 70m (2)[18,18] 1965

Eurydice — Classic, and not getting any easier. The RH line. 1. (33m) Climb the crack leading steeply up L past BR to niche. Straight up line above. 2. (35m) Up around difficult overhang, then carry on till corner steepens again. Exit up R, then onwards to Bard Terrace. Either solo off, finish up *Bard*, or continue directly above *Bard*'s corner when crack closes, finishing easily on arête.

▲▲ 17 85m (3)[12,14,17] 1967

Checkmate — A bold exploration of the Bard Buttress arête. 1. (27m) Climb the 1st part of *Bard*, belaying at foot of juggy ramp. 2. (20m) Trav 6m L above the small bulge and climb straight up just L of arête to *Bard*'s 2nd belay. 3. (38m) Up 8m to niche which is capped by overlap. Scurry up L, step R and find easiest way through roofs.

▲▲▲ | 12 | 120m | (5)[12,12,12,12,12] 1965

The Bard – The immortal classic. Start at the lowest point at the toe of buttress on R. 1. (43m) Climb slab and step L to gain short L facing corner which leads to an easy ramp. Belay at top of ramp. 2. (12m) R around arête, and trav awkwardly L below large roof to exposed belay on nose. 3. (20m) Step up R onto improbable wall, and either continue traversing R and up, or go up first and then R, to gain bottomless chimney. Bridge this to a snug belay ledge. 4. (15m) L and straight up to a broad (*Bard*) terrace. 5. (34m) Either struggle up chimney corner or climb R wall to top.

The Bluffs

Perched high above the plains, the faces of the Bluffs provide an excellent stage on which to act out Arapilesian theatre (let's hope it's not a drama or a tragedy). The E faces consist of a two-tiered double block. The line between the blocks on the top tier is *Beau Bummel* 17. Descent is by abseil off the back into the notch (down **▲▲▲** *Missing Link* 17). To get to the lower tier either climb something on Tiger Wall or come up Alis, through Ali Baba's cave and onto the large ledge that runs across the top of the L of Tiger Wall (Flinders Lane). To get to the upper tier climb something, the midway crack *Ivan* 12 is the easiest (or come through tight squeeze slot *The Keyhole*).

▲ | 12 | 14m

Ivan – The R curving crack R of the chimney roof that splits lower tier.

▲ | 17 | 14m | 1966

Scorpion Direct Start – To the R is a bulging hand crack starting from top of pedestal.

▲▲ | 22 | 20m | 1974

Scorpion Corner – The beautiful corner to R. Rap slings at top.

▲▲▲ | 11 | 30m | 1964

Blockbuster – The shallow wide corner taking the middle of the L face.

▲ | 20 | 30m | 1976

Jenny Wren – Start up *Beau Brummel*, then trav R to arête past PR and BR (suss). Up (stepping R and back briefly up high).

▲▲▲ | 19 | 33m | 1968 {1974}

Quo Vadis – To the R a hard move past an old BR gets you to the superb curving crack.

▲▲ | 18 | 30m | 1966

Scorpion – The crack you can see from Horsham, stepping off R of ledge to start.

Castle Crag (and Tiger Wall)

▲▲ | 17 | 20m | 1976

Swinging – On the N face of Castle Crag, starting up the crack on R and climbing past 2BR. Chains up and R.

▲▲   11   20m   1964

Trapeze — Up to 1st BR on *Swinging*, then trav L for 4m, then up. Chains.

▲   19   30m   1984

A Cut Above — From trav on *Trapeze* climb diagonally L to ledge on arête, continuing L above space and up.

▲▲   25   25m

The Low Down — From the trav on *Trapeze* climb steeply up L past 2BR.

▲   29   25m

Nati Dread — Start 2m R of *Procul Harum* and follow BR through roof crack, moving R to join *Low Down*, following it L then straight up.

▲▲   26   25m   1966 {1978}

Procul Harum — Australia's first 26 and a gymnastic exercise. The roof-crack.

▲▲▲   10   170m   (7) 1964

Syrinx — On the huge Tiger Wall behind Castle Crag there is a giant R-facing corner that swings R at top. This is the classic *Syrinx*. It follow the corner to top and R before climbing a short wall and traversing back L to exit.

Death Row and Uncle Charlie's

Continuing along the walking track you come to a small triangle wall, Death Row pinnacle. (Descend down S shoulder and off back or rap off slings.)

▲▲▲   23   35m   1976

Birdman of Alcatraz — Is the arching L line up the centre of the face, gained by moving in L from guano. ▲ *Bad* 23 45m 1978 takes the thin crack R of *Birdman*, trending R into *Death Row* sentry box. Undercling, up hanging corner and then back R (above start). ▲ *Bent* 24 40m 1982 starts 2.5m L of *Birdman*, climbing seam to cross into *Bad* corner. Up this before undercling L into another hanging corner, then L below bulge to crack. Up past BR.

▲▲   18   45m   1967

Death Row — Up the L-facing corner crack, stepping R into bottomless sentry box. Bridge out and up onto wall. Follow line L and up through bulges.

A little way past Death Row pinnacle a well-defined path leaves the main one, heading uphill and passing to the L of a steep bulgy wall (*Punks*) on the S face of a buttress split by two clefts (which don't reach the ground) on the L (Uncle Charlie's). Don't bother taking the gear unless you have some time on your hand.

▲   31   35m   1994

Pretty in Punk — Starts on L of wall, slabbing (?) rising R past 3BRs to join *Punks*. Up this for a few moves then R to arête. 2BR rap.

| ▲ | 32 | 35m | 1998 |

Punks Addiction — More of a connection than a route. Up *Pretty in Punk* but continue up *Punks* instead of stepping R.

| ▲▲▲ | 31 | 35m | 1985 |

Punks in the Gym — An amazing piece of climbing and history. (See history.) Start in middle of wall and climb up and then L and up the wall past BR and a fixed wire.

| ▲▲ | 25 | 20m | 1982 |

Punks in the Gunks — Start as for *Punks*, then climb R across shallow arch (BRs and PR) to arête and rap.

| ▲ | 28 | 20m | 1995 |

Ciela — The overhanging R arête past BRs to chain.

| ▲▲ | 20 | 48m | (2)[20,17] 1974-77 |

Pearls Before Swine — 1. (15m) Start at L toe of Uncle Charlie's climbing up the slab to roof and through this into chimney cleft. 2. (33m) Up chimney a little then trav L onto slender buttress and up.

| ▲▲ | 25 | 55m | (2) 1979 |

Uncle Charlie's Right Nostril — The sustained crack to the R of underneath the R cleft/chimney. Continue up bulging crack on R of chimney (*Picking Winners* 2nd pitch 23).

| ▲▲ | 29/30 | 30m | 1984 |

Ethiopia — Climb *India* (below) but from the block where the corner squarely meets the little roof trav L to BR and up past 2 more BR to roof crack.

| ▲▲ | 28 | 30m | 1982 |

India — Up the crack on R of buttress then L to rest and up through bulge (past fixed gear and PR). Up short corner to block (at break) then trav R and up wide crack. 2BR rap. The crack through bulge to R is *Wisdom of Body* 30.

| ▲ | 24 | 30m | 1978 |

Nose Job — Slabby corner to nose R of *India*. Step R (crossing *Coming on Chris*) and up steep weakness. 2BR rap.

| ▲▲ | 16 | 25m | 1976 |

Coming on Chris — Climb R-facing corner on N rib of Uncle Charlie's till it ends, trav L across space and up to ledge. Rap off *Nose Job* anchor.

| ▲▲ | 25 | 20m | 1983 |

Spasm in the Chasm — A popular work-out. In the chasm between Uncle Charlie's and the Pharos, up to the R (S), past the flaring V-line (*Virginia* 18) is a well-chalked line (underneath chockstone). (3BR & 7 Rock).

Pinnacle and Watchtower faces

The broken Pinnacle Face lies between the Pharos Gully and the L Watchtower Face, and is the home of some classic very easy routes. *Tiptoe Ridge* takes the prominent blocky pinnacle (best seen in profile) rising to two-thirds height in front of the main cliff. To descend, walk directly away from the cliff (west), following the track for 100m or so, until the Pharos Gully tourist track appears down to your L.

▲▲ 3 120m   1963

Tiptoe Ridge – A pleasant ramble. Start high up on the terrace about 30m up and L of the prominent ridge. 1. (43m) Gain the ridge via a series of steps going up and R. Amble up front of pinnacle to belay on ledge to L (above start). 2. (27m) Climb up R and around to roomy ledge in the notch between the pinnacle and the main face. You can go to top of pinnacle, followed by an awkward move off the back or go all the way around to the R and step across the void onto the ledge. 3. (20m) Start a few metres L of the chimney and go diagonally L for 8m and then back R above the bulge. Up to belay in small scoop next to chimney. 4. (30m) Climb wall just L of chimney to ledge, and on up face till an escape gully leads off R.. ▲ *Ordinary Trees* 6 takes the chimney on the R (N) side of the pinnacle to join *Tiptoe* at the notch. ▲ *Introductory Route* 4, the first route at Arapiles, climbs a line 100m R of the ridge before traversing L to join *Tiptoe* at the notch also.

▲▲ 9 166m   (4/5) 1963

Siren – Arapiles' 2nd route. It is worthwhile working out this route from the ground. You are ultimately aiming for huge bottomless R facing corner that bounds L edge of upper half of the L Watchtower Face. To reach the bottom of that corner requires long pitch of a diagonal R traversing. 1. (25m) Running down L edge of LWF is flake chimney. Climb easily up wall 20m L of this to dead tree (1st pitch *Introductory Route*). 2. (35m) Move up to long, deep crack which leads to belay on arête, or alternatively climb edge out R of this crack. 3. (35m) Step R across void and trav up and R to base of huge corner mentioned above. 4. (50m) Corner is beautifully clean, and can be split into 2 pitches. Exit on L. Walk L along bushy terrace to scramble up short wall.

The Watchtower is the large buttress lying between the two smooth faces, L and R respectively. To descend from these routes either walk N along under Kitten Wall (above R face) and down well defined path at R-hand (FI) edge or find abseil (2x45m) from ringbolts 20m N from the Watchtower.

▲▲▲ 10 123m   (4) 1965

Arachnus – The beginner's classic and just as enjoyable if you've been climbing for years. At base of Watchtower are 2 deep cracks which fizzle out into blank rock. *Arachnus* takes the R-hand one; it's 9m R of the L-hand crack (which is the ▲▲ *Watchtower Chimney* 12 111m 1965) and about 5m L of the undercut R arête. 1. (40m) Climb deep crack (5m) till it ends, then trav 4m R, up over disconcerting bulge and follow crack to large ledge with cosy niche at back. 2. (35m) Innumerable variations exist for this pitch. (This is *Minerva Variant*.) From niche, step R and climb wall, then diagonal R to an overhang and up to ledge (can belay here). Up overhanging crack, then balance carefully R (you can also go straight up from overhanging crack at a grade harder). Up to stunning belay in scoop which overlooks R Watchtower Face. 4. (48m) Move L out of cave for 6m, then follow your nose up exhilarating wall. Communication to your second is almost impossible from the top.

▲▲ `17` `100m` (4) [12,14,16,16] 1965

The Watchtower Crack – An old style wide crack classic. Starts at R side of *Watchtower*. 1. (33m) Climb slab just R of corner till good ledge on L can be gained. 2. (20m) The main corner and then L-hand line to good cave. (3–4) 47m Climb 4m to roof and around it (past old BR runner) and then corner.

▲▲ `18` `106m` (3) [12,18,17] 1966 {FFA late}r

Skink – 1&2. (65m) Approach it by 1st 2 pitches of *Watchtower Crack* then trav R across exhilarating easy wall to gain base of sickle-shaped corner. Up to tiny ledge. 3. (41m) Follow corner with detour out R by flake if necessary.

▲▲▲ `21` `90m` (2) [21,21] 1982

Auto Da Fe – 2 brilliant pitches that give steep climbing on small incuts with 'adequate' protection. Start at clean streak 12m R of *Watchtower Crack* (at cairn). 1. (40m) Hard move off ground then up streak to ledge (FHs). 2. (50m) Climb straight up through an overlap an follow streak through bulge. Veer L into *Skink* at level of flakes on L wall. Swing L on these to arête and then straight up.

▲▲▲ `16` `100m` (3) [16,16,12] 1975

Brolga – Exquisite. Starts from platform below wide natural water streak. 1. (30m) Climb easy rock veering R. At about 13m tricky move back L regains streak which is followed direct to sloping ledge. 2. (40m) Straight up appealing rock passing small ledge and on to bigger one. 3. (30m) Step R off ledge and up wall, finishing on R.

Henry Bolte (Doggers Gully)

A deep shaded wall that points S over the R Watchtower Face and can either be accessed by the track up this (on R) or from the summit car park below fire spotting tower. From car park walk L up the management road to the communications tower, following a path down to the R (FO) or S of the tower. Walking E will bring you to the cliff at the top of *Kachoong*. When you reach the edge of the cliff the top of the buttress to your L (FO) is above the face, and there is an observation gallery buttress to your R. Most routes have rap anchors at or near top.

▲ `18` `10m` 1986

Get Your Bloody Fingers Out of My Nostrils – The easiest line on the wall. The chalked holds on L of cliff.

▲ `22` `12m` 1982

Follow Your Nose – Start up *GYBFOOMN* and make tentative trav R past BR and then up.

▲▲ `26` `18m` 1984

The Fortress – To R is a well-chalked line past 2BR. At jugs after crux head R and up (or pumpy L and up *Follow Your Nose*).

▲ `29` `22m` 1998

Gridlock – A direct variant on *Slinkin'*.

Left: French climber Catherine Destivelle hanging out in Sydney, the ultimate Australian city for urban climbing and bouldering. The route is *Clocks* 22, a toy climb on Ball's Head, on the north side of Sydney Harbour.

Right: Robyn Cleland checking details for her forthcoming guidebook to the atmospheric Point Perpendicular. With the ocean crashing below and the sky wrapped all around, this climb is named for the last thing you want at this cliff—*Heavy Weather* 19, Windjammer Wall.

Left: Mountains maestro Mikl Law on pitch four of his new Grose Valley extravaganza, the 190-metre *Red Edge* 23, with the typical Blue Mountains' escarpment of Mount Hay in the background. With pitches of 23, 24, 22, 26 and 24 this climb typifies the long, adventurous nature of the Grose.

Right: Steve Monks on the classic *Disco Non-Stop Party* 25 at Pierces Pass—the only accurate part of the name is the word 'non-stop'. Representative of routes in the Grose Valley, it is a rap-in, climb-out affair, following a line of carrots up 'interesting' rock.

Left: One of the Thompson's Point developers, Rod Young, on the route *Cowboy Junkies* 26. As with most Nowra climbs it is sporty, short, and pumpy—an energetic and dynamic climb in contrast to the languid brown river just below.

Below: The UK's Mike Weeks on the crux, pitch seven, of another piece of John Fantini magnificence, *Overture to the Sun* 26, on Bungonia Gorge's impressive South Wall.

Above: Chris Warner on *Space Wasted* 23, on the Central Slabs at Booroomba Rocks in the ACT. The slabs below and left show just what this area is famous for—long, mind-frazzling excursions into the world of friction.

Left: Steve Monks stunned the Australian climbing scene in 1988 with his freeing of *Ozymandias* on the imposing North Wall of the gorge at Mount Buffalo. He followed that up with his incredible 1996 *Free Eliminate to Ozymandias Direct* 28, and is seen here on pitch six (28).

Right: Julian Saunders on a route he conceived and bolted but then had to leave for Dave Jones, the sustained and run-out modern classic *Daedelus* 28 on Taipan Wall (above). The long, sandstone routes on this wall are some of the finest in the country.

Below: The flat Wimmera plains stretch out below the remnant quartzite escarpment of Arapiles. At the very top, on the back of Bluff Major, Anna Jensen picks her way carefully up the classic *Missing Link* 17.

Right: Tim 'Tadpole' Balla demonstrates how to climb the cracks of Frog Buttress on the classic *Satanic Majesty* 23. This area in southern Queensland has hundreds of pure jam cracks awaiting eager hands.

Below: Malcolm 'HB' Matheson finds himself in a *One Way Street* 21 on the premier feature at Moonarie, the Great Wall. To the left, the sweep of the wall holds many equally superb climbs on exquisite, red desert sandstone.

Left: With the Indian Ocean far below, Amanda Watts climbs *Dessert* 24 at Willyabrup in the Margaret River region—an aptly named climb in an area famous for its eateries.

Below: The smell of ozone and the roar of the ocean is a pervasive presence at West Cape Howe. This long, 70-metre-high, black dolerite cliff is arguably the best sea cliff in Australia and one of Western Australia's finest climbing areas.

Above left: Despite the sameness of the moves, there is no time to get bored on the amazing cracks of Frew's Flutes in Tasmania, where Roxanne Wells stretches on *Defender of the Faith* 21. This is the place to come for traditional crack climbing.

Above right: The most photographed and described route in Australia, the Totem Pole on Cape Hauy, and the scene of British climber Paul Pritchard's unfortunate misadventure. Here Roxanne Wells is on pitch two of *The Free Route* 25.

Below: Steve Monks studies the route ahead on the long, dolerite columns of Mt Wellington, perche high above Hobart. Traditionally area of crack climbs, Sam Edward 1995 50-metre classic *After Midnig* 23 showed that the future was to be found in bolted arêtes.

▲▲ 28 25m 1984

Slinkin' Leopard — Seminal and stolen. Start 3m R of the *Fortress*. Stick-clip 1st BR and climb across R to slight rest. Up past 2BR, L to dyno into crack weakness and up.

▲ 31 20m 1992

Zorlac the Destroyer — Jerry Moffat's contribution to antipodean pain. Up R (past BR) from 3rd BR on *Slinkin'*.

▲▲ 31 20m 1986

Lord of the Rings — (See history.) Follow *Wackford Squeers* (below) to 2nd BR then up line of ring-BR. A direct (32?) climbs up from *Going for the One* (below) and into line past FH.

▲▲ 26 30m 1983

Wackford Squeers — Start 5m R of *Slinkin'* (just above pine). Up past BR to break then trav R (2BR) to limited rest. Up and at the bulge either straight through or R and up. *Straight Outa Compton* 28 climbs up from *Going for the One* (below) and climbs (closely) to the L past 2BR.

▲ 20 40m 1977

Going for the One — Starts at obvious weakness R of *Wackford*. Across wall to big flake system, then up onto juggy wall.

▲▲ 25 25m 1983-92

Henry Bolte — Superb thin face climbing. Starts R of *Going for the One* below big (for this wall) ledge. Up to ledge and BR then to next ledge (small wire) then up past 2BR to break (cams). Either up or R and up. Chain.

Kachoong area (Northern Group—Echo Crag)

From communications tower walk to the cliff top and N until you can get down. Then come back S under the cliff. Or scramble up from below (to S). There is a vague terrace that runs along under these walls from *Honeycomb* to *Kachoong*. High Dive Gully is accessed from above, by scrambling down to S (L–FO).

▲▲ 22 30m 1976

Honeycomb — Off the L end of the terrace is an arête. Scramble around this from R and belay on small stance. Up and then L to gain and climb steep finger-crack through overlap and up.

▲ 16 36m 1967

Nativity — Start as for *Honeycomb*, stepping L to surmount overhang via one of two weaknesses. Gain a corner which is followed for 4m. Now trav R across wall to prow, and up.

R of *Nativity* is a wall with a square cut corner on its R-hand side (*Lone Pine Corner* 8). R of this again is a deep chasm (opens out S). In the top half of this (approached from top as described above, the gully itself is dangerous) are a number of steep, pumpy climbs.

▲ 23 10m 1982

Cellular Destruction — The last word in pump. Start from R and go up and out.

▲▲ 27 15m 1985

Power, Corruption and Lies — But wait, there's more. Start 1m R of *Cellular*, traversing R (past BR) before heading up to 2nd BR and letterbox slot (#2cam). Up through bulge to join *Cellular*.

▲▲ 28 25m 1988

Lats in the Belfry — Starts in *High Dive* and climbs straight up middle of wall, joining PC&L.

▲ 29 25m

You're Terminated — Climbs the arête just R of *Lats*. Start up *High Dive* and climb up past 2BR to join PC&L. Watch the swing.

▲ 23 25m 1982

High Dive — Starts down in the gully where lots of chalked holds point the way out to a big horizontal break. Trav R then crank to break. Place pro (ignore *You're Terminated* BR) and move R (crux) around arête.

▲ 20 · 13m 1967 {1978}

A Taste of Honey Direct Start — The steep orange crack at bottom RH side of *Taste of Honey* gully.

▲▲▲ 21 27m 1968 {1975}

A Taste of Honey — The climb does not start in the gully proper but from a small ('photographer's') ledge. Either rap in, do *Direct Start*, or scramble up to stance from gully around R (grade 6). Up wall for 5m then trav L under roof and up corner to a magic thread at roof. Finger trav across break to arête then up.

To the R of High Dive Gully is an obvious triple stepped roof, the Kachoong area.

▲ 21 25m 1985

Dr Paul and the Amazing Dancing Gnome — Start as for *A Taste of Honey* but continue straight up gorgeous orange wall trending slightly L to major horizontal break up high. From there, either step R (22) and up to finish, or go L 1m to jugs.

▲ 18 25m 1966

The Golden Echo Variant — Start up *Direct 19* (the obvious wide line through off-width roof on L) for 5m, trav R and up little corner below highest roof. Step R around its lip, to finish back L.

▲▲ 18 25m 1974

The Golden Echo — Trav straight out R from the *Taste of Honey* stance to corner level with bottom roof to PR. Up corner to middle roof and trav R with delicious exposure.

▲▲▲ 21 25m 1968 {1975}

Kachoong — Don't forget the camera. Starts from high ledge on R. Clip PR and up seam to roof, where there is a mediocre rest on R. Now swing across roof on 2 curving flakes to lip with elusive hold. ▲ *Right Hand Variant* 21 25m 1968 {1975}, the original, goes L for a move at the ceiling into a short hanging corner and up this past an awful old PR.

QUEENSLAND

One of the more surprising aspects of Australia is that it is a continent, and there is a large variation in climate thoughout the country. This means that when it gets cold and wet in the temperate south you can pack up and head north for Queensland, a place always prefixed by the word 'sunny'. And this is what a lot of climbers in the east of Australia do in winter, pack up and head for the sunshine state. The temperature in winter (May–Sept) rarely gets below 20°C in the day, but in summer (Nov–March) the humidity can make climbing unpleasant, especially in the heat of the day. The further north you go the more tropical it gets, and that includes a wet season (Jan–March).

Queensland is a huge state, its mostly dry interior fringed by a lush coastline. Most of the population, and therefore the developed climbing areas, are in the south-east corner, as is the garish Surfers Paradise and theme park strip. There are beautiful forests in Queensland but unfortunately the state also has the highest rate of land clearance in Australia. If you are travelling, you must visit the beautiful beaches of the Whitsunday, the huge sand island, Fraser Island, and of course the Great Barrier Reef that runs along most of the north-east coast. And for a climber there is the chance to stop and sample the delights of the modern crags around Townsville.

The cliffs of Queensland represent a variety of styles. Frog is almost totally a jamming cliff with hundreds of fine rhyolite crack lines up to 45 metres. Further south, Girraween (which can get cold in winter) is a granite area with crack, slab and face routes on its large domes and numerous smaller tors. Much of the rock in southern Queensland is on ancient volcanic plugs, which gives varied (if sometimes loose) climbing. The cliffs of the Glasshouse Mountains definitely fit into this category, as does the huge cliff of Mt Marroon. Kangaroo 'Roo' Point in the heart of Brisbane was probably like this once but numerous ascents and council clean-ups have made it fairly tame. The worries of protection, traditional to many Queensland areas, have been banished with the development of bolted routes in areas like Urbenville, about 14km from Woodenbong (south of the border on the Mt Lindesay Highway and strictly in NSW), the sandstone crags of Brooyar near Gympie, and the area of Serpent, 140km north Brisbane in the Blackhall Range.

One of Queensland's great cliffs, Western Wall, is currently closed to climbers, as is its neighbour Shady Buttress. Crookneck, an impressive pinnacle in the Glasshouse, has recently been closed as it is deemed 'dangerously unstable'. (True, but so were a lot of the people who climbed there.)

In the north there is the incredible potential of Mt Stuart, the urban delights and worries of Castle Hill, and the hedonistic beach climbing of Magnetic Island, all close to Townsville. Further north there are a number of climbing areas close to Cairns.

Kangaroo Point

Long before the Sydney sea cliffs were developed, Kangaroo Point in Brisbane defined urban climbing. Over the years it has become even more urbanised and controlled, to the point that it is really just an outdoor climbing gym with council supplied gigantic concrete anchor-bollards at the top of the 20m high cliff face and almost unnatural grass at the bottom. There are barbecues, night-lights and the river.

Geology/type of rock/quality: The rock is volcanic tuff and not the best quality. It has a quarried texture and is often sandy but has been so well fondled, chipped and glued that it is now reasonably solid.

Grades: 3–26.

Height: Up to 20m.

Number of routes: Over 250.

Climbing style: There are mostly face climbs. Few people lead anything here that does not have bolts, though most of the climbs now do. You'll need brackets. Like gyms, it's predominately used for top-roping (and, sadly, abseiling). The crag is most popular with top-roping beginners who do low quality routes in the 14–17 bracket, though most of the better climbing is found on grade 20+ routes.

Season: It is OK to climb here most days in winter (May–Sept) but summer gets way too hot and humid in the middle of the day. Don't despair though, because the lights mean you can climb until 2–3am. Don't get there too late or the best routes will already have top-ropes on them.

Location/access: Roo Point is on the southern bank of the Brisbane River, E from the Captain Cook Bridge in the suburb of Kangaroo Point (directly across the river from the CBD). From Main St, go R into River Tce which turns into Leopard St, 2nd R into Ellis St, then onto Lower River Tce. Parking can be hard to find on weekends. You can walk (10–15min) from the Vulture Street railway station. Or along Lower River Tce from the River Plaza Hotel ferry terminal.

Camping and local amenities: There are no camping grounds in the vicinity but lots of backpackers' hostels etc. and lots of amenities.

Transport: Virtually anything you like.

Guidebooks: The most current guidebook is *Kangaroo Point Climbing Guide*, Darrin Carter (self-published) Brisbane, 2000 (a re-worked version of Neil Monteith's 1997 guide).

Information: Brisbane climbing shops (see Appendix 1).

Bouldering: There are a few problems here which can be found online (see Appendix 3).

The classic climbs are:

13	**Adam's Rib**
13	**By Ignorance**
14	**Anonymous**
16	**Halva**
17	**Bum Full Of Fists**
17	**Pterodactyl**
19	**Chubba Chips Mods**
20	**Squawk**
21	**Idiot Wind**
21	**The Stoats Stepped Out**
21	**A Dingo Got My Floater**
22	**Fowl Deeds In The Chookhouse**
23	**Cucumber Castle**
24	**Wages of Fear**
25	**The Olos Slab**

Frog Buttress (Mt French)

Frog Buttress is without doubt the premier crag in Queensland, a position that is continually reinforced by increasing access restrictions to other good cliffs. It is popular in winter with hordes flocking from the south to take in the sunshine and smooth cracks. In the process more than a few Australian climbers have learnt to jam here. There are few finer climbing experiences in Australia than jamming up a line in the warm afternoon sunshine, looking out over the forest and patchwork fields below.

Frog Buttress, near the town of Boonah, is properly known as Mt French and is now part of the Moogerah Peaks National Park. The 45 hectares of park has 40 hectares of rare fassifern scrub below the escarpment. The smallness of the cliff is more than compensated by the density and quality of the lines.

Geology/type of rock/quality: Rhylolite, a smooth volcanic rock that forms in columns with fine cracks. Most of the looser face holds have long since gone from Frog. **

Grades: Grades at Frog range from about 9 to *Whistling Kite* 31, but there are not too many climbs of quality under 15 and though many of the harder climbs are excellent the bulk of the best routes here are from 18–23.

Height: Up to 45m.

Number of routes: Over 400.

Climbing style: Naturally protected jam cracks though some of the more modern faces are bolt protected (mostly carrots).

Brief history: Frog has a rich history, being the focal point of Queensland climbing for the best part of 30 years. Local legend Rick White first investigated the cliff in 1968, climbing *Corner of Eden* (2 aids—Rick freed it in 1973 at 20), and the following year over 50 routes were established. White continued to dominate the scene for much of the early '70s with ascents like *Odin* in 1971 and *Child in Time* in 1973 (Henry Barber freed this at 22 in 1975). Ted Cais was also active with ascents such as *Black Light* 21 in 1973 (FFA Ian Lewis 1975). As with most Australian cliffs, Barber's whirlwind tour changed the face of the cliff. He established Australia's first 23 with his ascent of *Deliverance* (*Insomnia*, the other contender, has subsequently sunk to 21). He also freed *Satanic Majesty* at 23 and *Conquistador* at 21. Visitors continued to push the pace at Frog (although locals like Robert 'Squeak' Staszewski and Fred From were also active). In 1978 Kim Carrigan added *Paranoia* 24 and Greg Child established *Decade* 22. In 1979 another whirlwind tour passed through the cliff, this time by Tobin Sorenson (USA) and Jon Allen (UK). They freed routes such as *Tantrum* 25, *Green Plastic Comb* 25 and *Barb-wire Canoe* 25 and added *Catcher in the Rye* 27 and *Guns of Navarone* 23. Carrigan returned to repeat these routes and added to them with *Future Tense* 26 (1981) and then in 1982 added *Stand in Line* 27 and *Brown Corduroy Trousers* 28. His last important addition to the cliff was the 1984 freeing of *The Lord's Prayer* at 27. Kevin Lindorff had dropped up from Victoria in 1983 and bagged the incredibly bold (read dangerous) *Flange Desire* 27. During the '80s local climbers like the Camps (Stuart and Scott), Paul Hoskins, John Pearson, the Bieske boys and Chris Frost continued to plug the gaps moving out onto the walls and arêtes, but it remained to more visitors to add routes in the upper grades. This included Steve Mayers (*Time for Tea* 27, 1987), Mike Law (*Debrilla* 28, 1988), and from the UK Nick White (*Pokomoko*, with aid) and Paul Smith (a controversial free ascent of *Whistling Kite* 31, 1988).

Season: The best time to visit this Queensland crag is between April and September. In summer it is too hot and humid for all but the keenest local. The cliff faces W.

Location/access: Frog (Mt French) is just outside the little town of Boonah, 100km SW of Brisbane. You can get there from the Cunningham Highway (15) which runs from Ipswich down into NSW, turning L before you reach Aratula, or you can come in from Beaudesert S of Brisbane on the Mt Lindesay Highway (13). On the S edge of Boonah is the famous Dugandan Hotel. You turn R here (if coming through Boonah) and follow the signs up to the camping area which is at the back of the cliff.

Camping and local amenities: Camping is currently allowed at Mt French, although sites are limited. There are toilets and water. Pre-booking is almost essential, as is payment in advance (telephone the ranger). Firewood collection is forbidden so it is best to bring a stove. There is accommodation in Boonah in the caravan park, or in pubs. Most supplies, including fuel, can be bought in Boonah, but many things are cheaper to buy in Brisbane.

Kent's Lagoon, near Kalbah, is the best spot to go for a swim, although Lake Moogerah, further south, is also an option.

Transport: You must either bring your own car, hitch or arrange a lift in Brisbane.

Guidebooks: *Frog Buttress*, Scott Camps, A Wild Publication, Melbourne, 1989.

Information: Climbing shops in Brisbane (see Appendix 1); the Ranger, Moogerah Peaks National Park, tel: (07) 5463 5041 or fax: (07) 5463 5042.

Follow the path to the top of the scree slope and make your way down. This gives you access to the middle of the cliff. I will describe the routes to the L (FI) of the scree slope R>L and then describe those to the R (FI) L>R. Many of these routes are marked, particularly the older ones.

| ▲ | 12 | 7m | | 1969 |

Parson Pleasure – The first route of any substance. A short, juggy groove to ledge.

| ▲ | 20 | | 1972 {1973} |

Egotistical Pineapple – Technical crack and face climbing immediately L.

| ▲ | 20 | | 1975 |

Plummeting Pineapple – 2 corners L.

| ▲ | 20 | |

Close to the Edge – A long V-groove up to and around bulge on the R. Exit L at top of V-groove.

| ▲ | 16 | 38m | | (2) 1968 |

Liquid Laughter Layback – Climb 3 successive cracks past ledges to the base of a V-chimney. Belay on top of pillar. 2. Crack.

| ▲▲ | 16 | 18m | | 1970s |

Borderline 29 – From belay on *Liquid Laughter Layback* climb out to crack on L arête (FI).

▲▲▲ 24   1969 {1978}

Impulse – Impressive cracked face L of *Liquid Laughter Layback*. Up this to large ledge on R.

The next section of cliff, up to *Satanic Majesty*, has a number of climbs including the following recommended routes:

▲	19	1976	**Southern Comfort**
▲	16	1973	**Forked Tongue**
▲▲	14	1969	**Theory**
▲	16	1969	**Castor**
▲	22	1979 {FFA later}	**Steel Fingers**

▲▲ 23   1973 {1975}

Satanic Majesty – Start up manky groove (*Our Father*) then trav L to the base of fine diagonal. Up this to steep handcrack.

▲ 27   1969 {1984}

The Lord's Prayer – The thin crack up the face to the L past PR.

▲ 21   1973 {1975}

Badfinger – The crack to the L. Hard start leads to offwidth and then up finger crack to ledge. Up crack past tree to exit.

▲▲ 26   1981

Future Tense – L again is a thin seam however it is best to start up *Blood Sweat and Tears* to the L. From tree on *Blood Sweat and Tears* move R then up exposed line.

▲▲ 15   1969

Blood Sweat and Tears – The long steep groove to L.

▲ 20   1971 {1975}

Cannabis Crack – Impressive corner to L reached by bouldery start.

▲▲▲ 30   c. 1990 {1990}

Pokomoko – Long sport arête to rap.

▲▲▲ 31   1971 {1988}

Whistling Kite – The hardest route on the cliff to date. A spectacular crack past a 'reinforced hold' and 2BR and fixed wires.

▲ 19   1973

Inquisition – Line to L. Bridge to a bulge and up short crack to large ledge. Up wide crack above to finish.

▲▲ 25   1975

Carrion Comfort – L again is the shallow V of *Catcher in the Rye* 27 and L again is this leaning corner.

▲▲ 21 | 1973 {1975}

Venom — 6 climbs to the L is this route, the original 'overhanging, diagonal, glass smooth off-width' thrutch, finishing up short bulging finger crack.

▲▲ 17 | 1969

Resurrection Corner — Aesthetic twin crack corner to L, above hard bouldery start (climb in from side).

▲▲ 28 | 1988

Debrilla — The beautiful and hard arête to the L past BRs and fixed wires.

▲▲ 22 | 1973 {1975}

Child in Time — One of the cliff's classics and more sustained than most. The excellent crack to the L.

▲▲ 21 | 1973 {1975}

Black Light — Ditto. Starts to the L past V-groove. Up thin crack and subsequent corner.

▲▲ 25 | 1983

Hard Nose — L again is the fine blade arête of *Hard Nose*. Start up *Black Light* until you can pull L onto arête and clip BR. Up past 3 BR and finish up *Black Light*.

▲ 26 | 1989

Hard Nose Direct Start — Better is the direct start up the arête past BR to join original.

▲ 20 | 1970 {1973}

Erg — Another fine line to the L, from hand crack to chimney. Start on pillar to L or climb direct at 22.

To the L of these climbs are quite a few more of which the best are:

▲	18	1971	**Dave Manks Electric Gorilla**
▲▲	22	1984	**Tight Lips and Cold Feet**
▲	19	1980	**Peaches and Cream**
▲	22	1981	**Yodel Up the Valley**
▲	11	1969	**Condor**
▲	15	1969	**Mechanical Prune**
▲	21	1978	**The Stars Look Down**
▲▲	22	1986	**The Acorn Tree**

▲▲ 20 | 1973 {1974}

Rickety Kate — A fine corner accessed from the top of the cliff, from the tourist lookout. Walk 30m N along a little track and you will see the back of a shattered pillar. Abseil down gully to base of corner.

▲	14		1969	**Iron Butterfly**
▲	14		1969	**Electric Lead**
▲	16		1970	**Materialistic Prostitution**

| ▲▲▲ | 24 | | 1983 |

Plate Tectonics — Only five climbs from the L-most end of the cliff is this classic route which climbs a twin-edge corner and then steps off R to a blunt arête at BR. Continue up arête past BR and PR. L to short widening crack.

This brings us to the end of the L part of the cliff. We pick up descriptions (L>R–FI now) from the **Scree Slope**:

| ▲▲ | 13 | | 1968 |

Clockwork Orange Corner — Just R of the scree is a classic small clean corner with a slightly overhanging crux.

| ▲ | 14 | | 1968 |

Orchid Alley — To the R past small pillar is another fine corner which is climbed to the tree. The L of 3 cracks for best finish.

| ▲ | 10 | | 1968 |

Strawberry Alarm-clock — To the R is an easy chimney with a large block at 9m. Not much pro.

R of this are a number of climbs. The best are:

▲▲	24		1985	**Down With His Pants**
▲	22		1979	**No Return**
▲▲	25		1982	**Life at the Top**
▲▲	27		1987	**Time for Tea**
▲	25		1984	**You Climb This, I'll Climb Something Else**

| ▲ | 14 | | 1969 |

Electric Flag — The excellent long groove. Finish up crack on L and short chimney to ledge. Then groove past overhang.

| ▲▲ | 24 | | 1978 |

Paranoia — The smooth groove.

| ▲▲▲ | 24 | | 1978 {1979} |

Worrying Heights — The steep and thin corner.

| ▲ | 24 | | 1987 |

Ginger Bitch — The exposed arête above the line 1m R (*Quite Contrary* 23) past 2BR. Can be done as variant finish to *Insomnia*.

▲▲▲ 20 1968 {1970}

Piranha – The long steep groove, starting up fingery start before stepping L into groove at the obvious ledge. Crack and juggy corner.

▲▲ 21 1975

Insomnia – The incredible crack to the R. After large ledge take off-width to easy exit.

▲▲ 22 1971 {1977}

Epic Journey – R of *Insomnia* is a corner with a large ledge at half height (*Fluid Journey* 21). R of this again is the elegant twin-crack system that deteriorates higher up.

▲▲ 27 1981

Stand In Line – Start from ledge as for *Epic Journey*. Step R off the ledge and into the thin line leading to PR. After this it is run-out until crack widens to accept wires. The crack thins higher to leave bouldery finish.

▲ 25 1973 {1979}

Green Plastic Comb – The cracked arête to R. Finally crack trends R into gully.

▲ 26 1988

Sadhana – Direct finish which doesn't go R to gully instead climbing arête past BR. Runout to top.

▲ 27 1982

Handy Andy – 1.5m R of *Green Plastic Comb* is groove with 2 PR.

▲▲▲ 28 1969 {1982}

Brown Corduroy Trousers – R again, past dangerous blank corner of *Flange Desire* 27 (1983) is a twin seam line up a concave wall.

▲▲ 25 1970 {1979}

Barbed Wire Canoe – Sustained open-book corner to a prominent flake up high.

▲ 24 1976 {1976/8}

Wild One – Steep flared hand-jamming crack. R of *Barbed Wire Canoe* is thin black corner (*Chook Fear* 26). Either climb this for a few moves and stem R into this line or climb thin crack direct (hard).

▲▲ 21 1969 {1975}

Cock Corner – Steep corner to R. Bouldery layaway problem to finish above ledge at 2/3 height.

▲ 21 1984

I'm a Mop – From ledge on *Cock Corner* step down R to exposed arête and up it past BR to tiny cracked corner.

▲▲ 25 1988

Stonkers and Steroids – The arête R of *Cock Corner*. Clip first BR with stick, then past four more BR to join *I'm a Mop*.

▲	20		1969 {1974}

Cock Crack – Marked AA—originally called *Artificial Aurora*. The next crack R of *Cock Corner*.

▲▲	16		1986

Satan's Smokestack – The classic four-sided chimney to the R. Face climb up widening crack to get into chimney. At top continue chimneying or climb nice rib on R.

▲▲	19		1968 {1970}

Infinity – To the R is a great jam crack with an obvious diagonal part through a bulge. Either climb corner to R to start (recommended) or tackle off-width.

The next section of the cliff has some superb climbs, the best being:

▲▲	22		1979	**Lonely Teardrops**
▲	24		1969 {1980}	**Quietly Superior**

▲▲	12		1969

Witches Cauldron – The old-fashioned classic chimney and groove.

▲	19		1970	**Humility**
▲	17		1969	**Chocolate Watchband**
▲	18		1970 {1975}	**Gladiator**
▲	23		1981	**Midnight Lightning**
▲	19		1976	**Plume**
▲	20		1976	**Termination**
▲	14		1976	**Faki**
▲	22		1978	**Old Guard**
▲	20		1974	**Juggernaut**

▲▲	19		1971 {1975}

Sorcerer's Apprentice – Start off the L end of Warlock ledge (see below), behind large eucalypt (tree). Face and crack climbing leads to a good rest at half height followed by a sustained hand crack.

▲	20		1975

Dream of Purple Peach Popsicles – Sustained thin crack leading to easy chimney.

▲▲	22		1975

Yankee Go Home – The superb thin crack splitting smooth wall. There is an abseil chain at top.

▲	18		1969 {FFA later}

Warlock – Bouldery start can be avoided by starting in *Yankee Go Home* for 3m until you can pull into the twin crack groove (capped by enormous chockstone) at R.

▲▲	23		1980

Day of the Jackal – The arête R of *Warlock* to stance. Then up to short orange V-corner capped by small roof. Up this and around R just beneath roof to a rest on L wall of *Thor*. L into exposed position to finish up hanging flake on arête. Best with double ropes.

▲▲	20		1970 {1975}

Thor – The line to R is sustained. Pull onto wall at sharp jug to gain line then up this to overhang and corner above.

▲	19		1971 {1971}

Odin – The historical classic has lost some but not all of its appeal. Up line to 'magic block', hard move and then wide hand-crack to finish.

▲	23		1979

The Guns of Navarone – Stem up blank corner, pause on the *Odin* block if necessary, then hand trav R and out onto wall above.

▲▲	22		1978	**Decade** – Face to stance then thin line to top.
▲	17		1970	**If** – L and up line past PR.
▲	21		1979	**Androcles** – Direct start to If—the corner to L.

▲▲	20		1975

Short Order – Starts to R of smooth orange corner with PR at obvious finger-crack corner.

Through the next section of cliff the recommended routes are:

▲	17		1968	**Smoked Banana**
▲	22		1985	**Understanding**
▲	25		1969 {1979}	**Voices in the Sky**
▲	19		1969	**Magical Mystery Tour**
▲	20		1971 {1975}	**The Great Big Bright Green Pleasure Machine**
▲	21		1975 {1976}	**The One that Got Away**
▲	22		1988	**Bitter and Twisted**
▲▲	21	45m	1971 {1975}	**Conquistador**

This section of the cliff has a triptych of its most classic lines. This first route takes the obvious hand crack to slightly overhanging finger crack.

▲▲	20	45m	1975

Devil's Dihedral – Twin cracks to the R which merge higher up to form a classic crack.

▲▲	23	45m	1972 {1975}

Deliverance – The corner to the R, reached by bouldering up peg-scars.

The classics throughout the next section are:

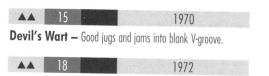

▲	17	1984	**Angel Rider**
▲	19	1976 {1979}	**Easy Rider**
▲▲	24	1984	**The Last Ungreat**
▲	24	1979 {1982}	**Gone and Forgotten**
▲	22	1976 and 1982 (a pillar fell off)	**Suicide City**
▲	23	1977	**Out on a Limb**
▲	25	1982	**Separator Direct Start**
▲	20	1979	**Footloose and Falling Free**
▲	14	1972	**Mr Bojangles**
▲	9	1969	**Short and Sweet**
▲▲	23	1982	**Ockerphillia**
▲	21	1983	**Oppenheimer's Monster**
▲	23	1983	**Garbage and the Goddess**

At the R end of the cliff is a small pillar, Devil's Wart. On it is the classic:

▲▲	15	1970

Devil's Wart – Good jugs and jams into blank V-groove.

▲▲	18	1972

Iron Mandible – Starts up prominent face-crack, with diagonal at top, four climbs R of *Devil's Wart*.

▲	16	1969

Neon Philharmonic – The 3-sided groove to ledge then bridge through bottleneck and around chockstone.

▲	17	1979

Neon Philarmonic Variant Finish – From the ledge above bottleneck trav R around arête to next crack.

▲	21	1983

The Anti-From – Exposed face climbing up rounded arête to L of *Neon Philarmonic Variant Finish*, starting from same ledge. ▲*The Direct* climbs up past BRs to arête at 24 (1984).

Girraween

All the eastern states have a granite play area and Queensland is no exception, with the Girraween National Park fitting the bill perfectly. It is almost into NSW and to get there from Brisbane you have to go up onto the plateau that runs through New England. The main feature of the park are two huge domes, the Pyramids, from whose top you can look south into the similar NSW area of Bald Rock National Park. Because it is higher (800–950m above sea level) Giraween can be cooler than most southern Queensland cliffs. As well as the domes there are numerous smaller tors and boulders all through the area. Its granite slabs and faces make a pleasant change from all the volcanic cracks and steep stuff.

There is a **bolting ban** on the Pyramids, Castle Rock, Sphinx Rock, Turtle Rock and Mt Norman and unfortunately **climbing is banned on the First Pyramid**. Please be careful with your climbing at Girraween because the Queensland National Parks Service are extremely sensitive and have a 'ban now, talk never' attitude when annoyed. There are over ten separate areas within the park where climbing is possible and well established. To find the easiest ways to these areas get a map from the Ranger's office. All these areas have well maintained walking tracks to them. Other areas in the park include Shark's Fin, Mt Norman, South-west and Middle Bald Rocks, Scattered Rocks, Crocodile, and the Scull Caps.

Geology/type of rock/quality: A course-grained granite (Stanthorpe Adamalite) ***
Grades: Up to 25.
Height: 10m on the tors, up to 70m on the Second Pyramid.
Number of routes: Hundreds.
Climbing style: The best routes are bolt protected slabs and faces—you need to bring bolt plates. But there are also some fine cracks like Scimitar, so a traditional crack rack is needed for these.
Season: It can snow here, and does get to below freezing at night in winter, but the summer days can still be hot. However, it is often cooler and more pleasant than Frog etc. Autumn (Feb–April) is nice here, as is spring (Sept–Nov).
Location/access: Girraween National Park is accessed from the New England Hwy (15) 26km S of Stanthorpe (which is roughly 260km SSW of Brisbane). The turn-off to the park is between Ballandean and Wallangarra. From the hwy a sealed road leads into the camping area (9km).
Camping and local amenities: There is a visitor centre (tel: 07 4684 5157) and two camping grounds with hot showers. The park service suggests that campers book in beforehand, especially if it is a long weekend or school holidays. The information centre is open 2–4pm weekdays and earlier on weekends. All supplies can be bought in Stanthorpe.
Transport: You must either bring your own car, hitch or arrange a lift in Brisbane.
Guidebooks: There is no real guidebook to Girraween unless you can find one of the rare, mid '80s, Scott Camps guide sheets to the area.
Information: The Ranger, tel: (07) 4684 5157 or fax: (07) 4684 5123.

Second Pyramid

Walk up to the First Pyramid and around to the Second Pyramid. On the wall between the two is an obvious large flake system, the classic:

Late Afternoon Flake

Just R of this, the classic L-wards rising sickle-shaped crack (FFA by Tobin Sorenson and John Allen in 1979) is:

About 50m R of Scimitar is an obvious slab with a thin seam which turns into a small corner system up higher. This is the classic:

▲▲▲ | 14 | 55m | (2) {1973}

Roarke's Rift — Descent off the top is either by soloing down the side facing the First Pyramid or scrambling and rapping down a gully on the opposite side.

Castle Rock

The routes on Castle Rock (2.6km from camping area) are on a beautiful orange-streaked slab on the E side. When the walking track first hits the rock of Castle Rock skirt around R for a couple of hundred metres to the first routes. The obvious orange, easy angled slab with one bolt is *Imagine* 13. L of this is an easy 15, *Dribbly Drop*. The next orange steak R of *Imagine* is the superb *That Gigantic Pygmy Possum Fossil* 19 with four BRs. R of this is a bolted overhung arête:

▲▲ | 24 | 55m | 1984 | **German Quality**

R again is an evil overhung thin corner crack by Geoff Weigland called *The Bat* 24.

Sphinx Rock

The 20+ routes on Sphinx Rock (3.5km from camp site) are mostly well protected and of quality but may be off limits currently. **Ask the Ranger before you climb.** The first block you hit has two good routes. The slabby N face is *Winter Daydreams* 15 M1, a route which has a ridiculously hard aid move off a bolt and hooks to gain the easier slab. Round L from this is a beautiful arête, *Space And Energy* 24, with 3BR. Behind this is a narrow ravine which has nine routes. The two best climbs on the eastern side are *Snow White* 15, the obvious vertical route with heaps of chicken heads, and *Vagabond* 21, the R-wards rising route on thin holds with a juggy finish. Opposite these on Sphinx Proper are a number of possibly undergraded routes. The R most is *Burnt Logs* 24, then *Around The World* 22 and, on the overhung wall 40m L is *Vakula The Smith* 24.

On the other side of the block from which Snow White climbs are two classic face routes—to the L (3m R of the obvious chimney on the eastern side of the boulder) is the classic arête:

▲▲▲ | 23 | 15m | 1985 | **Alex in Wonderland**

To the R of this is the great face route:

| 22 | **The Queen of Spades -** Belay and rappel bolts on top.

Turtle Rock

Turtle Rock (45min walk) is one of the more user-friendly areas in the park and is spread out over a large area, with a variety of different grades and protected climbs. From the tourist track go up into the gully to locate a good wall on the R side that has many short routes with bolts. The great big face about 70m L of the first route with three FH's is *Charapace* 17. Another 50m L again is the classic *Wading Ape* 15 which you need to rap in from the summit to start (unless you do the direct start at 20). L again of this route about 50m is an awesome red overhung wall with two hard classic 24s, the L one is:

▲▲▲ 24 30m 1986 **New Paths**

Mt Maroon

The popular winds of climbing fashion have blown cold on this area in the last decade. The potential for new hard routes and access problems on other crags has not been enough to lure climbers up to this grand cliff, replete with Queensland climbing history. The committing and daunting nature of climbing here has kept the crowds at bay. Perhaps times will change again and for that reason I have included it in this guide.

Geology/type of rock/quality: Volcanic plug rock.

Grades: 14–25.

Height: Up to 110m.

Number of routes: Over 100.

Climbing style: Face—mostly naturally protected.

Brief history: Rick White added some extremely difficult aid routes such as *Anti-Christ* A3+ here in the '70s, and in 1972 climbed what was then the hardest climb in Australia, *Vahalla* 22, a 30m (free pitch) on the E face of Mount Maroon. Rick described the route as 'a committing and unpleasant climb—very hard to protect before the days of small camming devices'. It takes a fiercely leaning corner and 'essentially goes nowhere'. No-one has yet freed the upper roof pitch so in effect it is a free pitch rather than a climb, although with a modern chain philosophy this is not a problem. Tobin Sorenson stopped off in 1979 to free *Nympho* at 25.

Season: Same as Frog, see p.131.

Location/access: S past Moogerah Dam and onto Cotswald Rd. Follow this until you get to picnic table. From here, jump the fence and walk past the water tank and up the ridge. This gets you to a saddle at the top of Viewpoint buttress. The 110m E face can be seen from here. L from Viewpoint gets you to Waterfall Wall.

Camping and local amenities: Camp at picnic tables.

Transport: Own vehicles.

Guidebooks: None.

Recommended routes:

▲	16	**Ruby of India,** East Face
▲	20M1	**Phaedra,** East Face
▲	22	**Valkyrie,** East Face
▲	22	**Valhalla,** View Point
▲	18	**Sticks and Stones,** View Point
▲	16	**Jezebel,** View Point

The Glasshouse Mountains

North of Brisbane, the volcanic plugs of the Glasshouse Mountains rear picturesquely up from the rich coastal plain. Once on the rock, though, the beauty of the area is often forgotten in a wave of fear that comes washing in on a tide of loose rock, poor protection and exposure. Fortunately, not all the climbs have this aspect to them and, as a result, coupled with the proximity to Brisbane, the cliffs of Tibrogargan, Beerwah and Mt Ngungun are reasonably well frequented. **Coonowrin is officially closed** to both climbers and bushwalkers, due to loose rock.

Geology/type of rock/quality: Trachyte—varies between plugs with Tibrogargen the best of the lot. Beerwah is very soft and flaky, and Ngungun's rock is soft to moderately hard * to **

Grades: Up to 24.

Height: Up to 500m on Mt Beerwah.

Number of routes: There are hundreds of climbs scattered through the Glasshouse.

Climbing style: Various, face climbing on bolts and natural gear. Except on the short sport bolted routes expect serious and committing climbing. Remember that a lot of these climbs were put up by real climbers, who knew no fear—not just wore the T-shirt.

Season: Same as Brisbane, see p. 129.

Location/access: Drive north from Brisbane for about 55km and take the Glasshouse Tourist Route (signposted) to the L. This takes you through Beerburrum to the township of Glasshouse.

To get to Tibrogargen turn L (Barrs Rd, signposted 'Forestry Nursery') about 6km before reaching the town. Go under the bridge and along the dirt track past the nursery, and take the signposted L-turn towards the mountain. The poor track continues past at least one brown and yellow national park sign saying Mt Tibrogargan. Park in the car park on the L. The track (15min) leads to the E face from the warning sign. Depending on what route you are doing, walk either R (towards *Wasp* 7) or L (towards *Carborundum Chimney* 11). The wall 15m L of this is Insurrection Wall. All routes on this wall are bolted with fixed hangers but require supplemental natural gear and all finish at rap chains. If you walk R for about 10 minutes (past the NE shoulder) when you get to the apron of rock at the base of Tibro, you will see the FHs of Shadow Glen, a quaint little area with 15 nice, bolt and naturally protected routes. See Lee Skidmore's online guide (Appendix 3).

Mt Ngungun is located about 2km west of the Glasshouse township, off Fullertons Rd via Coonowrin Rd out of the town. Drive along the dirt road and park in the nice car park. Follow the walking track for a few hundred metres to the first areas (Flat Battery Wall and the Pillar). Down R of the Pillar are the Lower Main Cliffs, and up the track further past the cave are the Upper Main Cliffs.

To get to Mount Beerwah take Coonowrin Road, turn L (Old Gympie Rd) at the end then next R (dirt) towards Mt Beerwah picnic area. To get to Thanksgiving Wall walk R when you hit the apron of Beerwah for about 300m or until you start to see FHs. To get to Short Cool Ones, walk L for a few minutes (about 100m) until you come to the clean, easy-angled slabs where you hit the rock apron of Beerwah. Down further L from Short Cool Ones are some longer routes. For Fern Wall, walk approximately 700m R from where tourist track hits the base of mountain (about 400m R of Thanksgiving Wall) and after passing numerous slabs you will reach an area with ferns and big roofs above the track.

Camping and local amenities: There is no camping allowed in the Glasshouse National Park. There are a couple of caravan park/camping grounds between Brisbane and the Glasshouse. There is also a free rest area with toilets and water just near Beerburrum. Although supplies are available from the small local towns it is better to bring things from Brisbane.

Transport: Own vehicle.

Guidebooks: A new guide by Lee Skidmore will hopefully be out soon. Ask in Brisbane climbing shops (see Appendix 1).

Information: Glasshouse Mountains National Park, tel: (07) 5494 3983.

Tibrogargen

▲▲▲   15   **72m** (5) c1960s

Trojan – The old easy classic. Start at the top L of 'the scrub'. Access the scrub via the Caves Route. 1. (14m) Climb the slightly overhung (in parts) wall on slick, orange rock. 2. (14m) Walk across a ledge for about 10m and then climb up about 3–4m into a cave. There is a single BR with ring in the cave for the belay (find other gear in crack of 3rd pitch). 3. (15m) Up the finger crack/corner. You can walk R along the ledge and escape via a 50m free-hanging abseil. 4. (15m) Crack corner. 5. (15m) Avoid the chimney and instead climb the nice crack to the L. From the top walk down on the W side (40mins).

The sensational yet rarely repeated 'adventure' climb *Out of the Blue and into the Black* 24 goes up to the R of *Trojan* and R again is the equally impressive *Raptures* 24.

Insurrection Wall

FH with natural gear to chains. (R>L).

   20   **20m**

First Contact – Slab to overhung wall. Up (2 FHs).

   18   **25m**

Insurrection – 5m L. Slab to leaning crack up white rock. Up this for 5m, then up passing 3 FH's to chains.

   21   **25m**

Insurrection VS – 5m L. Stickclip first FH and pull onto bottomless wall. Up R below bulge to second FH. Meet original at top of white rock. Continue.

   20   **25m**

Nine Month Sojourn – 8m L at blocky orange corner. Demanding start then L to meet *Leaving on a Jet Plane* at the roof.

▲   20   **25m**

Leaving On A Jet Plane – 2m L on far L of wall. Up superb, bulging stone past 2 FHs to roof (FH). Up wall above (2 FHs and gear) to chains.

Mt Ngungun

This is a good intermediate area with routes mostly in the 10–17 bracket. There are also bolted sport routes from grade 13–23. The four 45m classics in a row on the Upper Main Cliffs—*Carpe Jugular* 17, *Visions Of A Transmitter* 18, *Ensorcelled* 17 and *Icehouse* 15—all offer excellent climbing.

Mt Beerwah

Beerwah is the largest Glasshouse Mountain (500m). There are a few aid routes of about A1 and A2 that go through either side of the white roofs including *The Stainless Anticlimb* (A1) aka *The Beerwah Bolt Route* and 20m L of this is *Tribute* (A3). Between the two is *Crack Of Dawn* (A3+), Queensland's equal-hardest aid route (with *Antichrist* on Mt Maroon).

Development of smaller portions of ground-level Beerwah slabs has been going on since 1995. The most significant of the new development is that of Short Cool Ones, Thanksgiving Wall and Fern Wall.

Mt Stuart

Mt Stuart is a large mountain (22km SW of Townsville) with communication towers on top that sticks up above the surrounding coastal plains (584m). It offers the best climbing in northern Queensland with commanding views of the dry northern bush and super-blue coral sea. Add to this five minute access and good rock and you have all the makings of a great crag. The hill is about the size of Frog Buttress, but with routes up to 90 metres.

Most of Mt Stuart is on army land. Climbers currently have to **obtain a permit to climb** on Mt Stuart (and Castle Hill). They are free and available from Townsville City Council—Parks and Gardens, tel: (07) 4727 8952. Failure to do this may result in the cliff being closed.

The new area in the Townsville climber's wonderland is the boulders of the Herveys Range (see Appendix 3). Almost in town is the block of Castle Hill, which, though not of the quality of Mt Stuart, still has quite a few climbs. There are also other minor crags like West End Quarry, University Wall and Kissing Point scattered around the town.

Geology/type of rock/quality: Good medium grained granodiorite ***
Grades: Up to 26.
Height: 10–100m.
Number of routes: Several hundred.
Climbing style: Natural protected climbs on cracks and corners with some bolted face routes, carrots and hangers.
Brief history: Climbers have been enjoying the tropical delights of Mt Stuart for at least 20 years. In the early '80s, the local military began to use it for training and by 1986 had added 20 climbs to the Playground (up to 17). The earliest recorded route at Mt Stuart was *Cannonball* 17 by T. McOwen, Dave Hall in 1982.

In 1989 new members of the local James Cook University Rock Climbing Club, Scott Johnson, Allan McGill and Mathew Swait, began to further develop the cliff, adding 60 climbs in the next three years, up to 25. Since then development has continued. Mark Gommers got in on the act in 1990, as did local Andrew Doubleday, and more recently webmaster Lee Skidmore. There are now 150 climbs at the Playground and almost the same number in other areas.

Season: Because of the semi-tropical climate, the normal Australian winter (May–Oct) is perfect here. Its altitude means that in winter it can be cooler than down in the town. The rest of the year can be hot and humid. Most of the cliff goes into shade after midday which can make climbing possible on moderately hot days. The L-hand side of the Playground is called Windy Corner and gets more shade, but can get cold.

Location/access: There is a road that runs up to the top of the mountain. To find it head S on Charters Towers–Bowen Rd which becomes the Flinders Highway (78). About 15km S of town turn R (signposted) to Mt Stuart. It is about 10km to the top. When you are close to the top, instead of turning sharply L and going all the way to the picnic area and summit, turn R and park off the side of the road—don't obstruct the gate. Follow the track past the fence for about 5 mins until you reach the top (about the middle) of the cliff called the Playground. It is the most popular and most easily accessible area. The lower Playground is down to the R (FO) and below that the Pinnacle. The Fortress is below the Playground and to the L (FO) is Nameless Wall, The Main Faces, Colorado, The Neutral Zone, Wall of the Four Winds (the Great Wall is under this), Remembrance Wall and Acacia Wall (Butterfly Wall is lower here).

Access to the base of the Playground is by walking down either L or R down the easy track. Many routes are initialled at the base in paint, but this practice is now frowned upon. The Pinnacle is conspicuous from the top of the Playground. It is best accessed (as per the Lower Playground) by following the track downhill from the far L (FI) of the Playground. Scramble down the gully until you can gain the Pinnacle ridgeline at a small saddle. There are chains at the end of the top of the Pinnacle (use backup BR if rapping).

Camping and local amenities: Camping isn't allowed on Mt Stuart itself but there are a number of caravan parks down the hill. The nearest is Sun City at 119 Bowen Road, Rosslea. There are backpackers' hostels and hotels in Townsville, as well as all your shopping needs. Climbing supplies may need to be brought with you or try Adventure Camping Equipment (see below).

Transport: Own vehicle.

Guidebooks: *A Climber's Guide To Townsville and Magnetic Island*, Doug Hockly, self-published, 1999. Also useful web sites (see Appendix 3).

Information: Try Adventure Camping Equipment (see Appendix 1); or the Ranger, tel: (07) 4774 1382.

Playground (L>R):
(Those routes marked i are initialled.)

▲▲	23	16m	1991	**A Separate Reality**
▲▲	19	20m	1991 i	**Fist Full Of Ants**
▲	19	20m	1991 i	**Simple Pleasures**
▲▲	22	18m	1993	**Shadow of a Doubt**
▲▲	24	15m	1991 i	**Tit For Tat**
▲▲	24	20m	1998 i	**Salt in the Wound**
▲	11	18m	1994	**Happy Wanderer**
▲	13	22m	1985	**Holiday**
▲	21/22	21m	1991	**Joy Boy**
▲	25/26	18m	1999	**The Missing Link**
▲	25	15m	1991 (sport)	**Eclipsed**

▲▲	21	22m	1991 i (faded)	Yankee Logic
▲	21/22	22m	1991 i	Black Magic
▲	23	22m	1994 i	Voodoo
▲	17	22m	i	Cannon Ball
▲	18	22m	i	Hard Rain
▲	15	24m	1989 i	Under The Cling
▲▲	15	25m	1989 i	Under The Cling – ZZ finish

Other areas:

▲▲▲	25	35m	1991, The Pinnacle	Physical Meditation
▲▲	24	30m	1991, The Pinnacle	The El Nino Effect
▲▲	22	50m	1991, The Pinnacle	Romancing The Stone
▲	20	50m	50m (2)[20,19] 1991, The Pinnacle	Megalith
▲	19	35m	1991, The Pinnacle	Non Son Girate
▲▲	21	25m	1995, The Fortress	Rock Sex Variant Start
▲▲	22	80m	1991, The Neutral Zone	Beam Me Up Scotty
▲▲	23	65m	1991, The Neutral Zone	Cosmic Messenger
▲▲	23	80m	(2)[32,20] 1993, Lower Colorado Wall	A Few Good Men
▲	21	25m	1998, Lower Colorado Wall	The Fifth Element
▲▲	23	15m	1998, Lower Colorado Wall, Classic sport climb	Tristar
▲▲	22	50m	(3) [21,22,20] 1998, Upper Colorado Wall	Immortality
▲▲	24	50m	(3)[22,24,21] 1991, Upper Colorado Wall	Siddhartha
▲▲▲	18	90m	1996, The Great Wall, The best middle grade multipitch on Mt Stuart	Deliverance
▲▲	23	25m	1998, Wall Of The Four Winds	Ride Like The Wind
▲	22	25m	1997, Wall Of The Four Winds	Against The Wind
▲	22	25m	1996, Wall Of The Four Winds	Gone With The Wind
▲	19	25m	1997, Wall Of The Four Winds	Candle In The Wind

Castle Hill

About 1km from the centre of Townsville is Castle Hill—one local has described it as 'a pile of choss, but a really good one'. Its position compensates a little for the quality of the rock. Be careful you don't drop rocks onto tourists. There are a number of good climbs here from 12–25 on the L side, the best being the sport climb:

▲▲	23	10m	1997	Have a Nice Day I'm Off to New Zealand

There are also three multi-pitch routes:

▲▲	18	70m	1993	Vision
▲▲	19	115m	1998	

Transmogrifier – The classic, with its 45m first pitch.

Saint and Sinner – A line of bolts passing a large painted 'Saint' figure, 3 pitch.

Magnetic Island

The idea of a 'tropical island' has almost mythological resonance, conjuring images of hula skirts and pina coladas. Magnetic Island is only a short ferry ride from Townsville and is certainly tropical. It has good beaches and lots of rock to climb and boulder on. Pack your own grass skirt and cocktail shaker though. One of the more popular areas, Rocky Bay, is a nudist beach so the grass skirt is optional. The high point of the island is Mt Cook (494m) so if you don't want to get cold in NZ bag a summit here.

One of the more modern climbing areas in Australia, Magnetic Island does offer good quality granite climbs (not many) and boulders, often with soft sandy landings. It is more of a climber's than a tropical paradise. And if you get bored, take a dip, do some snorkelling, or unpack that cocktail shaker.

Geology/type of rock/quality: Granite ***
Grades: Up to 26/27.
Height: Up to 15m.
Number of climbs: Not many, about 10.
Climbing style: Granite face climbing and bouldering.
Brief history: Though Andrew Rule started with *Crimson Tide* (the rest subsequently freed by Mark Gommers in 1995) Magnetic Island has only been developed in the last few years when Doug Hockly and others began to visit the island.
Season: Like Mt Stuart, the normal winter (May–Oct) is ideal, and if it is hot there is always the option of the water. Beware of box jellyfish or 'stingers' (see p. 10) which can be fatal.
Location/access: You need to take a ferry out to the island. Magnetic Island Ferries (tel: 07 4772 5422) leave from the ferry terminal near the Great Barrier Reef Aquarium in Townsville and from a terminal at the breakwater on Sir Leslie Thiess Drive near the casino. It costs about $20 return to Picnic Bay, $15 for students. The trip takes about 15 mins. You can buy ferry and accommodation packages.
Rocky Bay is the first bay to the N (anti-clockwise) from the village of Picnic Bay. Alma Bay is about halfway up the E coast and Arthur Bay another 2km along from there. You can walk, take a bus, or if there's four of you it's cheaper to take a taxi.
Camping and local amenities: There is lots of good accommodation, pubs, bikes and mokes for hire on the island, as well as restaurants and a decent bus service. In Picnic Bay there are shops but prices are probably dearer than Townsville.
Transport: Walk, hitch, hire a moke or bike or catch the Magnetic Island bus service that runs 12–18 times a day (meets the ferries and stops at most accommodation). Fares are quite cheap ($8 full day pass).
Information: Try the Magnetic Island Tourist Bureau Information & Central Booking Office, tel: (07) 4778 5256; Adventure Camping Equipment in Townsville (see Appendix 1); Magnetic Island National Park, tel: (07) 4778 5378.
Guidebooks: *A Climber's Guide to Townsville and Magnetic Island*, Doug Hockly, 1999.
Bouldering: There are lots of boulders and some would say potential. Some of the harder problems are: *Reeven* V5/V6 and *Little Fervour* V5, both at Alma Bay.

Recommended classics at Rocky Bay (R>L):

▲▲	26/27	8m	1999	**Brudl**
	15	14m	1999	**Why Aren't They Naked?**
▲	22	12m	1999	**Natures Finest**
▲	23	7m	1999	**Curlew**
	20	7m	1999	**Not Without Jase**
▲	22/23	10m	1995	**Crimson Tide**

Cairns

Few people travel all the way up this end of Queensland to go climbing. A lot of people come up here to see Cape York, visit the Great Barrier Reef or just to hang out in the tropics. If you are here, and are a climber, you will be pleasantly surprised to find that there is a fair bit of rock around, with quite a few routes.

The cliffs are divided into three main areas: those accessed from Cairns (includes Barron Gorge Power Station and Trinity Beach bouldering), those from Kuranda (27km from Cairns— includes Barron Falls, Glacier Rock and Rob's Monument) and those accessed through Mareeba (37km from Kuranda—Davies Creek, Forest Domes, Turkey Hill, Mount Mulligan, Granite Gorge and Emerald Creek).

Barron Falls is the main area. It's in the Barron Falls National Park (follow the signs from Kuranda, about 6km). From the lookout where the shelter is, go over the fence and follow the narrow track down to the gorge (about a 20 min walk). There are more than 40 climbs (up to 30m) from 12–23+ including: *Head over Eels* 20, *Diving Board* 15, *Peanut Butter Spider* 17, *Tag Team* 19, *Cucumber Castle* 21, *Upwardly Mobile* 22, and *All Chalk and No Action* 23.

Trinity Beach has bouldering and reportedly a 12m-high grade 28/29. Turkey Hill is located 6km outside Mareeba (less than 1hr Cairns) and is adjacent to the road. A 10 minute walk leads to granite boulders and slabs. There are over 30 routes between 10m and 20m high. Visit Lee Skidmore's web site for details (see Appendix 3).

Geology/type of rock/quality: Various.

Grades: Up to 29 (reportedly) at Trinity Beach.

Height: Up to 50m at Barren Falls, Glacier Rock and Forest Domes, and 150m at Mount Mulligan. Mossman Gorge Bluff has been described as a 250m mini-version of El Cap.

Number of routes: Over 100.

Climbing style: Various.

Season: Cairns is quite tropical and thus has a wet season Nov/Dec–April/May (with Jan–March in particular) when it can be, as you might suspect, quite wet. And it is hot with daily temperatures in the mid to high 30s. It is slightly cooler and drier in 'winter' (June–Sept). In mid summer watch out for cyclones which can bring high winds and a lot of rain to the coast.

Location/access: Various, see the guidebook at Lee Skidmore's immortal.net web site (see Appendix 3) for different areas.

Camping and local amenities: Various options. Towns like Kuranda, Mossman, Mareeba and particularly Cairns have accommodation and all necessary supplies.

Transport: Own vehicle. Buses run to the various local towns. Areas like Barron Gorge and Trinity Beach are quite close to Cairns and could be reached by taxi, bus, or bike.

Guidebooks: See the guidebook at Lee Skidmore's immortal.net web site (see Appendix 3).

Information: Try Cairns climbing shops (see Appendix 1).

WESTERN AUSTRALIA

For most Australian climbers, Western Australia seems like a long way to go just to go climbing. Even if you live in the state, the long distances are still daunting. As a result, the majority of climbing has occurred within a certain radius of Perth. There are acres of unclimbed rock in the state, particularly in the north (although there is the potential for similar access restrictions to the Northern Territory).

There is a wide range of excellent climbs, including hard sport routes in the local quarries, the hedonistic delights of Margaret River to the south, the new pumps of Kalbarri to the north, and the excellent sea cliffs and mountains clustered around Albany, 400km south-east. One cliff which is worth visiting, although it is not described in this book, is the granite dome of Peak Charles (near Norseman), a mere 600km to the east of Perth and a favourite area of a small and dedicated band of Kalgoorlie Climbers.

Perth

Perth is a beautiful city, overlooking the wide Swan River and lined to the west with some of the best city beaches in the world. If you can drag yourself away from the beach and cafés, however, there is quite a bit of climbing to be had in the quarries and gullies of the hills that lie to the east of the city (see map, p. 152). There are Mountain, Stratham's and Boya quarries and the Toodyay, Spring Creek and Darlington boulders, Churchman's Brook and Mt Randall, among others.

If the climbing does not grab you, then perhaps the bouldering will. Some excellent granite bouldering exists on the low outcrops around Kalamunda, Darlington, Mt Randall, Toodyay and Jon Forest (where problems can be attempted whilst holding a cold pint). Underground topos are available from the Rockface Climbing Gym (see Appendix 2).

Problems range from V0–V10+ with some daring highballs for those with shockies for ankles. A wide variety of styles includes arêtes, slabs, gut scumming mantles and delicate faces, with a strong emphasis on footwork and technique rather than raw gumption.

Some of the best areas/circuits are marked with white arrows and must dos include: the 'Sunday Circuit', Piesse River Valley, Kalamunda; Trackside, Piesse River Valley, Kalmunda; the 'Happiland Circuit', Spring Creek, Kalamunda ; the Mountain Quarry Circuit; and the Toodyay Circuit

The Quarries

The quarries are just that, empty pits of quarried granite nestled in the hills. The easier climbs can unfortunately be on quite poor rock but with modern sport routes things are looking up, albeit at harder grades. These modern climbs have made the quarries more of an outdoor climbing gym, with many holds either glued on or drilled into the rock.

Geology/type of rock/quality: Granite *
Grades: Up to 30.
Height. Up to 30m.
Number of routes: 100 (approx.).
Climbing style: The older climbs tend to be crack routes with more modern sport bolted face routes.
  Older bolted routes were generally done with carrots.

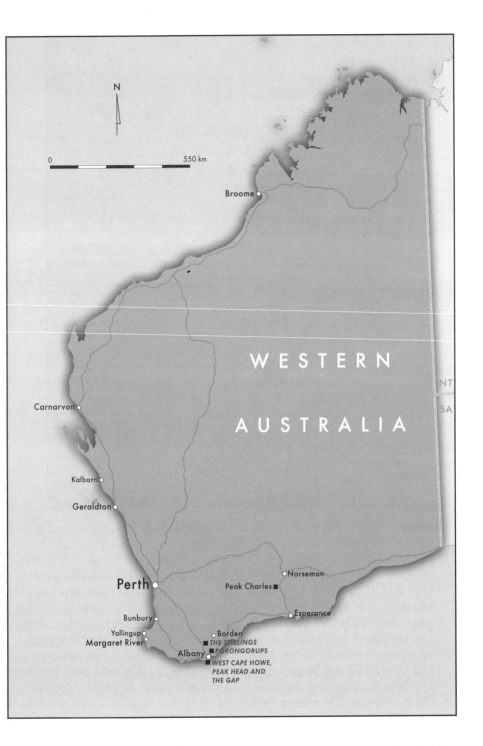

N

0 ————— 550 km

Broome

WESTERN

AUSTRALIA

Carnarvon

Kalbarri

Geraldton

Perth

Norseman

Peak Charles ■

Bunbury

Esperance

Yallingup
Margaret River

Borden
■ THE STIRLINGS
■ PORONGORUPS
Albany
■ WEST CAPE HOWE,
PEAK HEAD AND
THE GAP

NT

SA

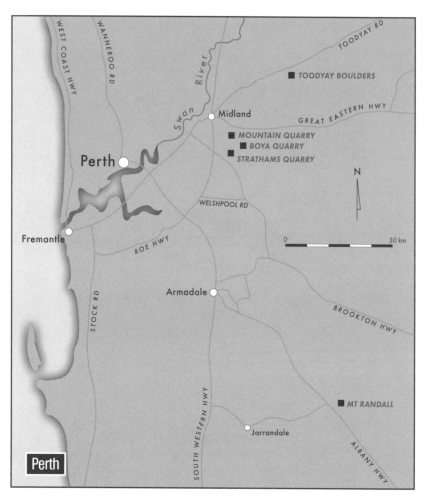

Brief history: Climbing in Perth started with Mike Adams' ascent of Back Slab in Mountain Quarry. The Climbers' Club of Western Australia was formed in 1968 and the group, mostly ex-British climbers, used the quarries as training for longer climbs in the Stirlings, to the south. In 1975, Robin MacArthur discovered Churchman's Brook and it was here in the mid '70s that Warren Lees climbed *Up for Grabs* 22. Lured by an article by Lees, NSW climber Mark Colyvan turned up in 1983 and bagged the FFA of *Skywalker* 23 in Mountain Quarry. Throughout the '80s, local activists like Ron Masters, Dave Waglands and Peter McKenzie began to find and develop cliffs close to Perth. In 1988 Mike Law visited, 'manufacturing' several 25/26s in the area. In the '90s locals such as Shane Richardson (*City Limits* 26), Anthony Bell (*Cranial Void* 27 and *Black Ambience* 29), Gerald Chipper (*Cardio Funk* 29) and Derek Toulan (*Sweet Pea* 28) added increasingly hard climbs, often with drilled or glued-on holds (all these last routes are in Mountain Quarry). In 2000, Boyd MacNamara manufactured *Ersatz* 30 to Stratham's Quarry.

Season: Although it can get extremely hot in Perth in summer, making the quarries unbearable, the other three seasons are good. Climbing is possible in winter, unless rain starts the cliff seeping.

Location/access: To get to Mountain Quarry (east of Midland in the suburb of Boya) turn R into Scott Rd (heading E on the Great Eastern Hwy—2km after Roe Hwy), then 2nd L into Coulston Rd, continuing to follow this at the roundabout. The quarry car park is 100m past the bus stop on the N side of Coulston Rd. Bus 322 will drop you at this stop. From the car park a short 300m walk takes you into the quarry. Skywalker Wall is at two o'clock (NNE).

Camping and local amenities: There is no camping in the quarries but lots of accommodation options in Perth.

Transport: Own car or public bus (see access).

Guidebooks: *Perth Rock: A Topo Guide to Rock-Climbing around Perth*, Shane Richardson, Stone Productions, 1996.

Information: Perth climbing shops (see Appendix 1). Note: Cars are often broken into in the parking area of Mountain Quarry. Take care.

Mountain Quarry

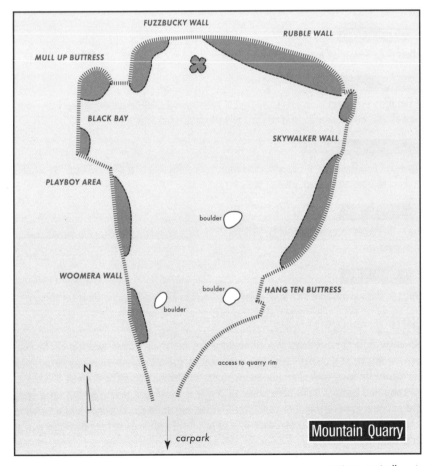

This is the best, largest and most historically important of the Quarries, with some of the state's hardest climbs and some easier top-rope problems. There are also 50+ problems V0–V8. A good bouldering circuit exists to the R (350m) of main entrance.

Going anti-clockwise from the quarry entrance:

		24	16m	1988
		27	16m	1993
▲		29	20m	1995
		28	22m	1994
		29	18m	1997

Hang Ten – The line of 4BR on R of triangular buttress.
Cranial Void – Line of 5BR L of *Hang Ten*.
Black Ambience – 6BR L of *Cranial Void*.
Sweet Pea – 6BR to L of *Black Ambience*.
Cardio Funk – L of *Sweet Pea*. 6BR to rap.

| | | 22 | 25m | 1988 |

Urban Ethics – Take care. Skywalker Buttress is the next one left (with the obvious L-ward facing roof crack on it). In the middle of the wall it is possible to scramble up to a high point. *Urban Ethics* climbs up L from here, then straight up (past pitons and BR).

| ▲▲ | 23 | 40m | (2) {1983} |

Skywalker – The obvious roof and up arête. Take large cams.

| ▲▲▲ | 23 | 30m |

Fringe Benefits – The line L of *Skywalker*, swinging L to underneath roof at half height (level with *Skywalker* roof), PR and BR. *No Wasted Space* 25 takes the line of bolts straight up, where FB swings L.

| | 21 | 23m | 1989 |

Mull Up – Mull Up Buttress is the tall one with a little pinnacle on top. The climb takes a line of BR and natural gear up L 3rd of wall, through small roof, passing L of another roof to BB.

| | 17 | 28m |

Playboy – The obvious V shaped corner L of the Black Bay. There are also easy top rope problems on this wall. Take care on gravel exit.

| | 26 | 15m |

City Limits – Woomera Wall is the small blank orange wall to your L as you enter the Quarry. The line of 3BR.

Kalbarri

A world away from the southern WA climbing areas and their winter weather is the sun-drenched sandstone of Kalbarri. Here, in a gorge cut by the Murchison River, are climbs of a different nature to most WA climbing areas: steep, sandstone sport clips. Areas like the Z-bend, D-Loop and Hawk's Head offer some of the best modern climbing in WA, in a truly beautiful national park setting. The town itself, at the mouth of the Murchison, is a peaceful tourist town, with great beaches and coastline; as beautiful a place as any to relax after a hard day's cranking.

Geology/type of rock/quality: Sandstone of varying quality.
Grades: Up to 29. Mostly from the mid-teens to mid-20s.
Number of routes: Up to 100.

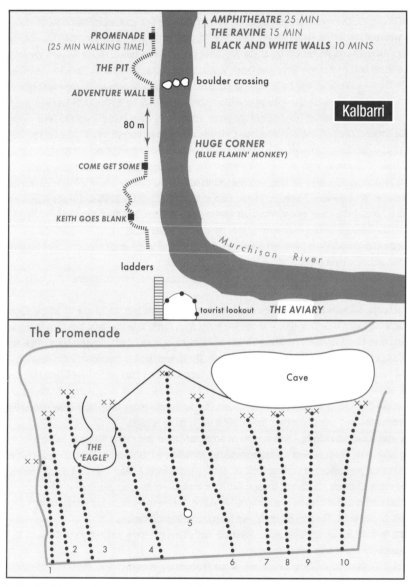

1. *It's a Boy* 24
2. *Heavy Petting* 24
3. *Root Canal* 27
4. *Glass Slipper* 28
5. *Homophobia* 28
6. *Bustin' Down the Door* 27
7. *She Magic* 26
8. *Super Funky* 25
9. *Fuck the Law* 24
10. *'Mikl's Route'* 25

Height: Up to 166m in the Amphitheatre, but mostly under 50m.

Climbing style: Sport routes from the mid-teens to mid-20s and naturally protected climbs.

Brief history: Climbers began to come to the gorge in the mid '80s, with Dave Waglands and others opening the Aviary and Left and Right Tourist Walls, doing routes like *Keith Goes Blank* 15 and *Keith Goes Boating* 13. The area slumbered until 1994 when Anthony Bell knocked off half a dozen routes in a weekend, including *Feral Dog Boy* 18 at the Pit. Ben Jones and David Brereton then did the classics *Akira* 18 and *Wicked City* 21 at the Amphitheatre. The direction of future Kalbarri climbing was realised best by Andrew Torbe and Derek Toulalan who journeyed up from Perth to add bolted climbs like *Love Muscle* 26 and *Rattler* 23. The Promenade began to be seen as the superb sport cliff that it was to become with the opening of *Bustin' Down the Door* 27 by Perth's Chris Jones.

In 1995 the UK's Adrian Wood visited the gorge, establishing often bold classics like *Homophobia* 28, *The Temple of Doom* 25 and 20 *Hot Potatoes Christians are Afraid to Touch* 25. Wood's climbing partner Julian Symmons also contributed with serious routes like *Reverend Chipper* 24 and *Sunnycide* 24.

Shane Richardson, who would later corner the guidebook market in the state, started to seriously develop the area in 1995, adding *Crankshaft* 24 to the Pit and *She Magic* 26 to the Promenade. He also added *Tripped Up* 24 and *Rippled Reflection* 25 to the Black and White Wall, both classics. Around the same period Victorian roof-meister Malcom 'HB' Matheson dropped by and bagged the huge 9m ceiling of *Kalbarri Gold* at the modest grade of 26.

Since this period, Chris Jones has developed the upper end of the grade spectrum, and his own abilities, adding climbs like *Jizz Lobber* 29 and *Glass Slipper* 28.

Season: It is possible to climb all year round in Kalbarri but it can be very hot in summer. Pick your cliff and hunt for shade.

Location/access: Kalbarri is about 530km due N of Perth. The town is 57km to the W off the Great Northern Highway. Travelling time is about 5–6 hours from Perth. Take the Great Northern Highway (95) and then Brand Highway (1). About 100km past Geraldton, turn L and follow the signs. An entry fee of $8 per vehicle is payable to the National Park. The Hawks Head is 3km down a dirt road (signposted to the R). About 20km into the National Park, turn R at the T-intersection and follow the road to the end at the Z-bend and Loop access. From here follow the footpath descending into the gorge. Go L at the first fork and climb down the ladders that access the gorge floor. Walk downstream for 10 minutes on the L side of the river (take middle tier if water is high).

Camping and local amenities: There are lots of accommodation and eating places in Kalbarri itself, along with most needs (unless it's more strength), including a bush nursing post, medical centre, police station, post office and banking facilities. At the parking lot at Z-Bend there are BBQs and toilets, but no water. Climbers are allowed to camp (with permission—contact rangers first) at the Pit.

Find food in Kalbarri town, or stock up in Geraldton. For cheap seafoods and salads, Finley's BBQ Restaurant is a must. The area is also known for its superb surf locations.

Transport: Own vehicle or hitching. Buses (Westrail) and planes (Western Airlines) go to Kalbarri. The local coachlines have trips out to the gorges.

Guidebooks: *Northern Rock*, Shane Richardson, Stone Productions, Subiaco, 1996. There are also some new routes online by the CAWA (see Appendix 3).

Information: National Parks information, tel: (08) 9937 1140; the Ranger, tel: (07) 9937 1192.

Bouldering: There is excellent bouldering in the gorge including areas of the Pocket Roof. This will be perhaps the future direction of Kalbarri, with vast potential for thousands of problems.

The Promenade

The Promenade (see topo, p. 155) is described as 'one of the most beautiful and steepest walls in Western Australia', an area for advanced climbers only. Good routes include: *Heavy Petting* 25, *Root Canal* 27, *Bustin Down the Door* 27 and *She Magic* 26.

On the trad front there are some very bold routes that have been done, one of the best being *20 Hot Potatoes Christians are Afraid to Touch* 25, in **The Ravine**, 30min downstream from the Promenade. It is on the opposite side of the river in a very obvious chasm. Trav in from L.

Main Face (left side)

This is the prominent orange and grey south-facing wall on the L as you look down from the lookout. From the base of the ladder, walk across and scramble up to the ledge. Descend from routes by following ledges R (FO) to scramble down gully.

Routes (L>R):

▲	20	20m	1989

Brother James — The white/grey lichen streak. Straight up past 2BRs (crux at 2nd) on thin moves to gain the juggy wall above. Straight up to finish.

▲▲▲	15	28m	1985

Keith Goes Blank — Steep and intimidating. Start off the boulder (the first moves off the boulder are about 17 but can be avoided by stepping further R). Follow the obvious L trending central crack. At top of crack, move L 2m and up to top.

▲	21	28m	1991

Quel Homme! — Start 3m R of *Keith Goes Blank* below a short flake at 6m. From the top of the flake, head straight up and through the roof.

Other recommended routes (see topo, p. 155):

▲	24	60m	1996, The Solarium	**Transformer**
▲	22	80m	1996, The Solarium	**Weird Sins**
▲	24/25	30m	1996, The Solarium	**Unknown Pleasures**
▲▲	26	23m	1994, The Pit	**Love Muscle**
▲	19	40m	(2)[19,12] 1998, Mad Cow Walls	**Enter Caveman**
▲	13	25m	1996, Mad Cow Walls	**Mad Cows and Englishmen**

The Amphitheatre

About 45 minutes walk downstream from the Z-Bend Lookout is a massive amphitheatre on the R side of the river.

▲	21	166m	(5)[21,14,-,14,16] 1994

Wicked City — Near the R (upstream) end of the amphitheatre two cracks start together at the ground The L one is sickle shaped and ends after 3-4m. The R one continues up through stepped roofs. 1. (28m) Up crack, through roofs, to ledge. 2. (20m) Off L end of ledge and up through big grass patch to corner. Up corner (beware large loose block) to main ledge/cave. 3. (50m) Move belay to L end of cave. Step down onto a traverse ledge and follow it around through thin section to ledge. 4. (18m) Up R leading ramp from centre of ledge then up slab to traverse L in crack to ledge at top of chossy pillar. 5. (50m) Up from L end of ledge where orange and white walls meet for 4m, then a R trending ascent of the excellent wall to belay in scoop under summit roof/lip.

▲　　18　　99m　　(3)[18,18,11] 1994

Akira – is the crack to a short chimney/flake, starting about 15m L of *Wicked City* and 8m L again is *Quedge* 17 105m (4)[17,17,10,14] 1997.

Margaret River

I have always maintained that a good climbing area should be surrounded by fantastic forests, great surf beaches, excellent gourmet restaurants and wineries. Sadly, so few are. However, around the town of Margaret River, south of Perth, there are cliffs that fulfil these criteria. The traditional climbing areas are the orange gneiss of the pretty Willyabrup, Moses Rocks and Cosy Corner. Willyabrup is a great little cliff, on a particularly scenic coastline, which is undercut partly by a series of roofs. This means there is a good variety of climbs here, from long corners to short, steep cracks.

In the area there are also the more modern sport climbing areas, the 'tufa dripped and stalactite laden sweatfests' of Bob's Hollow and Wallcliffe, which have ushered in a resurgence of interest in the area. Oh, and the wineries and cafés of course.

Access to Bob's Hollow is currently not officially permitted, along with the other cliffs in the Leeuwin–Naturaliste National Park, however discreet climbing (no bolting) is unofficially allowed.

Geology/type of rock/quality: Various—Willyabrup is granitic gneiss ***, Bob's Hollow limestone **, and Wallcliffe limestone **
Grades: Up to 28.
Height: Up to 40m at Willyabrup.
Number of routes: Within a 40km radius of Margaret River there are more than 200 routes.
Climbing style: Varies from mainly traditional at Willyabrup to sport at Bob's Hollow and Wallcliffe.
Season: All year round.
Location/access: Willyabrup is approx. 230km S of Perth. Take the Bussell Highway (1) S through Bunbury and after Busselton take the Caves Road (250) toward Yallingup. 16km after the Yallingup turn-off, turn R onto dirt road to Willyabrup Downs (signposted, opposite Gralyn winery). Two km and three bends later park and walk across paddocks to the coast. These paddocks are privately owned by the Cullen family (Cullen Wines) and **permission must be obtained**, tel: (08) 9755 5277 or fax: (08) 9755 5550. The vague path brings you behind and then S of the cliffs.

Wallcliffe is located on the banks of Margaret River, near Prevally Park. Take the Wallcliffe Rd W out of Margaret River, crossing the Caves Rd and R onto Surfers Point Rd after 3km. After 500m turn R again into Rivermouth Rd. Follow this to parking area. A track leaves from 30m S of the car park on the E side. Follow this up the river to the cliff, on the S side of the river.

Bob's Hollow is a very overhanging limestone cliff on the coast S of Margaret River which features over a dozen W-facing 1- and 2-pitch routes. It is in two parts: a smaller N crag with a large cave in which the fishermen sleep and the larger S crag with all the routes. Take Hwy. 1 S past Margaret's River to Cave Road. Just after the cave parking lot turn-off (on the L side), take the next road to the R. Park on the road if you don't have a 4WD, and follow a pronounced trail leading to the beach. Head L toward the cliff. Alternatively, walk S for 40min along beach from Conto Springs.

Camping and local amenities: There are a number of caravan and camping grounds up and down this section of coast, and at Margaret River. There is officially no camping at the cliffs. Local towns of Yallingup and Margaret River have fuel and supplies, though it is cheaper to bring stuff from Perth or larger towns like Bunbury.

Transport: Own vehicle or hitching.

Guidebooks: *Margaret River Rock, A Topo Guide to Rock Climbing in WA's South-West*, Stone Publications, Subiaco WA, 1996.

Information: The Augusta–Margaret River tourist bureau, tel: (08) 9757 2911) Local CALM Office, tel: (08) 9757 2322 or fax: (08) 9757 2930.

Bouldering: There is lots of good bouldering in the area. Chris Jones has established problems up to V7 at Merchant Rock, near Conto Springs.

Classics at **Willyabrup** include:

▲	26	25m 1986	**KGB**
▲	25	40m 1986	**Delving Devoids**
▲▲	24	30m 1986	**Heavy Metal**
▲▲	24	25m 1985	**Dessert**
▲▲	23	20m	**Well Stoned**
▲	22	25m 1983	**Blondes Have More Fun**
▲	21	20m	**Green Stone**
▲	21	30m 1985	**Stainless Steel**
▲▲▲	20	40m 1974	**Mobjob** – the mighty corner that splits the undercut Steel Wall.
▲▲	19	17m 1985	**Totally Awesome**
▲▲	19	18m 1978	**One for the Road**
▲	18	20m 1986	**Baited Frenzy**
▲	17	30m 1983	**Golden Buttress**
▲	16	17m 1985	**Heaven Calling**
▲	15	13m 1985	**Setting Sun**
▲▲	14	30m 1973	**Banana Split**

Bob's Hollow

▲▲	25	25m 1994	**Hollow Promise**
▲	24		**Altered States** – In the central section of the cliff.
▲	21/22		**Sunset Stroll** – (L of huge arête at S end)

Wallcliff

▲	23	10m 1991	**Kyle**
▲▲	24	18m 1993	**Fun, Love and Joy**
▲▲	27	25m 1993	**Bee Free**

Albany

If you want to choose an Australian town in which to live, and you are a climber, for variety you would be hard pressed to go past Albany, about 400km south-east of Perth. On the down side, however, are its remoteness and fickle (often miserable) weather.

The granite boulder studded town of Albany lies on the beautiful King George's Sound on the southern coast of WA. Within a short distance from the town there are areas like the short and ozone replete granite sea cliffs of the Gap, with its sea-level starts amid gigantic crashing waves, and the longer granite routes of the giant egg of Peak Head. As well there are the large, rough granite domes and boulders of the Porongorups (40km N) and the long black sea cliff of West Cape Howe (see below for separate description). Further out (70km N) there are the tall peaks and faces of the Stirlings of which Bluff Knoll is the tallest with its 320m face.

West of Albany are a number of good cliffs not described in this guide, including Elephant Rocks near Denmark, the 'must see' big granite dome of Mt Frankland near Walpole, (34 climbs, grade 4–25, 15–160m), and the cliffs of Thompson's Cove in the Nuyts Wilderness Area (7.5km walk in, 21 routes, grade 5–26, 5–25m).

Geology/type of rock/quality: Mostly Granite (except Stirlings which are not described) Up to ***
Grades: Up to 26.
Height: Up to 320m in the Stirlings. Routes at the Gap are shorter (20m) and the Peak Head routes up to 100m or slightly more. Routes in the Porongorups vary from 200m to 10m.
Number of routes: Many hundred.
Climbing style: Various. Short granite flakes, cracks and walls at the Gap. Long slabs and walls at Peak Head and in the Porongorups. Long faces in the Stirlings and short granite aretes at Castle Rock in the Porongorups.
Brief history: Refer to guidebooks.
Season: Being on the south coast of Australia, Albany has a similar temperate climate to Victoria or Tasmania. This means that winter (May–Sept) can be cold (down to 0°C at night, average 16°C day) and wet. The coast can be windy. Summer temps average 25°C, so the sea cliffs can be a beautiful place to cool off. Autumn is the calmest season. Note: on all sea cliff areas it is advisable to keep one eye on the sea at all times. Unpredictable king waves randomly batter this coast and regularly whisk away unsuspecting tourists. Be careful.
Location/access: From Albany, head E towards Esperance then after about 10km turn L towards Porongorup and Stirling national parks. The road continues to Borden. Heading N, The Porongorups are on your L after about 40km. The most accessible routes are on Castle Rock, a tourist lookout that is easily found. Climbs are described anti-clockwise around the lookout, starting in the narrow gap just before the ladder. The Stirlings are about 70km N.

To get to the Gap and Peak Head, head out of town (S) along the Frenchman Bay Rd into the Torndirrup National Park. The Gap is 16km out. You can't miss this one, just follow the tourist buses.

Also accessed from Frenchman Bay Rd are Family Rocks, Blow Holes, Peak Head and Salmon Holes. All of these cliffs are classified as being in an 'Adventure Climbing Zone' which means no new bolting may be undertaken.

To get to Peak Head, drive 20km S of Albany on Frenchman Bay Rd and turn R into Stony Hill Rd. Just before the car park there is a short gravel track (on L) that leads to a smaller car park. Follow the path from here for 2.5km down to the Head, which takes about 45 minutes. The path heads E towards the end, before the last steep sand ridge and rise to the Head. From the slabs at the back find the summit cairn. The best climbs are on the W and S faces.

Camping and local amenities: Camping is not permitted within the Torndirrup National Park but there are plenty of camping and other accommodation facilities in Albany itself. The town is quite large and has all the amenities anyone could want, including pubs and a live band scene. There is good camping within the Porongorup and Stirling national parks.

Transport: The oldest European settlement in the state, Albany is about 400km SE of Perth, a 4.5hr drive down the Albany Highway (30). It is also possible to get there by bus from Perth or towns like Denmark or Manjimup (coming from Margaret River). You can also fly into Albany from Perth. There is no public transport out to the crags so unless you want to hitch a ride with tourists, it's best to have your own vehicle. A 4WD is best for the access to West Cape Howe—it's a long walk in otherwise.

Guidebooks: *South Coast Rock: A Guide to Climbing WA's South Coast*, Richardson, S., Stone Productions, Subiaco, 1998.

Information: Regional and District Office, tel: (08) 9841 7133 or fax: (08) 9841 3329; Rangers at Porongorups, tel: (08) 9853 1095; Rangers at Stirlings, tel: (08) 9827 9230; Torndirrup National Park, tel: (08) 9844 4090. The Albany Tourist Bureau is in the old Railway Station, freecall: 1800 644 088 There is a climbing wall at the Albany Leisure Centre in Barker Road, tel: (08) 9841 2788, which hosts monthly meetings of local climbers.

There are a number of granite cliffs along the coast in the Torndirrup National Park (accessed from Frenchman Bay Road), including Family Rocks, The Gap, Blow Holes, Peak Head and Salmon Holes. Mermaid Point is further W near Cheynes Beach in the Waychinicup National Park. All of these cliffs are classified as being in an Adventure Climbing Zone which means no new bolting may be undertaken.

The Porongorups

This area of coarse-grained granite is only 30km N of Albany. There are excellent climbs on the huge **Gibraltar Rock**:

▲▲▲ 18 130m **Dinosaur**
▲▲▲ 17+ 200m **Dockyard Wall New Version** – established 1974, rejigged and bolted 1992.

The most accessible routes are on **Castle Rock**, a tourist lookout that is easily found. Climbs are described anti-clockwise around the lookout, starting in the narrow gap just before the ladder.

▲▲▲ 22 20m 1983

Meaningless – Start at the arête 2m L of *Guinevere*. Up the arête past 3 BRs (all on the LHS).

On west side of the summit catwalk is a large square bay, the LH corner is *Guinevere*.

▲	15	18m	1981

Guinevere – Up the corner.

▲▲▲	18	10m	1990

Arm Aggression – Obvious arête on block between *Guinevere* and *Sir Lancelot*. Climb past 2BRs to bolt belay on top.

▲	17	18m	1981

Sir Lancelot – The RH corner of the bay.

▲▲▲	24	25m	1992

Karma – The impressive arête 4m R of *Sir Lancelot*. 7BRs. Can be easily accessed by 'very cool' cave/tunnel slither. Look closely!

▲	18	6m	1990

Merlin – There is a block from which you start *Meaningless*, this block is 1m R as you face the cliff. Below this block is an arête. Up arête, past two BRs to belay bolt at top.

▲	22	20m	1988

Vous – Arête on the south-east corner of 'the castle'. Climb the arête, 4 BRs.

▲	22	25m

Plains Dweller (Top Rope) – Excellent slab climbing up rounded nose on the south-east corner of 'the castle' below the lookout fence.

The Gap

You can't say you've climbed at Albany until you have climbed at the Gap. Despite the fact that the climbs are only short, the crashing sea, the ozone, the gawking tourists and the fear of king waves taking you off the belay makes for the total sea cliff experience. It's 16km out of town off the Frenchman Bay Road. You can't miss this one, just follow the tourist buses.

There are over 130 routes here, grades 4–26, 10–30m. Many of the Gap routes involve abseiling into the boiling sea, or at least down close to it. If you are not confident leave a fixed line and take prussiks or ascenders. There are quite a few boulders to play on in the area but watch the landings!

To the R (FO) of the Gap are:

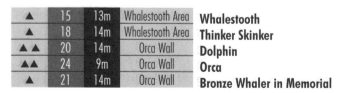

▲	15	13m	Whalestooth Area	**Whalestooth**
▲	18	14m	Whalestooth Area	**Thinker Skinker**
▲▲	20	14m	Orca Wall	**Dolphin**
▲▲	24	9m	Orca Wall	**Orca**
▲	21	14m	Orca Wall	**Bronze Whaler in Memorial**

▲	16	10m	The Bowl Area	**R.I.P. Corner**
▲▲	23	12m	The Bowl Area	**Softly Softly**
▲▲	24	12m	The Bowl Area	**Don't Petal Me**

Amityville Wall

This cliff is accessed by abseil to the wave platform (or a small ledge 6m above) and is about 20m to the left (facing out) from the Natural Bridge. It is split by a large crack and a corner.

▲	20	22m	1983

The Amityville Horror — The corner to pillar and then up wide crack in corner to finish

▲▲	19	16m	1983

Over Indulgence — The R trending flake system, just R of *TAH*.

▲▲	21	16m	1991

Noosa — To the R of *Over Indulgence*, on the same block, up a crack and then the series of flakes just to the left of the arête.

▲	16	16m	1983

One Step Beyond — The pikers variant on the arête, heading out of *Noosa* when the crack blanks out, around to the R side of the arête into hand crack.

▲▲▲	15	22m	1986

Surf's Up — 3m R of arête is a seam. Enjoy.

▲	20	25m	1991

Val Halla — R of *Surf's Up* is a corner (*Welsh Corner* 13) and R of this another arête. Start at the arête and follows flakes up and left to ledge, then up flake in centre of the wall to top.

▲▲▲	23	25m	1990

Ivory Tower — This great climb starts at the arête, up layback flakes to roof, then over to a 7m off-width crack.

The next walls have these recommended climbs:

▲▲	24	40m	Sea-Wolf Wall	**Fear No Evil**
▲	15	15m	Sea-Wolf Wall	**J.C.C.**
▲	18	15m	Sea-Wolf Wall	**I am the Walrus**

Atolls Away Wall

Take the walking track towards the lighthouse and follow this for about 400m to the E. This will bring you to the Ampitheatre. To the right (facing out to sea) is the popular Beginner's Wall with its selection of easy climbs. To the left is Atolls Away Wall, with some of the better, harder climbs in the area.

▲	22	20m	
▲▲	25	20m	
▲▲	24	25m	

Listen to the Wind Blow
Just an Aleutian
Atolls Away

Also recommended are:

▲▲	19	15m	The Chasm	
▲▲	23	20m	The Block	

Laughing Matter
Rainbow Warrior

Peak Head

Peak Head is a great Humpty Dumpty egg of exceptionally good granite rising 100m out of the sea. There are about 40 routes, grades 6–22, up to 120m. It is an atmospheric place to climb and has some of the longest sea cliff routes in the area, with long cracks, flakes and slabs. Take full rack and a handful of brackets for the old bolts.

The best climbs are on the West and South Faces. To reach the former, find your way west around the bottom of the dome's cliffs, then head down a slight spur to the large boulders at the base of the cliffs. To reach the S face, abseil (35m) from the R-hand edge of the W face from the base of *Baylac*, down a corner (*Prelude* 12). It may be advisable to leave rap rope here for escape. This abseil puts you on Stirling Terrace, a rising R-wards traverse of the S face (take this carefully) which accesses the climbs.

▲	20	45m	1992

Skysurfer – 'Sporty run-outs on the easy sections' plus 6BR (and limited natural gear –take #2 friend). Sounds great! Cutting across the West Face is an obvious diagonal groove/crack. Make your way around the boulders at the L end of the face until under the L end of the groove. Join the dots.

▲▲	19	77m	(2)[19,7] 1992

Layers of Grooviness – Starts 4m R of *Skysurfer* at 5m tall split block. 1. (50m) Up this the follow quartz dyke past 2BR. Cross diagonal (BR) and follow groove/weakness (large cam + BR) to a small hole. Up past 2BR and gear to the L side of faint groove and 2BB. 2. (27m) Easy to top.

▲▲	22	70m	(3)[22,19,7] 1990

White Witches on the Cross – Superb climb up centre of West Face. 1. (23m) Starts up diagonal. R into small cave and up to guano streaked bulge. BR then R up system of flakes to BR. Up to belay on sloping ledge. 2.(20m) Diagonally L (runout) up a series of 'vague weaknesses' to dinner plate flake. Up this to BR. Finish up grey groove to 2BB. 3. (27m) Easy to top.

▲▲▲	18	96m	(3)[18,16,15] 1990

Baylac Direct – If cracks are your thing then this is for you. Start R of *WWOTC* on boulder terrace at L most crack. 1. (33m) Up crack that fades before horizontal break. Follow curving finger crack then up layback flake to small belay ledge. 2. (23m) Up short corner, follow crack to easy ramp and belay on pinnacle/block to R. 3. (40m) L of pinnacle onto slab. Then up trending R as angle decreases, on higher of two ramps.

▲▲	16	96m	(3)[16,16,15] 1977

Baylac – The first climb here and still a classic. Starts up the crack R of *Baylac Direct*. 1. (33m) Up crack to top of block, then up L hand crack to detached flake. Climb outside of flake, L across wall to another good layback crack, up this the R to belay of *Baylac Direct*. 2. and 3. as for that climb.

▲▲▲	17	91m	(3)[17,16.15] 1981	**Lucifer's Left Hand**
▲▲▲	18	91m	(3)[17,16.15] 1978	**Lucifer's Dream**
▲▲▲	17	91m	(3)[17,16.15] 1986	**Lucifer's Right Hand**

These three climbs all share some of *Baylac*, the first two doing both pitch 2. and 3. and *Lucifer's Right Hand* doing pitch 3. *Lucifer's Left Hand* (25m) climbs the chimney 4m R of *Baylac* that thins into a crack and leads into layback flake of *Baylac*. *Lucifer's Dream* (25m) Starts at the next obvious corner crack to R. Up corner crack until it narrows and swings L. Swap to large flake on L and layback up to *Baylac* belay. *Lucifer's Right Hand* starts as for *Lucifer's Dream* but 1. (25m) travs R at 15m to a belay on a small ledge below a crack. 2. (26m) (Up crack until it joins *Baylac*.)

▲▲▲	15	105m	(3)[15,15,15] 1978

Albatross – The old classic and a fantastic climb. Start at far R of West Face. 1. (42m) Bridge R into ramp/crack system. Follow this to where slab moves R reach a ledge. The gently sloping crack to sloping belay ledge.

Good routes on South Face:

▲▲	21	102m	(3)[20, 21,17] 1991	**Power of the Old Land**
▲▲	16	118m	(3)[16,15,15] 1992	**On the Lee Side**
▲▲	17	118m	(3)[16,15,17] 1992	**On the Lee Side Direct**

West Cape Howe

The long sea cliff of West Cape Howe, 35km W of Albany, is one of the great cliffs of Australia. At the end of 4WD sand tracks through the national park lie several kilometres of sea cliff battered by waves of the Great Southern Ocean that have rolled all the way from Antarctica. The sea is an overwhelming presence at this cliff and the continual crash of waves and smell of the spray permeates every part of you and the rock. The 70m dolerite cliffs are not columnar and offer wall, slab and crack climbing on weathered and rounded rock.

Geology/type of rock/quality: Dolerite/gabbro with granite intrusions. The former is dark with a rough texture. Good friction and cracks. The granite is rougher, steeper and the cracks coarser. **

Grades: 4–27.

Height: Up to 85m.

Climbing style: Naturally protected cracks and flakes on faces. Bolts on harder climbs.

Number of routes: Several hundred.

Brief history: Climbers started climbing at West Cape Howe in 1978 when Richard Rathbone, Mike Smith and Peter Ritson started doing a few easy routes here. Word got out and routes started to fall. Paul Woperis and Ritson bagged *Andromeda* 14 and *Another Side of Midnight* 14 and Smith climbed *The Climb* 18 on the Old Man of Torbay. In 1979, Warren Lees, who would do a lot to publicise the Cape with his article in *Thrutch/Peaks*, turned up and added *Plumb Jam* 18 and *Body Builder* 20. In 1980 he climbed *Vulture Street* and *Tombstone* (with a rest). Lee's article lured two climbers from the east across in 1983 and Mark Colyvan freed *Tombstone* at 20, as well as adding a forgettable 22. The resultant publicity of this tour in the climbing magazine *Screamer* saw more interstate climbers visiting. Dave Wagland and Mark Witham arrived and bagged *Convict's Corner* 22, among other things, and Kim Carrigan dropped in, adding his usual swag of routes including *Corruption in High Places* 23. Locals like Roland Tyson and Mike Arnold continued to add climbs. Then in 1988 Mike Law dropped by, and bolted and made his way up a number of climbs including the phenomenal *Vampire Street* 20, *Tights, Camera, Action* 25, and *The Gay Blade* 27. Photographer Glenn Robbins accompanied Law on this trip and his pictures interested still more climbers, including Louise Shepherd, Mike Broadbent, Doug Scott and Simon Yates. Development continued with new climbers like Alan Rokich and Shane Richardson, and older refugees from the east including Roark Muhlen, Gordon Brysland and Waglands.

Season: As for Albany.

Location/access: From Albany head W on the Lower Denmark Road and turn L at Cosy Corner turn-off. After 3kms turn R into Combes Rd then after 2.5km turn L into Shelley Beach Rd. The road is gravel but a 2WD car can get down to the beach. If you're in a 4WD take the 2nd turn-off to R (Dunsky's Rd) about 4km along Shelley Beach Rd. It is then 5km through sand to car park on the W side of West Cape Howe.

The area of Old Man is just W of here, the Black Wall, Southern Ocean Wall Raft, and others are to the S.

Camping and local amenities: It is possible to camp at the cliff but the guidebook does not recommend it, calling it 'grim'. It is not too tiresome to come from Albany, however, there are nice camping sites nearby at the beautiful Shelley Beach and Cosy Corner.

Transport: Short of walking in through the sand from the lookout car park above Shelley Beach (3.5km/1.5 hours), the only access is by 4WD (deflate tyres to 16–20psi to drive on sand and reduce damage to tracks).

Guidebooks: *South Coast Rock: A Guide to Climbing WA's South Coast*, Richardson, S., Stone Productions, Subiaco, 1998.

Old Man of Torbay

To find the semi-detached 50m high sea-stack of the Old Man of Torbay follow the old 4WD track NW then walk W along the cliff. To reach the climbs abseil down the corner (*Easy Rider* 6) to the R of the classic SW face of the stack, to a belay ledge just below a huge chock stone. The descent is via an easy scramble down the NE side to the chockstone that joins to the mainland.

▲▲	26	25m	1992

Dancing the Deep Blue — 2BR. From belay head out left along seam then up finger crack to sloping ledge. Climb arête. Lower arête still to be climbed—wait for a calm day!

▲▲▲	18	23m	1978

The Climb — One of the great local classics. Takes the obvious crack in the south-west face.

Black Wall/The Pyramid

The Black Wall is close to and SW from the car park, in the middle of it is a large (30m) triangular buttress with a flat top. Access is by 50m abseil (to the R facing out) to the wave platform.

| ▲▲ | 19 | 45m | 1989 |

Harry Humpkin and the Exploding Pumpkin – A thinly protected classic that climbs the middle of the ramp that is the L side of the Pyramid. ▲ *Gob Smackin* 15 1989 takes the arête of the ramp and finishes as for *Andromeda*.

| ▲▲ | 15 | 50m | (2)[15,15] 1978 |

Andromeda – 1. (30m) Takes the chimney on the left side of the Pyramid to the top. 2. (20m) Up the fine arête that diagonals gently R.

| ▲▲▲ | 22 | 50m | (2)[22,15] 1986 |

Flickering Indices – Worried about falling Indice? The first of the cracks on the Pyramid (L to R) is ▲ *Mistaken Identity* 22 50m. R of this is an excellent finger crack and face climb that takes the middle of the face before trending L to arête then up short crack R of chimney to belay. Finish up as for *Andromeda*.

R again is a crack that runs through a niche in the middle of the wall:

| ▲ | 22 | 50m | **Mandrake** |

| ▲▲ | 19 | 50m | (2)[19,15] 1986 |

Take the Plunge – Up the R most crack on the Pyramid to top. Finish up as for *Andromeda*. The R arête is ▲ *Point Taken* 22 50m that starts up *Take the Plunge* before heading R to the arête.

The Raft

One of the few areas of West Cape Howe with walking access to the base of the climbs, the Raft is also one of the most popular and developed with some 72 routes. The old 4WD track from the car park that follows the cliff south leads to the old car park at the top of the descent gully. From here a slight trail with some cairns leads W to the gully. When this opens out turn R (N) across broken ground. A short scramble leads down to the flat raft. There is a cracked, small, flat-topped square buttress at the N end, the Tombstone.

Around the corner from the Raft (can abseil in) is a large chimney gully, *The Mincer* 9. About 8m L of this (accessible in low seas) is:

| ▲▲▲ | 19 | 75m | (2)[19,17] 1993 |

Better than Chocolate – A superb climb. 1. (35m) Start up corner the around roof at 3m. Follow crack which doglegs R Up to belay at horizontal break. 2. (40m) Up wall to large detached flake on L of arête. Small bulge, flake and up blunt arête.

On the R wall of *The Mincer* is:

| ▲ | 16 | 65m | (3)[9,16,14] 1982 |

Striptease – Leaves *Mincer* at 9m from belay at chockstones and climbs the steep crack after leaving the gully at a horizontal break. From crack trav R to easier rock and back L to belay. The V groove to finish.

▲▲	20	60m	(2) [15,20] 1980 {1983}

Tombstone – The classic handcrack in the middle of the feature of the same name, gained by a 20m pitch that climbs diagonally L from chimney. The curving flake line R is ▲ *I Wanna Be A Cop Too* 21 60m.

▲	11	55m	(2) [11,11]

Plumbline – The obvious chimney R of the *Tombstone*. The ledge belay at 40m is after you have been forced onto R wall when chimney narrows.

R of *Plumbline* there are two cracks:

▲	15	55m

Coast to Coast – Starts 4m R and heads up into the *Plumbline* chimney at the end of the first pitch (40m).

▲	18	55m

Sleepwalking – Instead travs R where *Plumbline* chimney closes, and climbs thin cracks up wall past BR.

▲▲▲	17	50m	1980

Vulture Street – The 2nd crack is a classic. Climb the R crack past old PR into triangular niche (can belay here). Follow crack system to top. The harder ▲ *Vampire Street* 20 50m, with its bold start, climbs the face 3m to the R to the niche, then finishes up *Vulture Street*.

R again in the *Gay Blade* area with:

▲	25	50m	(2) [25,25] 1988	**Tights, Camera, Action**
▲▲	14/16	50m	(2) [14,14/16] 1978	**Gay Dawn**
▲	27	50m	(2) [27,16] 1988	**Gay Blade**

Other recommended routes at West Cape Howe include:

▲▲	16	50m	(2) [14,15] 1988, Ed's Ledge area	**Wire Flake**
▲▲	15	50m	1988, Southern Ocean Wall	**Carousel**
▲▲	21	50m	1990, Southern Ocean Wall	**Planar Craving**
▲▲	18	70m	1978, Southern Ocean Wall	**Plumb Jamb**
▲▲	20	65m	(2) [20,17] 1993, Styx Gully	**Five Star**
▲▲	24	80m	(2) [22,24] 1993, Throne of the Gods	**Corruption in Higher Places**
▲▲	25		1997, Throne of the Gods	**Elegantly Wasted**
▲▲	27		1988, Throne of the Gods	**Twitch to Glory**
▲	14	70m	(2) [14,12] 1985, Throne of the Gods	**Yellow Peril**
▲▲	23	85m	(3) [20,18,23] 1990, Earl Grey Walls	**Badlands**

THE NORTHERN TERRITORY

Australia's most famous and popular climb is in the Northern Territory. However, the chain-draped tourist route up Uluru (Ayers Rock), climbed daily by thousands of brightly clad tourists, dripping sweat and platitudes, is hardly an indication of the rock climbing the Territory has to offer. Despite a great deal of rock, the lack of a large local climbing population, access restrictions (largely due to the sacred nature of much of the rock to Aboriginal people) the remoteness of many areas and the climate (hot and dry or hot and wet) means that the huge potential of this state has not been greatly developed. Nevertheless, there are some beautiful climbing areas in an environment that is quintessentially (or mythically) Australian. Note that climbing in most of Kakadu National Park, the main part of Kings Canyon, Uluru and Kata Tjuta (the Olgas) is illegal for reasons of cultural sensitivity (in the case of King's Canyon 'danger to tourists'), these areas being spiritually significant to the traditional landowners.

The lower parts of the Territory, known as the Red Centre, are beautiful arid lands, where the light only adds to the redness of the rock, which though plentiful is not always of the best quality. The best is fortunately found in the deep, sheltered gorges (often with good swimming holes) that cut through the rugged ranges of the MacDonnell Ranges around the population centre of Alice Springs.

In the north, the tropical climate can sap the enthusiasm of the most ardent climber. Nevertheless, there are some remarkable areas of rock. Umbrawarra Gorge (230km south of Darwin) is one of the more popular areas and there is a similar area at Hayes Creek (170km). Or, visit Katherine Gorge or Kakadu National Park and just ogle the rock. For physical gratification, in Katherine Gorge there are a million boulder problems over deep pools (the freshwater crocs are relatively harmless!)

There is also climbing at Robin Falls, 145km south of Darwin on the Stuart Hwy, and 15km south of Adelaide River. On the R-hand bank, 120m downstream from the falls, there is a buttress 25m up from the river.

There is a lot of bouldering, even in places like Kakadu. But beware, many rocks, no matter how insignificant, house art sites which should be respected. Watch for silicon drip lines that are used to protect faint artwork.

The history of NT climbing is barely recorded, and many of the original ascents of climbs have vanished with the itinerant climbers who did them. In the 1960s, Alice Springs climbers began putting up routes nearby, including some at Stanley Chasm (now off limits). In 1972, Andrew Thompson and Keith Lockwood drove from Victoria to illegally climb the *Kangaroo Tail* or *Ngaltawaddi* ('Digging Stick') at Uluru. They were caught and ordered down but returned in 1973 to bag the route. In the '70s, Alice locals including John and Helen Griffiths and Keith Seddon added routes at Trephina and climbed Chambers Pillar. Local Alice climbers continued to climb routes, and a small number of Darwin regulars developed local (for want of a better word) areas in the north. This included Roark Muhlen in the early '90s and later Keiran Culhane, Damian Auton, Steve Thorton and Goshen McCormack, who started recording climbs. Currently, the dedicated local scene is continuing the work, with Jock Morse working on a visitors guide to the Red Centre's delights. In the mid '90s a circus of climbers from Victoria, which included Glenn Tempest, Simon Mentz and Malcolm Matheson, toured the area bagging many lines.

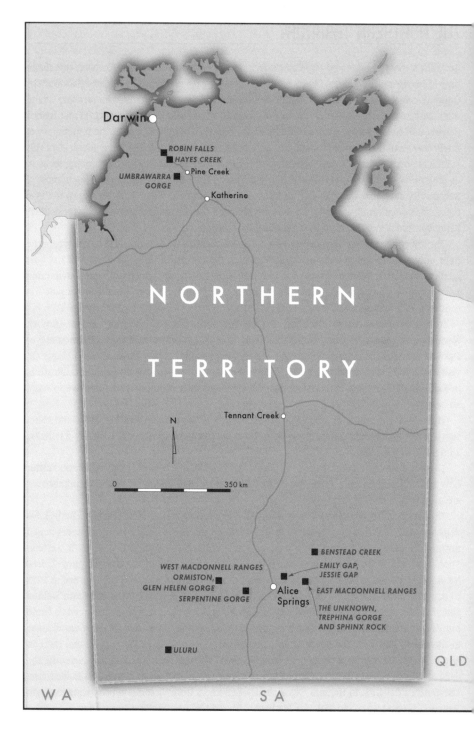

Darwin

ROBIN FALLS
HAYES CREEK
UMBRAWARRA
GORGE
Pine Creek

Katherine

NORTHERN

TERRITORY

Tennant Creek

N

0   350 km

BENSTEAD CREEK

WEST MACDONNELL RANGES
ORMISTON,
GLEN HELEN GORGE
SERPENTINE GORGE

EMILY GAP,
JESSIE GAP

Alice
Springs

EAST MACDONNELL RANGES

THE UNKNOWN,
TREPHINA GORGE
AND SPHINX ROCK

ULURU

QLD

W A   S A

The North (Umbrawarra Gorge)

Nowhere near as famous as some of the gorges in the Northern Territory, Umbrawarra still has quality rock faces above beautiful pools. Justifiably, its single pitch sandstone routes have made this the most popular area in the north of the state. Access is now restricted and climbers must obtain a permit from the Conservation Commission in Bachelor, tel: (08) 8973 8770.

Geology/type of rock/quality: Sandstone **
Grades: 16–22.
Height: 10–25m.
Number of routes: Over 20.
Climbing style: Mostly natural gear.
Season: Well into the tropics, Umbrawarra has a wet/dry seasonal range. During the Dry (April–Oct), though still hot (average temperature 28°C) it is possible to climb mornings and evenings in the shade. During the Wet (Nov–Mar) the humidity makes climbing extremely unpleasant even when it's not raining.
Location/access: Travel 230km S of Darwin on the Sturt Highway (1). Just 3km S of Pine Creek, turn off to the W and drive another 12km.
Camping and local amenities: There is a campsite (water, toilets, barbecues) at the gorge, plus limited accommodation and amenities in the town of Pine Creek. Better to bring supplies from Darwin or Katherine. Copperfield Dam, just out of Pine Creek, offers camping and a fabulous swimming spot.
Transport: Own vehicle essential.
Guidebooks: None.
Information: Darwin climbing shops (see Appendix 1), particularly John Fatora at 'Snowgum'. Note: drink lots of liquid when climbing in the heat. Take insect repellent and sunscreen, a hat and swimmers.

The Centre (around Alice Springs)

The Alice: what a fantastic place. Come for the climbing and stay for the experience. A strange, sprawling place in the centre of the magnificent MacDonnell Ranges, full of tourists wearing Aboriginal art T-shirts, sensible shoes and cameras. There are a number of camping grounds, hotels, supermarkets etc. here—the place to stock up before any trip out into the dry ranges. The Bardoppio Mediterranean Café down Fan Lane (arcade) off Todd Street Mall is the place to hang. Upstairs in the Alice Plaza (where the supermarkets are) is a fantastic museum which is a great place to chill (or at least stay cool).

Stretching east and west of the Alice are the MacDonnell Ranges, the scenery of Albert Namatjira paintings, through which cut several fantastic gorges. You'll need your own vehicle to get around but it is possible to hitch out to the more tourist frequented areas. You can take a fantastic 220km walk to the west, the structured Larapinta Trail, or do a variety of shorter walks.

In the West MacDonnell Ranges there are areas like Ormiston Gorge (climbing restricted) Ormiston Bluff, Glen Helen Gorge, and bouldering at Ellery Big Hole. In Serpentine Gorge there is the classic *Prenuptial Adventures* 23.

In the East MacDonnell Ranges there is climbing at Emily and Jessie Gaps (access will probably be restricted here soon due to traditional landowners' concerns), the Unknown (8km before Corroboree Rock), Trephina Gorge and Sphinx Rock (named after a roadhouse built for the film set of some Australian flop) near Ross River Homestead. The Unknown is a scary place with unlimited loose rock. It does, however, have two of the best lines around: *Superfreak* 20 and its twin, partly bolted. The setting is very reminiscent of Moonarie (10 minute trudge uphill).

There is also the limestone Benstead Creek (72km E of Alice) near Harts Range, which is thought to have the most potential with one unclaimed line (28 M0 currently) in the big cave described as two *Tjilkas* on top of each other. As with many cliffs in the area, the access situation is fragile and climbers should be discreet and polite with landowners.

One of the more popular areas close to Alice is the Stegar Rd cliff, south of the town, (aka Heavitree Quarry or the Quarry, though it is only on the way to the Quarry) with a great collection of short routes on 8 or so walls. The original 'High Wall' (bit of a walk up) has the best rock quality and a couple of excellent sports routes up to grade 24. The other crags have some nice natural lines currently up to 22, most of which have been led only last year. All up, there are now over 50 lines, only five minutes drive from town. The Stegar Road cliffs are on crown land so access is currently OK.

Other climbing areas close around Alice include Charles Creek (15+ climbs, 11–21), north of the Alice at the Telegraph Station Conservation Reserve.

Geology/type of rock/quality: Varies, mostly quartzite. Up to **
Grades: Up to 28.
Height: Up to 20m mostly but longer routes are possible at many areas.
Number of routes: Up to 100.
Climbing style: Generally face and corner climbing.
Brief history: See p. 169.
Season: The weather here is generally fine and winter temps (May–Sept) are ideal for climbing. The gorges protect you from the worst of the sun but in summer when temperatures can exceed 45°C it becomes obvious why the air-conditioned pubs are popular in the NT. Remember to drink lots of liquids (not just beer). It can get very cold at night so bring warm gear.
Location/access: See above for access to East MacDonnell Ranges. To access the West MacDonnells, drive W from Alice (head out on Larapinta Dr. and follow the signs). The road goes past the entrances to Stanley Chasm, Simpsons Gap, Elery Big Hole, Serpentine Gorge and on to Ormiston (130km W) and Glen Helen. To get to Ormiston Bluff, take the road into the gorge, and when you pass the grid you'll see the (dry) riverbed to your right. Look for a steep bluff on the other side, about 50m away. If you get to the Ranger's Station you have come too far, but this is the place to park for climbs in the Gorge itself—which are **currently restricted**. Tjilka Bluff is the large limestone cave about 2km in from the Ormiston Gorge turn-off. Tjilka Bluff has the Territory classic *Tjilka* 26 and a 24 to the left. The cliffs at Glen Helen are obvious from the homestead.
Camping and local amenities: There is a national park camp site at Ormiston (fees apply) but the nearest supplies (including fuel) are at Glen Helen Gorge, a few kms further on. The Glen Helen Homestead has campsites and other accommodation, depending on your budget. It also has meals and fuel. Tel: (08) 8956 7489.
Transport: Drive your own vehicle, grab a hire car in Alice, hitch or try and bluff your way onto a tourist bus.
Guidebooks: None as yet.
Information: The YMCA climbing wall can be a good place to meet local climbers; West McDonnell National Park, tel: (08) 8951 8211.

Ormiston Bluff

Ormiston is one of the Northern Territory's most popular crags, 130km W of Alice in the West MacDonnell National Park. There is a **no-bolting rule** in place which includes most national park controlled climbing areas. There are more than 30 routes here, grades 10–26, 10–25 metres.

▲	21	18m		1998

Old Favourite — On the left end of the cliff is a L-leading gully behind a huge dead tree (*Eat My Shorts* 8 13m) — chain 2m R at top. 13m R, from a gum, *Old Favourite* climbs up past two small ledges to BR then scoop (FH). Loose blocks and chain at top.

▲	20	20m		1995

Step Right Up — 6m R of *Old Favourite* is a crack to corner with 2BR, then to ledge. Step R onto face then climb past 3BR to easy ground. Chain on R.

▲	16	25m		1995

Sickle — On the buttress at the R end of the cliff is a 'large hanging dagger'. *Sickle* takes the crack below this for 5m then through overhang. Continue up crack, trav R under main (higher) roof then up to manky FH.

▲	20	18m		1995

Rock Shot — As for *Sickle* until above overhang the move R (ignore PR) to FH, then up past 2BR to chain.

▲▲	24	18m		1996

Rock Shot Direct Start — Start in obvious L-facing corner and climb up to major roof. Trav R along footholds to underclings then pumpy trav out the lip of the overhang. Move L and up to manky ring-piton (PR). Up to join *Rock Shot*.

▲	22	22m		1996

The Immortifier — To the R is a "major hand crack" on a prow above the creek bed. (*Wham, Bam, Thank you Jam* 18). *The Immortifier* starts off a block 3m R taking thin cracks to roofs. Up to ledges and easy cracks and then through top overhang to belay.

Glen Helen Gorge

Glen Helen Gorge is extremely user friendly, with both a swimming hole and a pub, and some argue the best rock close to Alice. It is past Ormiston Gorge—just follow the tourist buses. The sandstone climbs are mainly on the E side of the waterhole, which goes into shade after 2pm. There are approx. 20 routes, grades 8–22, up to 40m.

▲	19	40m		(2) 1996

Euro-dice — The big line on the east face.

Vomit Wall faces South; you have to swim or boulder through the waterhole to get to it.

On Vomit Wall there is:

▲	20	30m	1996

Downwind of Vomit – The handcrack at the L-end of the cliff, up to roof, then diagonally R to finish up crack.

▲	20	30m	1996

Hangover – 5m to the R of *Downwind of Vomit* is a prominent flake that makes a slightly overhanging layback.

▲	21	25m	1996

Hot Wet Canadian – 5m R again, before you drop into small gully, there is a thin crack on the R-end of the face. At the top trav R into *Chunky Little Boys* 16.

SOUTH AUSTRALIA

South Australia is the driest state in Australia. Like much of this continent, its landforms are old and weathered. The capital, Adelaide, is on the southern fringe of the state, a pretty city, dotted with churches and given to cultural performances. As with any large centre of population, the climbers of Adelaide have scoured every hillside and gully in the vicinity of the city, looking for the perfect crag. They have not found it, but they have turned up a lot of rock of varying quality. The most popular areas are the cliffs of Morialta and Norton Summit. Unfortunately, many of the cliffs around Adelaide, such as Rapid Bay, Myponga, and Belair are currently off limits to climbers.

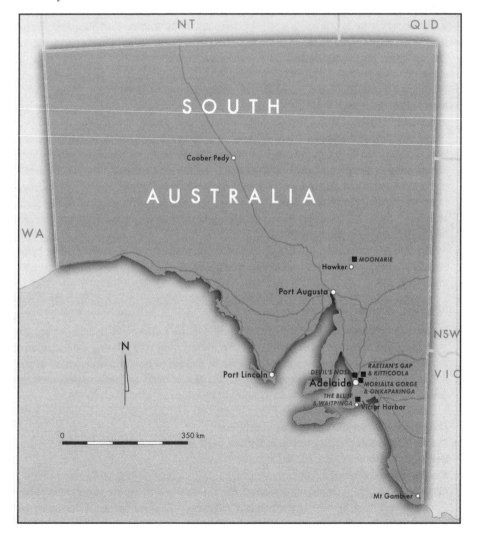

North of Adelaide is the small area of **Devil's Nose** with a few good routes, and to the north-west (near Palmer) the area of **Raetjan's Gap** offers a good alternative to Morialta in winter, with good rock and protection. The classic here is ▲▲▲ *Paradigm* 20 15m 1975{1977}. To the south of Raetjan's, **Kitticoola** is a good cliff though currently closed. South of the city, **Onkaparinga Gorge** (between Old Noarlunga and Clarendon) offers climbs in a 150m gorge, an attractive area that includes swimming holes for summer. It's quite sheltered and can get very hot in summer, but inversely is good on sunny cool days. The climbs are on a number of buttresses spread along the gorge and classics include ▲▲▲ *Bacchus* 14 23m 1972 and ▲▲▲ *Born Under Punches* 20 30m 1979.

Down south near Victor Harbour is some rare (for SA) granite climbing at **The Bluff**, on Rosetta Head (to the south). There are good slab, crack and face routes here, up to 25m. The classics include ▲▲ *Baudin* 14 25m 1977 on the Pleasure Dome, ▲▲ *Bandaid* 20 20m {1977}, Bandaid Wall, and ▲▲▲ *Richard's Route* 18 18m and ▲▲ *Hopes in Slopes* 22 25m 1979, at the Shaft Slabs Area. Further south again are the grand sea cliffs of **Waitpinga**, accessed through private property (be very good!) The best routes here are the thrilling traverses of ▲▲▲ *Flight of the Gull* 17 118m 1974 {1975} its extension, ▲▲▲ *Down to the Sea in Slips* 18 40m 1975, and ▲▲▲ *A Good Line* 18 110m 1975.

All these routes (and more, including banned ones) are to be found in *The Adelaide Hills: A Rockclimber's Guide*, Nick Neagle, Adelaide, 1997. Ask at any of the Adelaide climbing shops (see Appendix 1).

The vast bulk of the state is relatively featureless, however there is a chain of hills running from the coast and deep into the state. On the escarpment of this, or nestled in gorges cut by ancient streams, there are a number of fine cliffs. By far the most outstanding area is Moonarie, in the Flinders Ranges, 450km north of Adelaide (a 5–6hr drive), a large area of red sandstone ramparts standing proud above the desert plains. Moonarie is not the only cliff in the north, although it by far the best and most developed, and there are other areas like the excellent Buckaringa Gorge and Rawnsley's Bluff.

There is also the newer bouldering area of Yourumbulla Caves (signposted 10km before Hawker on the Quorn–Hawker road, i.e. on your way to Moonarie). See *Rock* 45, Summer 2001 for more details.

Morialta Gorge

Morialta Gorge's main attribute is its proximity to Adelaide's CBD—a 20 minute journey. The quartzite rock is of indeterminate quality, but nevertheless there is an amazing concentration of routes here. The proximity also means that it can be packed, with walkers and tourists as well as climbers. This popularity has also lead to a proliferation of tracks and national park signs and fences. There are even giant ring bolts supplied to belay from.

Geology/type of rock/quality: Quartzite, can be loose. *

Grades: There is a huge range in grades at Morialta. I have included routes from 8–28.

Height: Up to 21m on Far Crag and 30m at Norton Summit.

Number of routes: Several hundred.

Climbing style: Mostly face and corner climbing. Mostly natural gear, though the harder routes do have the odd bolt. There has been some retro-bolting. In general, much of the climbing at Morilata involves top-roping.

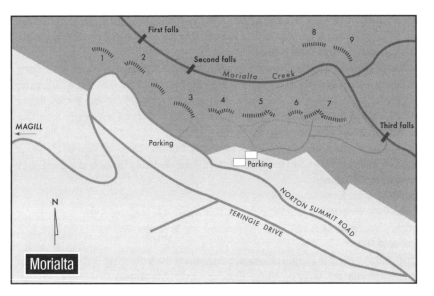

Morialta

Brief history: The history of Morialta is the history of the Adelaide Hills, and parallels that of Moonarie. Climbing started here in 1962 with members of the Adelaide Uni Mountaineering Club. By the mid '60s, climbers such as Ivan Dainis and Andrew and Glen Ward were active in the gorge (doing aid routes), and travelling to recently discovered Arapiles (and by 1968 to Moonarie). Climbers Mike Waite and Mike Ashton added a lot of climbs to Morialta, including Far Crag in the '60s.

In the early '70s, climbers such as George Adams (*Cioch*), Stuart Fishwick (*Golgotha*) and Richard Horn (*Illequipt* and *Asgard*) were climbing at Far Crag. In 1972 Colin Reece, a South Australian climbing icon, started aiding and climbing in the gorge (*Gladiator, Triad, Popular Misconception, Grurper* 22 and *Trout Fishing in America* 22 at Norton). The epidemic that was Henry Barber infested the gorge in 1975 and when the symptoms left he had freed *Bung* 20, *Cioch* 22 and *Barad Dur* 22. And in 1978 Kim Carrigan was lured to SA and added a swag of harder routes including *Bung Left Side* 24.

Other climbers resident in Adelaide at various times included Nyrie Dodd, Gary Scott (*Pizzazz*) and the ACT's pocket strongman Mike Law-Smith (*Bung Direct, FFA Geronimo's Caddillac* 25). Locals, the Shepherds (Lousie, Lincoln and Chris), along with honorary Shepherd Carrigan, set to work in the mid '80s at Norton Summit, establishing a set of good hard routes that include Lincoln's *North Terrace Stroll* 26.

In recent years young climbers like Stuart Williams (*The Stench before the Storm* 26, *Olympus* 28/29, *Following a Felch* 29), Jared McCulloch (*Shell Shock* 25—Norton), Matt Adams (FFA *Pergrine* 28— Norton) and Simon Wilson (*Elusive Muff* 27) have continued to push grades.

Season: Being a gorge, Morialta can be warm and sheltered in winter and at the right crag you can find shade in summer. Far Crag is popular for this reason. But if it is raining in Adelaide, it will be raining in the hills. Autumn and spring here, like most southern Australian crags, are the best time.

Location/access: Morialta is on the E side of Adelaide, in the hills. If you take Magill Road out, then 500m after the Tower Hotel (where Magill Road meets Penfold and St Bernard's Roads) turn L into Norton Summit Road. If you drive 5.9km (from the Tower) up this a fire track, with locked gate, cuts off steeply to the left. Park here with the other cars and walk down the track into the Morialta Gorge

Conservation Area. This is the best access for all the cliffs on this side of the gorge, which includes Billard Table, the Boulder Bridge and Far Crag. It is also the access for the cliffs on the opposite side of the gorge which include Thorn Buttress.

Continue along the fire trail adjacent to the fence, and about 300m from the second of the swing gates there is a grassy area (the fire track curves right here). Follow the obvious foot track towards the gorge which will bring you to the top of Far Crag, at the main descent, and at the L (FO) or downstream side of the cliff. As you walk left around the cliff the first wall you come to has a flake in the centre of it. This is *Asgard*.

Camping and local amenities: There is no camping at Morialta. There are, however, a lot of accommodation options just down the hill in Adelaide. There are quite a few cafés in the area and a fine pub at Norton Summit.

Transport: Drive or hitch.

Guidebooks: *The Adelaide Hills: A Rockclimber's Guide*, Nick Neagle, self-published, 1997.

Information: Climbing stores or online (see Appendices 1 and 3); Ranger, Morialta Conservation Park, tel: (08) 8280 7040.

Bouldering: Norton Summit is a popular bouldering destination. The Bachelor Pad is the latest hotspot with numerous problems, including *Madball* (sitdown start) V12 by Austrian Klem Loskot.

Far Crag

There is a descent at the left of the crag as well as the main descent to the right. I have described the climbs R>L (FI), as you approach them. Some of these climbs are initialled. All the climbs here can be done on half a rope so I have not given heights.

▲ | 16 | | 1970

Asgard – Flake in the centre of the 1st wall you come to. Up this past finger pocket to top.

▲ | 8 | | 1968

Al Sirrat – The blank looking arête L of *Asgard*.

▲ | 18 | | 1969 {1973}

Illequipt – Up the easy groove L of the arête of *Al Sirrat* to the small overhang then L and up the crack. L into groove at top.

▲ | 23 |

Illequipt Left Side – The thin wall with the black streak on wall to L, runners in *Illequipt*.

▲▲ | 15 | | 1968

Shedidit – The thin hand crack in the shallow corner on the arête R of the nice looking Bung Wall. This wall is the L-hand of three narrow parallel walls to the R end of the cliff.

▲▲ | 20 | | 1979

Bung Right – Up *Bung* to rest in centre of wall then branch R to finish up just L of arête.

▲▲ 20 1975

Bung – Up the wall to make a small deviation to the R where the crack begins, then step back L into crack. Poorly protected.

▲▲ 23 1968 {1984}

Bung Direct – Follow crack all the way.

▲ 24 1988

Bung Left Side – Centre of L side of wall using crack to L for protection.

▲ 16 1968

Ob-la-di – The centre route on the red wall above blackberries. Directly up wall above sharp blade.

▲▲ 16 1970

Golgotha – 1m to the L is a steep groove, to a ramp below double roofs, though these and finish with the hand crack.

▲▲ 12 1968

Sheoak Corner – Around the arête L is a large open corner just R of an olive tree beside track. It ends at a gum.

▲▲ 22 1970 {1975-79}

Cioch – Climb orange rock L of *Sheoak Corner* above olive tree on track. Up through a series of bulges past a old PR and BR under the roof. After top roof go L to gain headwall crack.

▲ 21 1983

Klutz Connection – Climb *Cioch* past the PR to the roof then L onto the black wall.

▲▲ 17 1972

Resurrection – The fine V-corner L of *Cioch's* roofs with a mantle to start.

▲ 15 1968

Lords Prayer – The major L-hand corner/chimney several routes L of *Resurrection*.

▲▲▲ 22 1970 {1975}

Barad Dur – The classic of the crag. L again is a steep juggy wall L of an undercut arête. This leads up past a big rattly block, then R and up to roof. L past BR and into the finger crack.

27 1994

Elusive Muff – The narrow wall between *Pizzazz* and *Barad Dur* with side runners. Included only because it is the hardest thing here.

▲▲ 23 {1980}

Pizzazz – Start as for *Barad Dur* (or L) and climb up to and up gently overhanging wall (slightly L past several BR. (hangers and nuts off bolts may be gone)

The Billiard Table

▲	19	1976	**Popular Miss Conception**
▲	22	1990	**Potluck**
▲	20	1979	**Up The Baize**
▲	20	1988	**Gang of Four**
▲▲	21	1983	**Fascination (LHV)**
▲▲	18	1965 {1971}	**The Billiard Table**
▲	19	1980	**Tilt**
▲	22	1991	**Resisting A Rest**

The Boulder Bridge

▲▲▲	16	1972-1977	**Muesli**
▲▲	21	1983	**Extra G**
▲▲▲	24	1985	**Extra G Connection**
▲▲▲	26	1972 {1992}	**Geronimo's Cadillac**
▲	25	1985	**Geronimo's RHV**
▲	11	1971	**Clea**
▲	15	1971	**Clea Direct Finish**
▲	16	1975	**Plexas**
▲▲▲	11	1971	**Balthazar**
▲	11	1971	**Big Sham**

Thorn Buttress

▲▲	23	1988	**Breathless**
▲▲	20	1970 {1977}	**Gladiator**
▲	24	1990	**No Mustard on Withdrawal**
▲	29	1991	**Following a Felch is No Part Fun**
▲	24	1988	**Hippy and a Wharfie**
▲▲	24	1988	**Pussycats and Crushed Kneecaps**
▲▲	22	1995	**Sardine**
▲▲	18	1973 {1973}	**Terrathea**
▲	24	1995	**Two Hour Hole**
▲	24	1973 {1979}	**Japetus**
▲	24	1981	**Japetus Direct**
▲▲	26	1988	**The Stench Before the Storm**

Norton Summit

In the next valley south of Morialta Gorge is an orange quartzite crag which has the most overhanging territory close to Adelaide as well as being the tallest local crag, with routes up to 60m. Access here is under strict conditions and is quite fragile. **Climbing is totally banned during the peregrine falcon nesting season** from 1 July to 30 November.

The Cave

	Grade	Height	Year	Route
▲	22		1972 {1979}	Grurper
▲▲▲	26		1982	North Terrace Stroll
▲	28	60m	1970 {1979–late '90s}	Peregrine
▲▲▲	27		1988 {1989}	Kensington Park Duck Massacre (aka The Hindley Shuffle)
▲▲	26		1996	Eddie Misses the Point
▲	26		1989	Tim in the Gym
▲	21		1988	The Natives are Restless

Above The Cave are:

	Grade	Height	Year	Route
▲	15	66m	1965	AUMC Route
▲▲	22	47m	1976 {1977}	Trout Fishing in America
▲	23	35m	1980	Endive

Moonarie

'The Moon' is not a completely unsuitable nickname for Moonarie, a series of cliffs that rim the eastern edge of the Wilpena Pound, in the Flinders Ranges National Park. By the time you get there you have left virtually all greenery behind and have driven into an area of quintessential Australian landscapes, red dirt, red rocks and stunted native pines. It is an area of subtle beauty unmatched by most Australian cliffs, of desert orange rock and sweeping dryland vistas. It is a truly beautiful place to climb.

Geology/type of rock/quality: Sandstone ***
Grades: Up to 28.
Height: Up to 130m.
Number of routes: 550+.
Climbing style: Moonarie has a lot of traditionally protected climbs although some of the more modern routes are bolted. There are a few old carrots but most modern bolts have fixed hangers. There are thin sandstone faces, long cracks and chimneys, big athletic roofs and funky things that are hard to classify.
Brief history: Climbing started at Moonarie in 1968 and over the next few years the usual motley crew of South Australian climbers, George Adams, Richard Horn, Stuart Fishwick and Doug McLean, added climbs throughout the walls, including *Pagoda, Thor* 15, *Duke, Robbing Hood, Spartan* and *Orion*.

Colin Reece began to show his potential in the '70s (*Sienna, Hangover Layback* 15) and interstate visitors started to drift in. Inveterate traveller Keith Lockwood dropped by with Andrew Thompson, as did Joe Friend, Kim Carrigan and the remarkable Henry Barber, though the latter's achievements were quite modest here compared to elsewhere. In 1975 Kevin Lindorff and Matt Taylor came over (*Casablanca, Stranger in a Strange Land* 19), Mike Law stopped by, with Mike Stone and Chris Baxter. Routes like *Medici* and *Machiavelli* were a result of this trip. In the late '70s Reece was again active (*Sweet Fire, Cold Blue Steel* and *Tim Tam* 16) along with locals Quentin Chester and John Marshall (*Trojan, Desolation Angels*). It is impossible to underestimate Reece's contribution to this cliff, establishing good climbs over three decades.

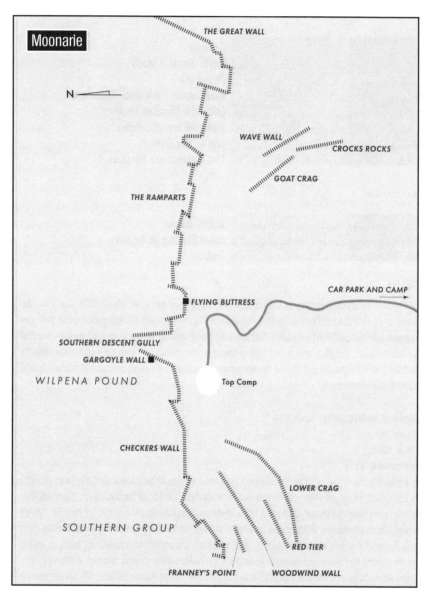

Moonarie

THE GREAT WALL

N

WAVE WALL

CROCKS ROCKS

GOAT CRAG

THE RAMPARTS

CAR PARK AND CAMP

■ FLYING BUTTRESS

SOUTHERN DESCENT GULLY

GARGOYLE WALL ■

WILPENA POUND

Top Camp

CHECKERS WALL

LOWER CRAG

SOUTHERN GROUP

RED TIER

FRANNEY'S POINT

WOODWIND WALL

Canberra climber John Smart upped the ante with his ascent of *Grand Larceny* 24, the freeing of *Desolation Angels* 22 and the route *Downwind of Angels* 19, the first of several excellent excursions onto the Great Wall. Legendary slow climber Eddy Ozols crawled up a few classics, including freeing the superb 1st pitch of *Fingernickin'* 24 and later the ascent of *Honour Amongst Thieves* 24. Ozols was one of many talented SA locals climbing at Moonarie in the late '70s and into the '80s. Others included Jon Chester, Neil Smith (*Nemesis* 22) and the Shepherd siblings (Louise, Lincoln and Chris). Lincoln Shepherd added the immaculate *Goblin Mischief* 23 and *Languish in Anguish* 25, Louise added

Another Excess 25 and *Upstairs Downstairs* 23 to the Great Wall and Chris found *Endless Love* 25, *Locomotive Direct Start* 25 and *Monopoly* 26. Carrigan was also particularly active during this period, freeing aid out of routes like *Rip Off* 25, *Robbing Hood* 24, *Curving Wall* 24, and establishing classics like *Insect Fear* 25. He pushed grades into the upper 20s with his ascents of *Ape and Away* 26 and *Full Torque* 26. NSW climbers such as Rod Young and Warwick Baird also visited, the latter finding *Barren of Emotion* 26.

After this period one South Australian took charge of Moonarie, establishing some of the finest routes here, and without doubt the hardest. Stuart Williams' contribution to Moonarie is indubitable, with excellent routes like *But Holland is a Country* 25, *Durban Poison* 25, *Captain Attrition* 28, *Womb Waltz* 28 and *Two Faced Guru* 27. Malcolm Matheson also made his mark on the cliff adding climbs like *Yerba Mate* 27, and Duncan Graham his with *Body Free Fall Direct Finish* 27. And during all this the hoards of unsung Moonarie climbers like Chris George, Mike Broadbent, Nick Neagle, Tim Day, Rob Knott, Rob Baker, Tony Barker, the eternal presence of Colin Reece and others, have continued to develop this awesome cliff.

Season: Moonarie is an outback area and although it could hardly be described as a desert, the climate here is similar to the more arid areas of Australia. Autumn (March–May) is the most popular time but Spring (Sept–Oct) is also good. It can get cold here in winter and the summer temperatures (40°C+) make climbing and camping oppressive.

Location/access: Moonarie is about 450km (5–6hrs) N of Adelaide and can be reached via Hwy 1 before turning east through Quorn and up to Hawker. A nicer drive is to come via Clare and Wilmington to Quorn. From Hawker it is 41km N towards Wilpena Pound (an impressive shallow dish ringed with escarpment) then turn L at the road (signposted) to Arkaroo Rock (just past Prelinna Homestead). After 800m (past two creek bed crossings) turn L onto wheel tracks (about 150m after road takes broad turn to R). Disregard the sign prohibiting camping as climbers have permission from the local landowner (do nothing to jeopardise this permission—see p. 8 for camping etiquette). Follow the rough track (gently) to the camp site against the national park boundary.

From this camp site a walking track (30–60min) follows cairns up to Top Camp, a flat rock at the base of the Southern Descent Gully and beneath the grand Flying Buttress. From Top Camp, Checkers Wall, with the great flake of Pagoda, is obvious to the L. Gargoyle Wall is up the Southern Descent Gully to the L. The Ramparts are around to the R and some way further past them the smooth and impressive Great Wall.

Camping and local amenities: Bush camping (see p. 8) is possible at the camp site where you park the car or up at Top Camp. There is a water tank in the Southern Descent Gully above here but water needs to be brought with you to the bottom camp. Fire bans are in force from 1 Nov to 30 April and fires should be undertaken with care at all times.

Hawker has petrol and a small supermarket, and Rawnsley Park Caravan Park and Camping Ground (5km before the Arkaroo Rock Road) has petrol and limited supplies as well as showers. To the north, the Wilpena Chalet has a hotel, tourist centre and shop (beer, supplies, ice, etc.).

Transport: Mostly by private car but there is a bus that runs between Adelaide and Wilpena Pound.

Guidebooks: *Moonarie: A Rockclimber's Guide*, Tony Barker, The Climbing Club of South Australia, 2000. (Also online—see Appendix 3.)

Information: The National Parks and Wildlife Service like to be informed of trips to Moonarie. You can ring the NPWS Hawker regional office, tel: (08) 8648 4244.

Bouldering: Hardly developed, though there are some on the Mushroom Boulder, 150m N of the walk-in track, above Lower Crag escarpment. Problems include Toni Lamprecht's 1992 problem *Acid Head* V9 (Australia's first V9?), *100% Rambo* V5 (L>R Trav) and *Savages* V7.

Checkers Wall

The steep walls above and to the L of Top Camp, with six distinct faces separated by large corners. Pagoda Wall is the fine wall with the large detached triangle flake on it.

▲ **24** **55m** (2)[24,24]1996

Criminal Streak — Starts L of *Free For All* (see next route). 1. (30m) Groove in black wall past 4BR to 2nd ledge. 2. (25m) Up the wall past 3BR to chains.

▲▲ **21** **90m** (2)[16,21] 1995

The Big Picture — At the L of Checkers Wall is a shallow corner L of a massive block. *Free for All* 19 starts here. 1. (45m) *The Big Picture* route climbs the first pitch of this (easily up, passing overhang on L , back R and up sustained corner) but continues up R to sloping ledge and belay below 1st BR on *Criminal Streak's* 2nd pitch. 2. (25m) Up 2m, trav L into discontinuous crack system and up past horizontal breaks. Rest ledge at 30m, then into R-leaning jam crack and up.

▲ **21** **60m** (3) 1999

Mr Ordinary — Starts on S side of detached block L of *Casablanca* (below). 1. (30m) Climb wall of block to big ledge and leave this at the L to climb arête past 6BR to anchors. 2. & 3. (30m) Scramble up easily to belay 8m R of *Criminal Streak* 2nd. Up past 3BR and scoops, to level with that route's chains. Trav to these and rap.

▲ **22** **100m** (2)[22,20] 1979

Feeding Frenzy — Start in the chimney 3m L of *Casablanca*. 1. (50m) Chimney the block, up the wall, then step R and follow the bulging line on the rounded holds until an easy crack. Up L to a mossy slab and belay in the corner. 2. (50m) L up the wall following the overhang, then a short white blank corner and hand trav L a metre and up a short white groove. Tend L to the top and final corner.

▲ **19** **100m** (4)[16,18,18,16] 1975 {1976}

Casablanca — L hand of the twin corners in the shady recess behind Pagoda wall. 1. (30m) Up the corner, continue past a ledge to another below a thin crack topped by an overhang. 2. (30m) 18 - Up the fine corner, pull around the overhang then up and move R to Spartan's 3rd belay. 3. (10m) Through the roof on awkward jams and belay under the overhang. 4. (30m) Trav L under the roof then climb diagonally L up the exposed wall to a ledge.

▲ **22** **120m** (5)[22,16,14,13,10] 1974 {1979}

Sienna — On the L side of Pagoda Wall. The thin crack leading into roofs between *Spartan* and *Pagoda*. 1. (27m) Up the crack, trav R under the roof and around the R edge to a vertical wall. Belay in a small cave. 2. (15m) Crack leading to notch on *Pagoda* flake. 3. (18m) L to the end of the flake, poor PR in place, then cross to corner, and down this to a ledge. 4. (30m) Up twin cracks, onto easier climbing and a ledge. 5. (30m) Continue up easier cracks.

Right of *Sienna* is:

▲	28	40m	1996	
▲▲	28	30m	1997	
▲▲▲	17	100m	(4)[10,13,17,12] 1969 {1976}	

Animal Attrition

Captain Attrition – R of Animal Attrition.

Pagoda – 1. (30m) Corner to ramp that leads up to a ledge under a roof. 2. (15m) L along the flake, climb the overhang, or squeeze behind it. Continue to the top of the flake. Thread belay. 3. (12m) Step back down to the top of the overhang on the flake. Climb the crack to a ledge. 4. (43m) Corner to a slab at the back and around R into the corner, then up.

▲▲	15		1977

Pagoda Variant – From the top of the flake climb up into the scoop and along R-ward curving crack back to the corner.

▲	19		1975

Pagoda Direct – The steepening corner crack and large roof above *Pagoda*'s first belay. Belay in the scoop above the roof. Continue up *Pagoda* corner.

▲	25	65m	(3)[23, 19,25] 1981

Nuts and Raisins – Start as for *Private Currant* 23 (the first horizontal crack leading L from top of *Pagoda* pitch 1). 1. (20m) Across *Private Currant* to the thin L leaning 2nd diagonal crack. Up, then R, then back L along main crack to the top of flake. 2. (25m) Up crack directly behind flake to ledge. 3. (20m) Up face to the roof crack, across this and up.

▲	18	70m	(2)[10,18] 1996

Hanging Fred Bonnet – A trav of the Pagoda Wall above *Private Currant*. 1. (25m) Up *Pagoda*'s 1st pitch until level with 2nd horizontal on L. 2. (45m) Trav L across horizontal and then slightly up to 2BB on a ledge beneath twin cracks (*Sienna Variant*). Up these or off.

▲	18	45m	2000

Blinding White Thought – The third horizontal on L. See above.

▲	24	55m	(2) 1995

Acid Rain – On the next wall is another big corner capped by roofs (*Oedipus* 17) 1. (20m) Climb 1st pitch of corner. 2. (35m) L across wall and up to chains (5BR). The ▲▲▲ *Direct Variant* 26 30m 2000 straightens out the original between the 3rd and 4th BR.

▲	21	75m	(3)[9,21,18] 1979

Crawling from the Wreckage – The crack on the L wall of *Oedipus* Corner (The major corner R of *Pagoda*). 1. (30m) As for first pitch of *Oedipus* but belay is level with wall crack. 2. (20m) Up crack to mantle into a scoop. Trav L at roof then up over a bulge or two and belay. 3. (25m) Through two bulges then trav R to the lip of *Oedipus* roof, then finish up *Oedipus*. ▲▲ *Crawling into Acid Rain* 21 25m 2000 is a composite route traversing L for 6m into *Acid Rain* (at 4thBR) from the 2nd horizontal off the crack in the 2nd pitch.

▲ `22` `110m` (5)[22,10,18,16,12] 1976 {1979}

Medici – Start R of *Oedipus* in the L hand of twin lines L of *Thor's* chimney. 1. (25m) A hard overhung V leads to a thin crack with a steep finish. 2. (20m) Up the crack and ramp and belay in base of crack in the R wall. 3. (25m) Up crack, step L and up to ledge, then move R to the main crack. Up wall 5 m, then trav R to a BB. 4. (20m) Two cracks leading to a slab. Trav L to a cave and pull through the overhang and go R into the corner (poor pro). 5. (20m) The corner to the top.

Right of *Medici*, through the double roofs, is:

▲▲ `27` `70m` 1998 **Yerba Mate**

▲ `15` `98m` (3)[15,10,12] 1969

Thor – Starts in a narrow chimney behind the squat buttress in the middle of Checkers Wall. 1. (30m) Chimney up to the roof, move L, and continue up the corner to the ledge. 2. (33m) Up the corner behind the ledge. 3. (35m) Up a series of steps above some trees and follow the bulging corner to a blocky chimney which leads through a narrow opening to the top.

▲ `22` `83m` (3)[22,17,12] 1980

Family Holiday – The wall L of *Pine Crack*. Start 3m L of *Pine Crack* in a corner with an overhang at 8m. 1. (30m) Up this to the wall with a scoop and thin flake, moving up R towards the belay ledge on *Pine Crack*. 2. (18m) Off the L end of the ledge, through the roof and up a mossy wall to *Thor's* ledge. 3. (35m) Continue up *Thor* to the roof.

▲▲▲ `19` `65m` (3)[16,19,19] 1977

Pine Crack – The line that bisects the wall R of *Thor*. Start behind the burnt pine. 1. (10m) Up the thin line to the ledge. 2. (35m) The crack past a bulge then the groove for 5 metres on the L, trav R to a steep crack which leads to a small ledge and BR and PR belay. 3. (20m) Up crack, move L out under the roof then up to *Thor's* ledge. Up.

▲ `22` `90m` (3)[16,22,13] 1977 {1978}

Desolation Angels – R of *Pine Crack*. 1. (15m) Up *Pine Crack* for 10m, trav R to a small ledge. 2. (40m) Up a thin crack, then follow main line to an overhang, L and up to another small ledge. 3. (25m) Up, L under the overhang and follow corner and chimneys to the top.

▲ `24` `100m` (4)[22,24,-,-] 1996

I Can Jump Puddles – Start 8m R of *Pine Crack* at a small flake and pockets at the R end of a low roof. 1. (20m) Up to roof, L at the horizontal and up to belay on *D. Angels*. 2. (45m) L-hand thin crack past 2BR, R into roof crack and up easy L-leaning crack on wall to belay. 3. & 4. Up to *Thor* ledge and up to top.

▲ `16` `70m` (2)[16,16] 1973

Asimov – Scramble up the bushy gully and belay at the base of the faint line to the R of the red wall under the huge roof above Top Camp. 1. (40m) Trav L along a narrow ledge. Up the steep flake crack for 24m then past the scoops and up to a belay atop the big block. 2. (30m) A short chimney to a dicey overhang and then a neat V-chimney, then up through the final overhang.

Gargoyle Wall

Compact wall on the L side of the Southern Descent Gully. Amble almost all the way up the gully until beneath the R end of the wall then clamber onto a terrace.

▲ 26 35m (2)[26,-] 1982

Full Torque — The big roof, high above Top Camp. Do the first pitch of *Asimov* to the rubbley ledge or trav in from the ground on the R. 1. (15m) Up the thin seam in the wall, hand trav R to the roof crack. Climb roof on technical finger jams (crux) then belay on the ledge. 2. (20m) Continue up to the top.

▲▲ 14 35m 1972

Corkscrew Retribution — The roofed corner at the L end of the wall. From the top of the corner make a move into the wide crack and up this.

▲ 19 33m (2)[19,13] 1976

The Prince — 1. (18m) Up the short corner crack R of *Corkscrew*. Undercling to the R and bustle up the edge. 2. (15m) Up the stepped corner on the R.

▲▲ 16 30m 1977

Tim Tam — Steep, straight line through a series of overlaps and ending with an overhang, R of the deep chimney/cleft dominating the L end of the wall.

▲▲ 13 40m (2)[11,13] 1969

Gargoyle — Halfway along the wall, beneath and to the R of a prominent nose. 1. (25m) Up the wall and mantel shelf your way up a series of ledges, continue up the corner crack on the L. 2. (25m) Climb wide crack and move R under the gargoyle, finishing in the crack on the R.

▲ 16 35m (2) 1977

Hunky Dory — 16 35m 3m R of *Gargoyle*. 1. (15m) Up crack to tiny blank corner then through the overhang to a ledge. 2. (20m) Climb the steep wall crack above the flake, trav L, then up through the break in the bulge to final short corner.

The Flying Buttress

The big buttress looming over top camp. Descent is a scramble over the boulders joining the buttress to the main face and then L (diag) up the easy exposed wall.

▲ 17 45m (2)[17,16] 1973 {1976}

Vortex — A striking line on the back of the Flying Buttress. Scramble up gullies. 1. (25m) The steep crack through scoops to a large ledge. 2. (20m) Corner and around overhang. Up to summit.

▲▲ 19 45m (2)[19,16] 1993

Buckets of Jism — Start as for *Vortex*, climbing the R-side of the arête past 4BR and up small open corner. Finish up *Vortex*'s 2nd.

▲▲▲   25   25m   1993

But, Holland is a Country – Takes the scalloped wall to R with BR to chains.

▲▲▲   15   105m (4)[10,15,15,12] 1972 {1973-75}

Flying Buttress – This classic climb takes the crack line that splits the front of the buttress directly behind Top Camp. 1. (20m) Gain the chimney at 20 m. Climb this to a belay underneath the overhang. 2. (35m) Move up and edge out through the roof, (the original line is via the wall on the R). Continue up to belay underneath the 2nd overhang. 3. (35m) Up the crack to a niche, move to the front of the overhang, swing out on a jug or two and up. Continue in the line to a belay beneath the summit overhangs. 4. (15m) Climb up R of the scoop, crawl back L at the top of it.

▲   12   60m   (2)[12,11] 1968

Ultion – The enjoyable line up the corner on R-side of buttress. Start in small corner before main line. 1. (35m) Up corner to cave. 2. (25m) Crack and corner to top.

▲   22   50m   (2)[20,22] 2000

Hold Tight – Face climbing up the black wall 5m R of *Ultion*.

The Ramparts

The name for the walls running R from the *Flying Buttress*. The first good wall is the Curving Wall, with the route of that name.

▲   25   55m   (2)[18,25] 1980

Insect Fear – Start at a large roof at the bottom L of *Curving Wall* (below). 1. (15m) Up to the corner, then either the face crack or ceiling into more of the corner. Climb over the roof, and belay on slab. 2. (40m) Climb the diagonal to mantle and jugs. Continue over roof, L across slab and on to top.

▲▲▲   22   55m   (2)[18,22] 1981

Expiry Date – 1. (15m) As for *Insect Fear*. 2. (40m) Up *Insect Fear* to 2nd finger pocket, then trav R to next crack which is followed to top, finishing up the steeply overhanging L facing corner.

▲   24   80m   (2)[20,24] 1976 {1980}

Curving Wall – Scramble 35m through broken mossy ground to base of the obvious crackline leading to a double barrelled roof on the clean concave wall. 1. (25m) The crack. Belay beneath the first roof. 2. (20m) Up the cracks through the double roofs and on to top.

▲▲   26   45m   1986

Barren of Emotion – 5m R of *Curving Wall*. Climb past 2 spaced BR. Take rest before the two tiered roof and then climb the final headwall.

▲   24   70m   1972 {1978}

Grand Larceny – Roofed corner above and L of *Orion*. From the top of *Orion's* 2nd pitch move L and follow the open corner. Move L under the overhang and up the blocks to a stance at the base of the thin corner. Up this (crux) and launch out under the roof. Finish up crack.

▲▲   **21**   **105m**   (6)[16,15,13,15,21,16] 1970 {1979}

Orion – L side of Garden Refuse Removed Cheaply Buttress (big buttress to R). 1. (30m) The corner. 2. (20m) The line to a ledge beneath the overhang. 3. (15m) The chimney and out through the overhang. 4. (15m) The corner leading to an overhang, and up this bottomless corner to a ledge. 5. (10m) The thin crack through a square cut overhang. 6. (15m) The delicate corner.

▲   **22**   **115m**   (4)[22,17,15,18] 1976 {1979}

Remnant – The wandering line up the front of GRRC Buttress. 1. (25m) The thin crack and out across the ceiling with PRs. Around and up into the line that curves L into a cave on the arête. 2. (40m) Trav up R out of the cave to the mossy central crack. Take this to a huge scoop. Belay in a crack at the ledge above and R. 3. (30m) L and up onto a block. L around the arête and into *Orion* (4th pitch). Up this to a neat ledge. 4. (20m) Crawl R inside the incut to a PR at the nose. Move out to a foothold and finish in the thin crack in the middle of the buttress.

▲   **25**   **25m**   1987

Cross Purpose – Start 5m R of *Remnant* and climb easily to the roof and BR. Up to lip and R to jugs. From a small ledge L a little into a small corner just R of *Remnant*. Out of this into corner and onto the headwall, then follow a thin seam and brushed line to a big ledge. Can rap off a bollard here.

▲   **24**   **30m**   1996

Space Madness – *Nemesis* to the 1st roof then veer L to BR. Up wall (BR) to belay as for *Cross Purpose*.

▲▲   **22**   **130m**   (5)[19,22,16,21,17] 1979

Nemesis – Start 5m R of *Remnant* under the roof. 1. (20m) Up the wall to a PR below the roof. Out through the roof on good holds then up the steep wall to a belay on the nose. 2. (30m) Into the chimney/groove then up onto the steep wall. Do several desperate, moves then trav L via the rising crack to a rest on the arête. Trav back R on the bottomless wall then up to a belay. 3. (30m) Up the R-hand wall of arête to belay at the chossy band of rock below a roof. 4. (25m) Through roof via horizontal break. Trav L and up on good holds 5m from the arête to a roomy belay on the arête. 5. (25m) Back onto the wall and climb the rising diagonal crack.

▲▲   **13**   **120m**   (4)[13,12,9,12] 1968

Garden Refuse Removed Cheaply – The R hand corner joining the buttress to the main wall. Scramble up and belay directly beneath the line. 1. (35m) Up, then step R under the small overhang, back L and up the line to a ledge, continue to a belay at the junction of the two corners. 2. (25m) Move carefully into the corner on the L and follow it to a big block. Over this to a ledge. 3. (30m) Up the bushy corner. 4. (30m) Climb the steepening corner to the top.

▲   **18**   **85m**   (4)[14,12,17,12] 1973 {1975}

Spartacus – The straight line bisects the wall between *GRRC* and *Kneedeep* Chimney. 1. (10m) Up slab through an awkward little roof and up the R facing corner to a ledge. 2. (15m) Bridge through roof via the R hand line. Belay under the overhang. 3. (20m) Move out L then up into the bottomless corner. Up the chimney. 4. (30m) Up the steep wall crack.

Sweeping Statement — R of *Spartacus*. 1. (20m) Climb the prominent brushed line up the steep slab to a BB 10m below the roof. 2. (35m) Continue up to the roofed corner. Clip PR but exit onto the face above this. Continue up to a ramp and trav R on small holds to a stance at the base of the L leaning seam. Follow past a fixed PR up the wall to a ledge. Double BB—rappel off or continue up *Spartacus*.

▲▲ | 25 | 100m | (3)[23,25,21] 1995

Jesus Loves Me, The Poofter — The face and arête R of *Sweeping Statement*.

▲▲ | 24 | 30m | 1983

Honour Among Thieves — Wall climbing past three BRs on the R wall of (*Kneedeep* 13) chimney, scrambling up chimney to start. Abseil off.

▲ | 20 | 105m | (4)[20,12,17,12] 1979

Balancing Bunnies (née **Cardiac Arête)** — Start up chimney or solo the corner around to the L, to a ledge at 20m. 1. (30m) Place high runner above orange scoop, hand trav R to a ledge on the nose. Up the line 15m to a weak flake and hand trav R to an incredible ledge on arête. 2. (20m) Up bulge and jugs to ledge beneath roof crack on the nose. 3. (30m) Scramble L and up wall L of the nose. Hand trav to a point above a roof crack. Up and move R steeply past thread and easily to ledges. 4. (25m) Climb easy blocks and small corner in the R side of a square amphitheatre.

▲▲ | 24 | 24m | (2)[24,??] 1982

Poodle Lust — R arête of *Kneedeep Chimney*. Starts just L of the arête proper. 1. (24m) A series of overhangs: at the last good horizontal swing around onto the L face. Up thin seam (crux) to the arête which is followed to semi-hanging belay at end of the *Balancing Bunnies* hand trav. To finish, go up *Balancing Bunnies* or reverse the hand trav L into *Kneedeep* chimney and downclimb.

▲ | 19 | 100m | (4)[19,13,17,12] 1969 {1976}

Duke — A spectacular roof and corner climb. Starts 5m R of *Kneedeep*. 1. (25m) Into the narrow chimney then head out through the roof crack then up to a ledge. 2. (30m) Continue in the corner, through an overhang and move up to a belay in the shade of a wide ceiling. 3. (25m) Climb the crack in the lofty ceiling then up the wall. 4. (25m) Easy blocks to a small corner in the R-side of a square amphitheatre.

| ▲ | 26 | 45m | 1997 | **Endaisle Man** |
| ▲▲ | 26 | 30m | 1998 | **Lactic Man** |

Both climbs find their way up here.

▲▲ | 19 | 100m | (4)[19,15,18,12] 1977

Stranger in a Strange Land — The irregular crack on the R edge of the monolithic red stone R of *Duke*. The crack develops into a chimney. 1. (35m) L hand corner, then L into the crack. Up this to the chimney and continue to ledge. 2. (30m) The corner, then amble through mossy territory to a ledge. 3. (20m) Up through the two overhangs. 4. (15m) Slightly L and finish in the small roofed corner.

▲ 17 100m (4) [17,17,16,12] 1977

Falling Monkeys – 1m R of *Stranger*. Fine corner following the huge flake. 1. (40m) R hand corner then L to the main line. The corner to the top of the flake. 2. (33m) Through the roof then the overhang, continue up moving L to ledge under *Stranger*'s roofs. 3. (22m) Up and trav L under first overhang to ledge. 4. (15m) Finish as for *Stranger*.

▲▲ 18 100m (3) [16,18,14] 1973 {1978}

Miles from Nowhere – Start from a grassy ledge at the base of the largest corner on the *Ramparts*. 1. (25m) Up the corner for 10m, L into another corner then back R and up the main line to a cramped belay. 2. (40m) Up into the L corner, revert back to the line and climb the steep thin corner crack through the orange bulge, then to the ledge. 3. (35m) Up the corners and behind the chockstone in the bottomless chimney.

▲▲ 23 50m 1992

Jenny Craig Moonarie Summer Camp, Activity One; The Endless Pitch – Up *Miles from Nowhere* for 15m then trav to the BR at the base of the thin crack on the R wall. To the top of the crack then up and R to the next BR. Up the thin flake directly above then R and to the tombstone shaped flake. Up the L hand side of this, then to the rap chains.

▲ 27 20m 1993

Lettuce Eating Poof – The smooth arête below *Live and Let Di*, on L side.

▲ 24 100m (4) [24,21,19+,19] 1981

Live and Let Di – R of *Miles From Nowhere*. 1. Through roof at start with BR runner and up flake on arête to belay at a small ledge. 2. Up detached flake then trav R to arête from top of flake to belay. 3. Scary, mossy climbing with little pro, up and veering slightly R, then back L to arête to go through a small roof. Belay above roof. 4. Wander up wall above, past a few ledges but no gear to top.

▲▲ 26 35m 1982

Ape and Away – Start as for *Live and Let Di*, trav R and then up in a diagonal line tending R-ward with PR to the same rappel anchor as *Endless Love*.

▲▲ 25 35m 1982

Endless Love – Central line between *Live and Let Di* and *Nervine*. Extreme climbing past a BR to a rest. From the overlap at 10m tend R and then climb the face near the R arête. Rappel from BR and PR.

▲▲ 12 115m (5) [10,12,12,9,8] 1968

Nervine – The R facing corner midway between *Miles from Nowhere* and the *Great Chimney*. 1. (20m) Start 8m R of the main line. Climb the short corner. Grovel L to belay in the chimney. (The direct start is graded 15). 2. (15m) The chimney and on through the overhang. Continue in the crack past one ledge to belay on a 2nd one. 3. (30m) Follow the corner to the base of the chimney. 4. (30m) The chimney. Continue in the same line to belay under another smaller chimney. 5. (20m) The chimney and easily to the top.

▲ 19 100m (4) [12,19,17,17] 1997

Every Fuckin' Day, Brother – 1. (30m) Up 1st pitch of *Nervine* and part way up 2nd to a small ledge with a bush. 2. (30m) Step R onto the face to join thin crack at the overlap. Up crackline to large ledge with dubious PR. 3. (30m) The face above into intermittent corner system on the pillar. Up to a tiny ledge on front of pillar. 4. (10m) 3m R on the horizontal then up wide crack and chimney into top of pillar. 2 raps to ground.

▲▲▲ 28 35m 1989

The Womb Waltz – The superb wall L of *Goblin Mischief* with 2BR to chains.

▲▲▲ 23 50m (2) 1982

Goblin Mischief – Superb snub buttress to the L of the *Great Chimney*. Start 3m L of *Fingernickin'* at a small roof. Straight up to a PR, then trav L 4m to a poor stance. Straight up to a 'hands off' rest. Trav L to the major arête and piton. Climb arête until holds veer L onto the face and another piton runner is reached. Move up to BR below another hard move then climb on to belay ledge with abseil chain.

▲▲ 25 45m 1995

Durban Poison – Another Williams' classic. Start as for *Fingernickin'* but head for blank corner at L of roof. Up corner past BR and arête past BR. Trav up and L to gain the 'backward 7'. On the L of this is a rest and BR. Up wall and arête past 5BR to *Goblin* belay. Rap off.

▲▲ 24 100m (4) [24,21,20,-] 1979 {1980}

Fingernickin' – Intense L wall of the *Great Chimney*. 1. (30m) Up the line to the 2nd ledge. BR and nut belay. 2. (25m) Up for 5m then L into another crack. Up to a cave, then onto the arête and up to a ledge. 3. (15m) Back into the chimney following the crack around the inside of the huge chockstone. 4. (30m) Amble to the top.

▲ 19 125m (5) [13,10,19,12,13,] 1977

Loco-Motive – Thin corner above and L of the chimney. Starts in the *Great Chimney* L Variant. 1. (20m) Up corner crack until it gets steep beneath chockstones level with ledge on the L wall. 2. (30m) L across the ledge around the arête to a corner with a PR (can belay here). 3. (20m) 6m up arête to horizontal. Hand trav L to a corner and straight up to a good belay. 4. (35m) Up the crack with chimney, weedy ledges and overhangs. 5. (40m) More. Finish up corner crack.

▲▲ 25 25m 1982

Loco-Motive Direct Start – Up *Fingernickin'* crack to roof then up thin corner L of roof. Past 2 BRs until original line is reached via a thin arête.

▲▲ 14 105m (5) [6, 12,–, 12, 14] 1968

Shangri-La – A long, sustained outing up the R side of the *Great Chimney*. 1. (10m) Up easy crack on L to ledge. 2. (35m) Climb chinmey and around the chockstones onto ledge. 3. (20m) Up into the grassy ravine and belay at shattered rib. 4. (28m) Climb the ridge on R of the overhung block and move R to belay on the rock strewn ledge. 5. (12m) The short corner.

▲ 20 100m (5)[20,20,16+,14,15] 1979

Wild Oscar – Disconcerting line on the R wall of the *Chimney*. Starts from a ledge at the base of the recessed corner. 1. (25m) Up the corner for 10m. Move L and up the finger crack. Pull L around the roof and into a groove on the chimney wall to hanging belay. 2. (20m) Continue up the groove to the base of the ravine in *Shangri-La*. 3. (13m) A few hard moves up the short crack on the R wall. Trav 5m to the foot of a tiny corner. 4. (30m) Up the corner, move R on jugs then L up a brief curving corner which leads to a wall and a big ledge. 5. (12m) The corner and an overhang.

To the R of *Wild Oscar* are the excellent routes:

▲▲	21	55m	1994	**Reality Factor**
▲	27	50m	1997	**Trouble and Strife**
▲▲	26	50m	1997	**Everyone Dies Alone**
▲▲	25	80m	1997	**Buzzard Arête**
▲▲	26	30m	1997	**Buzzard Direct**

A little further along, in **Callitris Corner**, is the classic:

▲▲ 15 90m (3)[15,15,15] 1973

Hangover Layback – Starts in a small corner towards the R end of the large mossy slab. 1. (25m) Around small overhang then thin crack and up to a ledge at base of steep wall. L to belay just L of flake on wall. 2. (25m) Up to flake and up it to ledge. 3. (40m) The crack, then hand trav R under overhang. On to ledge and up steepening crack to top.

Great Wall area

All the rock between Callitris Corner and the North Gully. Access to the terrace beneath the superb Great Wall itself is via a vague short corner R of the L edge of the wall (chain at top). An abseil chain is located near the tree close to the top of *Rip Off*, from where an abseil of 50m facilitates easy return to the terrace.

▲▲▲ 17 60m (3)[16,17,12] 1973 {1978}

Rush – Corner L of *Sorcerer's Apprentice* 16 which is the major corner line left of the Great Wall. 1. (25m) Climb the flake and continue up the corner past an overhang to a small stance. 2. (15m) Move up R into the cramped sentry box. Climb the overhanging corner to a ledge and move R into *Sorcerer's*. 3. (20m) The last pitch of *Sorcerer's*, up corner.

▲ 18 60m (2) 1997

Roaring – Offers airy moves up the R arête of *Rush*.

▲▲ 16 50m (2)[16,12] 1975

Outside Chance – Arête climbing on the L edge of the Great Wall. 1. (30m) From the L end of the terrace move across the wall to an airy position above the overhang. Up the arête. Belay on the *Sorcerer's* ledge. 2. (20m) Sneak L and finish up *Sorcerer's Apprentice*.

▲▲ 17 20m 1981

Buckley's — Better 2nd pitch to *Outside Chance*. Step R out of the belay cave and stretch up to the 2nd horizontal. Trav back L to the arête, then follow this to a ledge. Pull into the big scoop above R and exit at its top L.

▲▲ 19 55m (2)[19,19] 1978

Downwind of Angels — 20m L of *Robbing Hood* and 4m in from the L arête. 1. (45m) Up the wall on small holds to a hand crack. Continue past the horizontal break and gain the crack that leads up R-ward to the *Sorcerer's* ledge. 2. (10m) Trav 3m R to a thin vertical line. Up this.

▲▲▲ 25 40m (2) 1982

Languish in Anguish — Starts at the flake crack between two pine trees R of *Downwind of Angels*. 1. Climb flake to its conclusion, and up the pocketed face, past two BRs to large horizontal break. Another move upward, then trav L into the crack line. Up this to (*Providence*) ledge and belay. 2. Trav off L or continue up remainder of cliff.

▲▲▲ 24 50m (2)[24,19] 1969 {1979}

Robbing Hood — The main line L of the centre of the wall, past a couple of BRs. 1. (30m) Thin, sustained climbing up L of two old BRs. Gain crack and continue to ledge and BB. 2. (20m) Wide crack leading to a pine at the top.

▲▲ 24 45m (3) 1981

Hypertension — 5m R of *Robbing Hood*. First two pitches best combined. 1. (20m) Up thin crack past 2 BRs and PR. Trav L to belay in *Robbing Hood* at the 1st main horizontal. 2. (15m) Trav back R for 6m and up finger crack. Step L just below ledge and belay. 3. (10m) Finish up *Robbing Hood*.

▲▲ 23 45m (2)[23,19] 1981

Against the Wind — Take the corner flake R of *Hypertension*. 1. (30m) Climb flake until it expires then trav R past a BR runner into *Rip Off*. Climb *Rip Off* to (*Providence*) ledge and BB. 2. (15m) Continue up 2nd pitch of *Rip Off* to the top.

▲▲▲ 25 40m (2)[25,18] 1975 {1981}

Rip Off — Starts at the L hand base of the huge block. 1. (26m) Climb wall on the R side of the thin crack, follow it to a BR at 10m. The crack widens and the climbing eases to a narrow ledge with BR and nut anchors. 2. (14m) Straight up on horizontal cracks until a large horizontal incut is reached. The crack finishes at a tree near the rappel chain.

▲▲ 23 45m (2)[23,19] 1973 {1981}

Infirmity — Start from the apex of a huge block leaning against the cliff. 1. (35m) Up flake 1m R of the crack, using crack for runners. At 5m trav into the crack, up, and balance R onto a flake for rest. Up the flake for 2m and trav back to the line. Up the widening strenuous crack to belay in the large horizontal break. 2. (10m) Continue to top.

▲ 21 40m 1980

One Way Street — Starts from top of the large block. Follow a R leading ramp to a flake. Up this to another flake, trav 4m R and up another ramp past a BR. Finish up wall through two bulges to top.

▲▲▲ 22 45m   1980

Dry Land — An excellent pitch. Start just R of the huge boulder. Up a thin flake to a vertical crack, up this and follow the R-ward tending flakes to the top.

▲ 18 45m   (2)[18,17] 1979

Cypress Avenue — Crack at the R end of the wall. Solo 20m up *Chaullay*, (the gulch on the right of the wall) until underneath the start of the line. 1. (30m) Pull around bulge and follow crack to a belay in the horizontal break. 2. (15m) Climb crack through the two overlaps.

▲ 12 60m   (2)[10,12] 1968

Finale — The major chimney line 30m R of the Great Wall. 1. (35m) Up chimney with a gnarled tree sprouting from 6m up the route. 2. (25m) From the large ledge continue up and move around the chockstone. Take the steep crack on the L which eases near the top.

R of this are:

▲▲	25	30m	2000
▲▲	27	30m	2000

Body Free Fall from the Womb of Time
Direct Finish

TASMANIA

Tasmania, Australia's only island state, is a wonderful place and the climbing here feels completely different to most mainland cliffs. Here the majority of significant larger cliffs are in beautiful, wild areas and, as a result, some have major walk-ins. Consequently, most extensive development has occurred on the more user-friendly and accessible cliffs.

There are many good areas in Tasmania, including the high remote cliffs of Frenchmans Cap, Federation Peak, Mt Geryon and the Acropolis, the long cracks and corners of the Ben Lomond plateau, the numerous areas close to Hobart, the sport climbing conglomerate of Adamsfield,

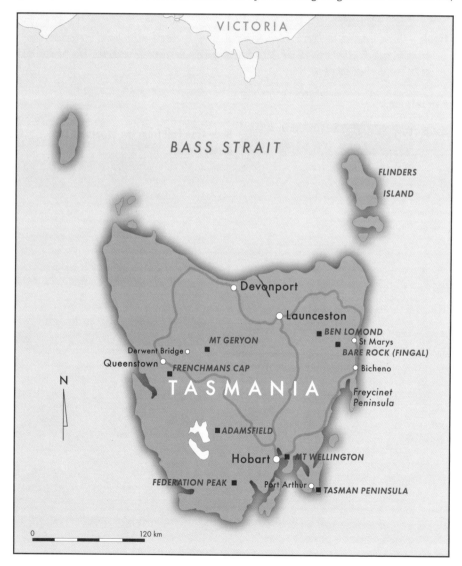

the brooding bulk of Fingal and the seaside granite of Freycinet. Areas such as Mt Wellington above Hobart, and Launceston's Cataract Gorge, offer both modern and traditional routes in abundance, close to town. The excellent and not so small crags around Hobart include Freuhauf, Kempton, Handsome Crag, Quoin, Lowdina, Proctor's Road Quarry, Rocky Tom and Gunner's Quoin. All of these climbs are described in *Craglets 5* (5th Edition) by Roger Parkyn and Matt Perchard, Climbing Club of Tasmania, 1997. They are more for locals, or visitors who can't get to the better cliffs like Coles Bay when the weather is not good on Mt Wellington.

There is a saying that 'dirty days have September, April, June and November, all the rest are dirty too, excepting February' which is a way of saying that as the most southern state, the weather here can be more miserable than the mainland. As a result, unless you live here, climbers tend to venture onto the rock over the summer months of January to March.

To get to Tasmania you need to either fly in or take a boat. You can fly into Hobart, Launceston, Burnie and Devonport. The large passenger ferry *Spirit of Tasmania*, and the new, fast *Devil Cat* both depart from Melbourne's station pier (the good thing about going on the boat is the ability to take a vehicle over). Contact Tasmanian Travel Centres (tel: 1300 655 145) for more information on getting to Tasmania. **Note:** Tasmanian national parks require an entry pass, costing $9.90 per vehicle or $3.30 per person per day, or $33 per vehicle or $13.20 per person for two months. There is also an annual option.

Mt Wellington (The Organ Pipes)

Few Australian capital cities have a quality cliff as near to hand as the dolerite columns of Mt Wellington. Unfortunately, Mt Wellington can also advertise its antagonism to normally sun-seeking climbers when it dons its mantle of winter snow. The dark rock of Mt Wellington, only 8km from Hobart's GPO, forms long columns on which multi-pitch routes are possible, in a style that generally involves a mixture of face-holds, jugs and jams. Surprisingly, there are relatively few pitches that involve pure jamming. The cliffs offer exposure, atmosphere and superb views over the southern capital.

Geology/type of rock/quality: Regular dolerite columns, hence the name. **

Grades: Up to 26.

Height: Up to 125m.

Number of routes: Over 300.

Climbing style: Mainly traditionally protected crack lines. There are increasing numbers of sport climbs at areas like the Lost World.

Brief history: Climbing started here in the '60s, pioneered by local Jim Peterson and Queenslander Ron Cox. In 1965 the Climbing Club of Tasmania was formed and when Victorian Reg Williams moved down the next year, standards increased and lines fell. *Opthalimia* 18 and *Moonraker* 16 date from this period. In 1968 John Ewbank also popped in and climbed *Icarus* 19, *The Shield* 20 and the classic *Centaur* 17, as well as others.

Henry Barber visited in 1975 and solo climbed *Double Column Central* 17, as well as establishing the grade 22 with *Savage Journey* at the Lost World crag nearby. Interstate hot shot Kim Carrigan combined with local Ian Lewis to climb *Tartarus* 20, and returned in 1978, with Mike Law and Greg Child hitting the crag blitzkrieg like, establishing several hard climbs including *Play Dirty* and *Sorrow*, both 23.

Not to be outdone, the local scene in 1981 produced Simon Parsons who bagged a number of classics, pushing grades to 24. His most endearing classic is probably *Sky Rocket* 20. His climbing partner Justin Kennedy stepped into the limelight in 1985 with *Second Coming* 26. Throughout the

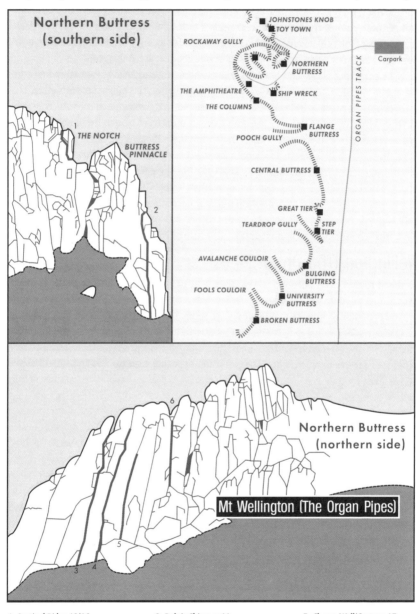

1. *Sentinel Ridge* 12/16

2. *Skyline Major* 14/16

3. *Pulpit Chimney* 11

4. *Pegasus* 12/14

5. *Chasm Wall/Centaur* 17

6. *Labyrinth* 8/12

'80s, climbers such as Garn Cooper, Nick Deka, Doug Fife, Dave Stephenson, Frenchman's Cap aficionado Peter Steane and his cousin Phil all helped to establish a number of fine routes.

With the '90s, bolt protected face and arête routes have started to appear, anticipated by Chris Shepherd's now rusted *Vanity* 25. A more modern classic in this style is Sam Edwards' bolted sport route *After Midnight* 23.

Season: It snows up here. It looks pretty, but unless you're counting on a winter ascent it will cool your climbing ardour. Spring to autumn (Oct–April) is the best time with Jan–March ideal. The cliff generally faces east. Head up early to catch the morning sun. Climbing in the afternoon, or on the south-facing parts of the cliff (where many of the best routes are), should generally be saved for the warmer days.

Location/access: From Franklin Square in the centre of Hobart travel S for 9.6km up Davey Street (this becomes Huon Rd). Just before the small town of Fern Tree, Pillinger Drive (signposted) heads off to the R and up the mountain. 4.5km of winding will get you to The Springs (picnic area and parking spots with access to Gorby's Corner and Sphinx Rock). Further on (2.7km) is a small parking bay on the L-hand side of the road. Above here, a few minutes scrambling up a vague track through scree and bush brings you to the Organ Pipes Track (see map, p. 198). Continue up the hill to gain access to Northern Buttress (the first piece of rock you come to) and The Columns. Flange Buttress can also be accessed this way. Alternatively, walk L along the Organ Pipes Track to access the other buttresses (including the Flange), heading up when you get under them. You can generally avoid unpleasant scrub-bashing by following corridors of scree and some formed pads through the bush.

The Ship Wreck is a prominent rock in the midst of a sea of scrub and tallus, approximately half way between Northern Buttress and Flange Buttress. It provides a good vantage point for identifying routes from The Amphitheatre to Flange Buttress, and is best accessed from the Northern Buttress track.

The Lost World is best accessed by continuing up the mountain for a few more kms to a big L-wards bend in the road. Follow the track (marked with red dots) through the bush to the R.

Camping and local amenities: With discretion you can doss at The Springs picnic area. There is water and toilets. There are also a few basic huts and shelters dotted around the mountain. There is no need to camp at the cliff though; that big, sprawling metropolis at your feet has a plethora of accommodation options, as well as most of your other needs. The closest camping ground is the Sandy Bay Caravan Park (1 Peel St, Sandy Bay), less than 3 km from the city (tel: 6225 1264), $9 per person per night for a camp site, though for what you're getting at this price you might be better off in a backpackers' or youth hostel.

Transport: Own vehicle or hitch. Buses to Fern Tree, route 47 or 48 (very infrequent on weekends) run from Franklin Square but you still need to hitch up Pillinger Drive. There are a variety of tour buses that run up the hill and for $20 you can get a lift up on a Harley. Hell, it's not far, you could walk! There are nice walking tracks from Fern Tree to the Pipes. Ask the locals or get a Mt Wellington Walk Map.

Guidebooks: *A Climbers Guide to the Organ Pipes*, CCT, 1992; *Craglets* (3rd, 4th and 5th editions), Roger Parkyn and Matt Perchard, Climbing Club of Tasmania.

Bouldering: Mt Wellington is generally not good for bouldering, due in part to the columnar nature of the rock and also to the bad landings.

Northern Buttress

The first major buttress which has shorter, sunnier and less serious climbs. It is divided in the middle by a gap in the ridge, the Notch. The pinnacle immediately L of The Notch is Buttress Pinnacle. The climbs to the R (FI) are on the Upper Cliff, and to the L, The Lower Cliff.

▲▲ `12/16` `84m °`   (6) 1968

Sentinel Ridge – Is an excellent excursion that's grade depends on which options you take. It follows the crest of the Upper Cliff.

The **Lower Cliff** (described R>L): A 45m abseil from Buttress Pinnacle down through the chockstones descends to the base of The Chasm (the major cleft splitting the north face), or rap 25m down the back of the buttress.

▲▲ `8/12` `56m`   1962–1966

The Labyrinth – Another classic easy route that has a number of options. Starts in the back of *The Chasm* in a dark chimney on the R and climbs various chimneys before following the buttress towards the Notch.

▲▲▲ `17` `48m`   1965–1968

Chasm Wall/Centaur – Climbs the wall between *The Chasm* and *Pegasus*. Climb up 5m to groove and follow this to a ledge R of *Pegasus*. Crack above.

▲▲ `12/14` `50m`   1961–1961

Pegasus – The squeeze chimney with 2 chockstones L of *The Chasm*. 1. (24m) Chimney to small stance on R. 2. (14m) Climb to top of The Great 'detached' Flake, then crack on R to ledge 5m up. 3. Either continue up crack and finish just short of Buttress Pinnacle (12m - 14) or trav L to wide ledge then follow skyline (8m - 12).

▲▲▲ `20` `45m`   1982

Subterfuge – L of *Pegasus* chimney is another, *Pulpit Chimney* 11. *Subterfuge* takes the buttress between the two. Climb thin crack through bulge and up to rest below small overhang. L past this and climb arête to top of Great Flake. Up wall above to *Pegasus* ledge.

▲▲▲ `17` `25m`   1972

Rasberry Jam and Crackers – This route takes the wall L of ▲ *Andromeda* 14 (the L-most major chimney on the North face of the Northern Buttress). Start on bottom L of wall and climb shallow corners. Spaced protection.

▲▲	`14/16`	`93m`	**Skyline Major**
▲▲	`9`	`120m`	**Skyline Minor**

Both take the ridge of the N Buttress.

The Columns

▲▲	`20`	`30m`	1975 (Amphitheatre Ledge)	**Resurrection Shuffle**
▲▲	`20`	`51m`	(2) 1968	**The Shield**

▲▲ `24` `55m`   (2) 1993

In Flagrante Delicto – [Bolts and cams up arête R of *Skyrocket*]

▲▲▲ `20` `60m`   (2) 1982   **Skyrocket**

▲▲	22	52m	(3) 1982

Killer Canary – [Rap down and do the top 2 pitches (37m) for a ▲▲▲ classic]

▲	17		(3) 1977 {'90s}
▲▲	13/15	118m	(4) 1962

**Double Column Central
Battlements**

▲▲	19		(3) 1978

Split Column – [Rap down and do the last 40m -1 pitch from the ledge]

▲▲	21	60m	(2)1978
▲▲	24	100m	(3) 1968 {1982}

**Holiday in Cambodia
Bismark**

Top-down access is sometimes best on the Columns, particularly for *Resurrection Shuffle*, *In Flagrante Delicto*, *Skyrocket*, *Killer Canary*, *Split Column* and *Holiday in Cambodia*. Drive to the Pinnacle, and walk down to the cliff.

Flange Buttress
To the L end is Pooch Gully and to the R end is the deep cleft of *Brown Madonna*. Rap off ledge above these routes, or continue up the last 50m of ▲ *Bert's Fear* 11, which follows the ridge, starting in chimney 10m R of the lowest point on the Flange.

▲▲	19	45m	1978

Brown Madonna – The chimney.

	26	55m	1996

Pleasant Screams – Two pitches of bolts up the wall L of *Brown Madonna*.

▲▲▲	23	50m	1995

After Midnight – The bolted arête R of *Digitalis*.

▲▲	18	62m	(2) 1977

Digitalis – Line downhill and L around corner with a loose block at 26m. 1. (36m) Climb to small overhanging chockstone, and over into offwidth. Up to large flake and belay. 2. (26m) Up corner, moving boldly L onto a series of ledges and up a groove past a large flake. Belay on top of Flange Buttress.

There are two bolted routes on the wall R of *Fiddlesticks*, which share the same bolted first pitch (this pitch has been led on natural gear without clipping the bolts). L>R:

▲▲▲	25	25m	1997
▲▲▲	23	25m	1997

**Neon God
The Holy Road**

▲▲▲	14	65m	(2) 1976

Fiddlesticks – Corner 26m uphill (R- Fl) from lowest point of Flange Buttress. Climb up to corner with twin cracks. 1. (35m) Up corner, belay in notch. 2. (30m) Up flakes on wall, R to regain crack line, and follow to large ledge.

▲▲▲	20	40–50	(2) 1969 {1979}

Precarious – This old aid line starts 9m L of *Fiddlesticks* and 7m R of the squeeze chimney of *Bert's Fear*. 1. (30m) Climb corner to ledge, R and up short face to ledge. 2. (10–20m) Either climb crack on L of ledge and up broken ridge to belay near large block, or, go L and up to tape abseil point.

More classics:

▲▲▲	18	89m	(4) 1973, Central Buttress	**Third Bird**
▲▲▲	18	100m	1978, Central Buttress	**Battle Cruiser**
▲▲▲	20	30m	1989, Central Buttress	**Space Cowboy**
▲▲	22	65m	(2) [20, 22] 1978, Central Buttress	**Starship Trooper**
▲▲▲	20	45m	(2) 1982, Central Buttress	**Improbability Drive**
▲	18	80m	(3) 1978, Great Tier	**Suicide Sadness**
▲	19	77m	(3) 1974, Step Tier	**Lone Stranger**
▲	15	90m	(4) 1966, Step Tier	**Moonraker**
▲	21	50m	1991, Step Tier	**Left Out**
▲	21/22	30m	1975, Lost World	**Atlantis**
▲	22	30m	1975, Lost World	**Savage Journey**
▲	23	25m	1978, Lost World	**Rosy Pink Cadillac**

Around the foot of Avalanche Couloir at the southern end of the Pipes (see map, p. 198) there is a fairly high concentration of quality but shady (sometimes frigid) routes—a great place for a warm day. The most obvious line is the corner of *Ozy* 16. The routes are described L > R. Descent from the following three routes is from the U-anchours atop *Carpe Diem*.

▲▲▲	22		(2) 1978

Blank Generation – The steep line just L of the arête at the base of the L side of the couloir.

▲▲	17	60m	(2) 1972

Chancellor Direct – The clean R-facing corner just up the couloir from *Blank Generation*.

▲▲▲	19	45m	1990

Carpe Diem – ▲ *Piping Hot* 20 is a R-facing corner capped by a roof, about 10m up the couloir, and set back somewhat. *Carpe Diem* is the terrific wall just L of this.

▲	21	30m	1994

Terra Nullis – The bolted face/arête about another 10m up the couloir.

The following three neighbouring routes are on Bulging Buttress but are accessed by sidling R from 50m up Avalanche Couloir.

SSSSI – The L-facing corner capped by a roof.

| ▲▲ | 24 | 35m | 1999 | **Mildly Amused** |
| ▲▲ | 22 | 40m | 1989 | **Beaten and Abused** |

These two routes share the same start, i.e. the flake and crack—3m R of *SSSSI*. Climb L at 6m and up bolts for *Midly Amused*. For *Beaten and Abused*, go R and up to 2nd horizontal. R, then up crack.

The following three routes on Bulging Buttress start below those above. L>R:

The Wizard – Corner crack through roof.

| ▲▲▲ | 21 | 30m | 1996 |

Cold Power – Line up overhung wall R of *The Wizard*.

| ▲▲ | 18 | 90m | (2)1975 |

Black Magic – Steep jamming up the middle of Bulging Buttress.

Tasman Peninsula

If ever there was a climbing area that was made famous by a photograph then it is the Tasman Peninsula, just outside Hobart. This area's most famous (and photographed) climb is the slender 65m dolerite pinnacle, surrounded by crashing ocean: the Totem Pole. Though originally aided by John Ewbank in 1968, it was Steve Monks, Simon Mentz and Jane Wilkinson's ascent of *The Free Route* 25 in 1995, and Simon Carter's photographs, that reawakened the world to this remarkable piece of rock. The UK's Paul Pritchard's accident here, the subsequent publicity and his award-winning book of the same name have done nothing but increase its profile.

The Free Route is not the only climb on the Peninsula, nor dolerite cracks and columns the only form of climbing. As well as this style of rock and climbing at Cape Hauy (where the Candlestick and Totem Pole are situated) there are overhanging sport climbs at The Paradiso on Mt Brown, multi-pitch routes on Mt Brown, and the eclectic Moai. Mount Brown has over 70 routes on dolerite (not columnar). There are three star single-pitch sport routes and three star trad routes up to 100m, grades 8–27.

Geology/type of rock/quality: Dolerite, weathered by waves and winds rather than alpine snow and ice.
The rock on the steep sections of The Paradiso is generally good, otherwise treat everything as suspect.
Grades: Up to 27.
Height: Totem Pole 65m, up to 120m elsewhere at Cape Huay, 300m at Cape Pillar.
Number of routes: About 100, spread through different areas with the most at Mt Brown.

Climbing style: Face and crack climbing. Mostly traditional, though there may be bolts. The Paradiso on Mt Brown is sport-bolted and a rarity because it is steep non-columnar dolerite.

Brief history: Ewbank and Kellar aided the *Totem Pole* in 1968. Reg Williams 'and party' first climbed the Candlestick in 1969 with a 2nd ascent done for TV in 1972. *The Free Route* was done by Monks, Mentz et al in 1995. The Jacksons started climbing in the Mt Brown area in 1994 and sport climbing came to The Paradiso in 1995 with the likes of Parkyn, Edwards, and Garry Phillips.

Season: Like most Tas crags, this area is best Dec–March. Remember though, the sea cliffs can be affected by wind, even on nice days. If the waves get up, access can be a nightmare.

Location/access: Port Arthur is just over an hour's drive from Hobart. Just before you get there turn L to Fortesque Bay. The Candlestick and the Totem Pole can be reached by an hour's walk to Cape Huay from Fortescue Bay. The Moai is the opposite direction around Fortesque Bay, past Waterfall Bay. South of Port Arthur is Remarkable Cave. Mt Brown or Dauntless Point is half an hour's walk S from the car park. After about 25 minutes, you come to a sandy creek, from where you follow the coast around, first passing Parrot Shelf Cliffs. The steep and juggy eye-bolted cliff you come to is The Paradiso.

To get to the abseil point for both the Candlestick and the Totem Pole walk past the Cape Huay warning sign at the end of the track. A vague track takes you down to where you can view the stacks. Continue down to a point lower than the Pole's summit, from where you can traverse across until you are closest to the summit. A full length abseil gets you down. Watch out for waves. There is a single BR belay.

Camping and local amenities: There is good camping at Fortescue Bay and maybe also at Mt Brown. The area has recently been declared a national park so entry fees now apply. There are caravan parks, a YHA, B&Bs and even more expensive options in the touristy Port Arthur. This is also the closest spot for most of your other needs though it can be more expensive than Hobart.

Transport: Own vehicle.

Guidebooks: *Craglets 5* (5th Edition), Roger Parkyn and Matt Perchard, Climbing Club of Tasmania, 1997.

The Totem Pole

▲▲▲	25	65m	(2) [25,25] 1995

The Free Route — 1. (25m) Hard to R arête. Carrots. 2. (40m) Follow 10 FH—there is some natural gear in last 10m.

The *Original Aid Route* A3 65m climbs straight up the middle of the landward face with a short excursion around the L arête a little past half height.

Mt Brown

▲▲	16	18m	Parrot Shelf Cliffs	**Low Road**
▲▲	20	15m	Parrot Shelf Cliffs	**Geronimo**
▲	22	25m	Paradiso	**Aquaphobia**
▲	23	20m	Paradiso	**Super Charger**
▲	23	25m	Paradiso	**Thunderbirds Are Go!**
▲	24	30m	Paradiso	**Offender of the Faith**
▲	27	27m	Paradiso	**Expendable Youth**

▲▲	16	30m	The Furnace/Land's End	**Stone Biter**
▲▲	17	53m	(2) , The Furnace/Land's End	**Inferno**
▲▲	15	105m	(4) , The Furnace/Land's End	**Dauntless**

Adamsfield

The steep and strenuous conglomerate boulders of Adamsfield are like mammals in a burning meteor-lit field of dinosaurs, a sport climbing haven in a world of naturally protected 'adventure routes'. Of course it depends who you talk to. With more than 60 routes here now, it is arguably Tasmania's premiere sport climbing crag. Despite being in the middle of Tasmania's south-west, the area is seeing quite a lot of activity due to the unique climbing offered.

Geology/type of rock/quality: These conglomerate boulders are steep, pocketed, and juggy.

Grades: 14–31 (*Roid Rage*) but mostly 23+. The easier climbs may have been sooled—don't expect protection.

Number of routes: Over 60.

Height: Up to 20m.

Climbing style: The climbing is very steep and strenuous, with lots of pockets and jugs, and is fully bolt protected. There is a 'no natural gear' ethic, for want of a better term.

Brief history: The area has been developed since 1994 by climbers such as Sam Edwards and Roger Parkyn.

Season: A good summer crag as high rainfall make it unsuitable in other months. Can be good in easterly weather when Hobart is drizzly.

Location/access: Adamsfield is on the end of the Ragged Range in the south-west, about two hours drive from Hobart. Head out on the B62 (then Gordon Road, B61) from New Norfolk, through Maydena and into the South West National Park (you do not have to pay the entrance fee as Adamsfield is not in the Park). Turn R 5km past the Scott's Peak Dam onto the gravel Clear Hill Road and follow this for 16km until you see a large boulder on the R, almost overhanging the road. Park 50m further on the L. From here walk up the slippery bank on the R-hand side of the road for 100m (blue tapes) to the first boulder, the High Wire. From here, head up the hill to the R to the top of the hill to Pyramid Rock and the Bear Pit. Follow the orange tapes L to the Trapeze. From the Pyramid 10min to the R brings you to the Rage Cage and Magic Mushroom.

Camping and local amenities: There is a flat camp spot 2km past the car park at the base of the hill and a good flat and sheltered camping area exists behind Pyramid Rock, but there is no water. There is also a swimming hole, and obviously water, 3km past the car park, 50m downstream from the bridge. The nearest town for supplies is Maydena but it's best to stock up in Hobart.

Transport: Own vehicle.

Guidebook: *Craglets 5* (5th Edition) Roger Parkyn and Matt Perchard, Climbing Club of Tasmania, 1997. Also online, see Appendix 3.

Bouldering: This is supposedly the best place for bouldering in Tasmania but information is limited. Ask any locals you meet.

On **High Wire** (L>R):

▲▲	25	15m	1995

The Great Houdini — The 'steep' black crack on the lower side of the High Wire boulder.

▲▲	29	15m	1998

Magic Potion – Very overhanging wall to rap.

▲▲	23	10m	1994

Dragging the Chain – Start off large pile of cheat stones, grab holds and climb past 3FH. Lower off top BR.

▲	24	15m	1994

Lithe and Svelty – Stick clip start, and lower off last BR.

▲	22	10m	1994

Materialisation of a Psychotics Dream – Face climb up L of the line FH a few metres R.

▲▲	23	10m	1994

Bitter Twisted Soul – Thin slab and face 3m R to rap anchor.

▲▲	18	10m	1994

Elvira Maddigan – The slab to R past 3 FH, then L to rap anchor.

▲	24	10m	1994

Caught in Disaster – 15m R on North Face past 2 FH (stick clip first). No rap chains.

Other Classics:

▲▲	21	12m	Pyramid Rock	Soft
▲▲	21	12m	1995, Pyramid Rock	Attack of the Deranged Mutant Killer Monster
▲▲	25	12m	1997, The Bear Pit	Morjabia
▲▲	25	15m	15m 1997, The Bear Pit	The Mike Tyson vs Macaulay Culkin Fight
▲▲	25	12m	1998, The Bear Pit	Temper Tantrum
▲▲	23/4	10m	1997, The Bear Pit	Get a Grip
▲▲	22	19m	1997, The Bear Pit	Couldn't Bear to Wait
▲▲	26	20m	1998, The Trapeze	The Velocity Vampire
▲▲	25	20m	1997, The Trapeze	The Aerial Ballet
▲▲	27	20m	1997, The Trapeze	Forearm Flameout
▲▲	26	20m	1996, The Trapeze	Redback Fever
▲▲	24	20m	1994, The Trapeze	Circus Oz
▲▲	26	15m	1997, The Magic Mushroom	Super Unknown
▲▲	27	15m	1998, The Magic Mushroom	Frequent Flyer
▲▲	23	15m	1997, The Magic Mushroom	High Voltage
▲▲	24	22m	1997, The Magic Mushroom	Snake Charmer

Frenchmans Cap

You have to want to climb on Frenchmans Cap. The large (350m) quartzite half dome-like cliff is remote, situated in the west of Tasmania at the end of a ten hour walk. But then I suppose if you whacked a huge, white monolith in a paddock near Melbourne it would not have the same atmosphere. The climbing would still be superb, though, and the weather might be better.

The cliff is at 1443m and looks out over some of the best alpine scenery in Australia; wild bush, rugged mountains and crystal blue lakes. Despite the effort involved in getting there, climbers still make the trip to sample some of the best long route experiences in Australia. Frenchman's is described as having 'a real mountaineering flavour due to its isolation, seriousness, height and the unpredictability of the weather'. Go prepared.

Geology/type of rock/quality: Quartzite of variable quality, from very loose, sometimes with bands of rotten schist, to immaculate. Sometimes it's wet and mossy, sometimes it's hard, compact and smooth as glass. It often has very sharp edges so double ropes are recommended. **

Grades: Up to 23 but the length and seriousness of the routes should be taken into account. Hardest route so far is *De Gaulle's Nose* 23, which I don't think has yet been led without falls despite strong ascents by the likes of Carrigan and Dave Jones.

Height: Up to 350m.

Number of routes: Some 60 routes from 25–500 metres, plus some variants.

Climbing style: Traditional face climbing, using flakes and cracks. There are few bolts and the odd piton. These are now often rusty and largely redundant with modern equipment.

Brief history: Lured by bushwalkers' reports of the huge white cliff, the first climbers arrived in the early 1960s, bagging some of the obviously easier lines: *Western Slab Route*, *Deceptive Gully* and *Solomons Sanctuary*. During Easter 1962, Peter Sands and Bob Lidstone climbed North-East Passage, finishing in the upper reaches of the East Face. In December of that year Doug Cox and Mike Douglas climbed the Pillar Face. In 1962 Gwendolen Buttress was climbed and a year later R Sykes and Mike Douglas (alt) were the first to broach the southern arête climbing Southern Parapet.

Then in 1965 the indomitable Bryden Allen with Jack Pettigrew did the first route up the imposing main face, what became known later as *The Sydney Route*, a far cry from its original French name *A Toi la Gloire* (thine be the glory—an attempt to subscribe to the French theme here).

In 1968, when a strong group of mostly Victorian climbers arrived and tackled the main faces, John Moore and John Ewbank climbed *The Chimes of Freedom*. Blessed with eight days of fine weather, the team added *Valerie*, *Waterloo Road*, *Fleur-de-lis* and *Tierry le Fronde*. Chris Baxter and Chris Dewhirst did the second ascent of *The Sydney Route*, adding *The Melbourne Variant* 16.

Members of this team returned in 1970 and 1972, strengthened with the inclusion of Dave Neilson, who, with Dewhirst and Ian Ross, added *Conquistador*. This classic route was climbed free (except for one or two points of aid in the last pitch) during the 2nd ascent by Adrian Herington and Phil Cullen in January 1983. The original route was finally freed at 21 in 1990 by Canberra climbers: David Jenkins, Rohan Hyslop and Lucy Collaery. Chris Dewhirst and Dave Neilson also did a mostly FFA of *The Chimes of Freedom* 17 and *The Sydney Route* 17.

In 1982 Kim Carrigan with American Evelyn Lees added *The Great Flake* 22, cracking the 'last great problem'. Carrigan returned in 1983 with Mark Moorhead to pick off *The De Gaulle's Nose Route* 23, an exceptional route.

By 1986 the Tasmanians Garn Cooper and Peter Steane began to fully realise the potential of the cliff, their first of many fine efforts, *The Ninth of January* 19, and in 1988 one of the classics of the cliff, *The Lorax* 20.

Adventure climber extraordinaire Steve Monks, with Simon Mentz, visited in 1995 adding *The Natimuk Route* 22. (Please note: locals claim that any more routes named after climbers' home towns will be ignored and descriptions burnt, no matter how good the route is, or how famous and hot the climbers are—use some imagination.)

Season: This is a cliff that is best visited during the stable months of Jan and Feb. The most settled weather occurs from mid Jan–April, but expect the worst no matter when you go. In autumn the shorter, cooler days can be an issue on the longer routes. Its prominence above the surrounding country means it makes its own weather, and it is usually a wild mix. It can snow at any time of year. Most people probably climb here during the holidays, Jan–Feb.

Location/access: Take the Lyell Highway (A10, towards Queenstown) W from Hobart. About 30km past Derwent Bridge (about 200km or 2–3 hours from Hobart) there is a sign-posted car park where the walking track to Frenchmans Cap starts. It is 25km from here to Tahune Hut, where most climbers camp. The track can be very boggy after rain. It takes about 40 minutes to get to the base of the largest cliffs from the hut. Be warned, vehicles left in the car park are often 'tampered' with, i.e. broken into. See under transport for other options.

Camping and local amenities: The Tahune Hut holds several people and there are tent sites nearby if you are willing to carry a tent in with all your other gear. There is also a hut at Lake Vera on the way in. Tasmanian National Park entry fees apply and a permit system may be introduced in the future. All food and fuel will be cheaper if brought from Hobart or Queenstown.

Transport: The odd bus goes past the walking track, but they tend to be expensive. You're probably better off hitching. If you drive, make sure it's somebody else's car so that it's not your problem when you stagger out onto the highway in the pouring rain to find the seats, wheels and motor missing. An alternative is to park your car at Lake St Clair and arrange transport with a commercial operator to the start of the track.

Bus companies and tours provide transport to the Franklin–Gordon Wild Rivers National Park. For further details contact Tourism Tasmania, tel: (03) 6230 8250.

Guidebooks: *Frenchmans Cap*, Stephen Bunton (included with Jan–Jul 1990 edition of *Rock* magazine. Also online, see Appendix 3.

Information: South West National Park, tel: (03) 6288 1283.

South-East Face
Routes are listed from L to R as viewed from Lake Tahune.

▲ | 10 | 200m | 1963

Southern Parapet – A great climb up the SW arête, on the L side of the SE face.

▲▲▲ | 17 | 270m | (10) 1968 {1970}

The Chimes of Freedom – The most sought-after route on the face, a test piece despite its modest grade. It takes the most plausible route up the L side of the face, utilising the obvious ramp in a L-facing corner. Start from a small col below the ramp. 1. (30m) Wander up steeply towards the ramp. 2. (30m) More easily to the base of the ramp. 3. (24m) Up to a grassy ledge with pandani—can be comfortably reached in 2 pitches. 4. (18m) (crux) Corner to small stance on R. 5. (35m) Corner-crack to base of a chimney. 6. (27m) The chimney or, preferably, its R arête, to a large ledge. 7. (20m) L and up with poor protection, aiming for the foot of the dark corner. 8. (18m) Ascend the corner before escaping R and up to a ledge. Head back L to a corner. 9. (35m) Follow the corner for 18m before escaping L over loose blocks. 10. (35m) L round the corner then easily up.

▲▲▲   17   380m   (13) 1965 {1970}

The Sydney Route — A classic of the cliff and its most often repeated climb. Start as for *Valerie* 16M4 400m which is the route that follows the prominent line of weakness carved deep into the R side of the SE Face. It starts L of the main buttress which is directly below the summit of Frenchmans Cap. Go up scree in the gully to find a vegetated crack and belay knob. *The Sydney Route* takes the next prominent weakness to the R. 1. (35m) Up the crack before heading R up the unpleasant ramp. 2. (35m) Go easily R through the obstacle course to the base of a chimney, pass a flake, and then scramble to the chimney top. (The real climbing begins here). 3. (18m) Diagonally L to a rocky terrace. 4. (35m) Diagonally R to a detached pinnacle. PRs. 5. (24m) Chimney for 12m then avoid the overhang by the rotten rock to the L of a small corner. 6. (30m) Up R to the chimney and climb it, then continue up the L crack. Head R and up to PRs and belay. 7. (30m) Up R to a corner past a PR. Sustained climbing past a ledge on the L for a further 6m. 8. (30m) Poorly protected. Trav 6 m L round the corner to a faint line. Climb up to a good ledge but continue 3m to the top of a block. 9. (20m) (crux—L'Escalier du Diable—The Devil's Stairway). Up across the L wall to the arête and a small ledge. 10. (35m) Tentatively down L into the chimney leading to the top. 11. (30m) Ascend the chimney, surmounting the large boulder. 12. (30m) Same again. 13. (30m) Up to jugs.

▲▲   14   62m   1975

The Sydney Route Direct Start — Avoids the unpleasant 1st two pitches of the original route. Starts on the grassy knoll directly below the route. Aim for the large chimney and the start of pitch 3. 1a. (27m) Up L following the obvious line. 2a. (35m) Up and L. Step on to the L wall and gain the large ledge. R to the big chimney and the start of the route proper.

▲   16   370m   (13)1966

The Melbourne Variant — Don't get lost like the first ascentionists. This route is a variant to the top 8th, 9th and 10th pitches of *The Sydney Route*. 8a. (22m) Trav L for 6m as for that climb's 8th pitch then continue traversing for a further 9m. Step down L to gain the obvious line with the overhang towering 15m above. 9a. (24m) Climb up and L for 5 m. Go round the corner and 9m up the wall to PR. Continue up to a good ledge. 10a. (30m) Up 5m to PR. Trav R to the overhanging crack. Up the filth to rejoin the original route in the exit chimney. 11. to 13. As for *The Sydney Route*.

▲▲▲   23   330m   (8) [-,20,21,23,21,-,-,-] 1983

The De Gaulle's Nose Route — The hard test-piece. Prepare to fall. *De Gaulle's Nose* is the main arête between the SE Face and the E Face. The 'nose' is the prominent roof seen in profile. Start 50 m R of the nose at a chossy corner at the top of the vegetated ramps. 1. (40m) Up corners to bushy ledge. L to trees. 2. (40m) L to foot of corners. Up past ancient PR and blocks to ledge. 3. (15m) Up shallow corner on R to horizontal break. 4. (50m) L to crack. Up past roof and up overhanging crack to ramp. Up crack on L to large ledge. 5. (50m) From L of ledge diagonally to shallow corner. Up then diagonally R to huge flake. 6. (50m) R to arête and up to large ledge. 7. (40m) Up front of buttress to ledge. 8. (45m) Up the nose. R into groove. Up to top (loose).

▲▲▲ 22 370m (9) [-,16,20,20,19,22,21,18,18] 1982

The Great Flake – The most obvious feature on the E Face. Start at the corner down and R of the flake. 1. (90m) Up to foot of corner. 2. (25m) Corner to ledge on L. 3. (40m) L for 8m then up to shallow corner. Up to small stance. BB. 4. (40m) Up flake (loose flakes). Follow ramp to foot of corner. 5. (40m) Up corner to roof. Undercling then up off-width chimney to bulge (need very large gear). R on to face and up to sloping ledge. 6. (40m) Round roof then off-width to bulge. R and up to shallow corner on arête. R for 5m. 7. (21m) Up corner for 5m. L for 8m into next corner. Up to ledge and PRs and belay. 8. (40m) Up short slab to top. Up wall to ledge. R to avoid roof then L to foot shallow corner. 9. (30m) Roof and corner to ledge. R for 5m then up.

▲▲▲ 20 385m (7) [-,-,20,-,-,19,18] 1988

The Lorax – An impressive route up a R-leading corner level with upper half of *The Great Flake*. Protection is sparse on pitches 6 and 7. Start 80m up, from top of the highest grassy ramp (about half way across the E Face). 1. (55m) Diagonally L up ramps for 15m. Up the wall L of prominent corner. 2. (50m) Up 5m then L and up 10m to the contact point of the steep white rock with the black rock. Diagonally R until 25m below Bus-stop Ledge (the main feature in the centre of the face). 3. (35m) Trav 10m L to cave. Up difficult overhanging crack to top of R-leading corner. 4. (50m) Trav 15m L along obvious ledge. Up corner to good ledge on L wall. 5. (37m) Step R round arête to large ledge. Up juggy wall and short, steep hand-crack to ledge below big black corner of *Conquistador*. 6. (38m) Up 5m then L 6m. Up short, bottomless corner with difficulty and wall above for 6m. L for 7m then up corner to ledge R of deep cleft. 7. (40m) From L of ledge up wall for 4 m. Step L and up corner. Pass small roof to gain ledge below black, mossy corner. Step up and R round arête. Trav easily R to top of small chimney.

▲ 19 55m 1997

The Lorax–Conquistador Connection – A worthwhile link pitch-and-a-bit from the top of pitch 3 of *The Lorax* to pitch 9 of *Conquistador*. Start: Climb the first 3 pitches of *The Lorax*. 1. (45m) Instead of traversing L head up R past some loose flakes and a terrific corner. 2. (10m) Continue up the neat little wall on the R to join *Conquistador* at the big long ledge.

▲▲ 20+ 360m (11) 1972 {1990}

Conquistador – A magnificent and serious route directly up the face. Start below the L side of Bus-stop Ledge. 1. (35m) Line of weakness. 2. (35m) The corner until it is possible to move R to a ledge. 3. (35m) Aim slightly R to a block in the corner. 4. (15m) Good holds lead to a 12m trav L to a good ledge. 5. (35m) Directly up the steep wall to small belay (PR). 6. (43m) Tackle the loose rock in the corner until the sanctuary of Bus-stop Ledge is reached. 7. (27m) Trav L on fingertips for 5m to reach the foot of a corner. Up this with PRs to BB. 8. (35m) V corner for 24m then continue to ledge—PR and belay. 9. (35m) L along ledge to corner. Up this to big ledge. Keep going until it is possible to step on to the R wall – PR and belay. 10. (40m) Up then R and delicately up to a small ledge atop a detached block. Diagonally L for 6m to PR and belay. 11. (24m) (crux) Up to the loose blocks, and L then back R with improving pro.

Other recommended routes:

▲	16	295m	Terray's Tower Area	**Waterloo Road Direct**
▲▲	19	160m	Terray's Tower Area	**The Ninth of January**
▲▲	16	147m	Tahune Face	**Tierry le Fronde**

▲	16	45m	Tahune Face	**Tierry le Fronde Direct Start**
▲	17	25m	Tahune Face	**Tierry le Fronde Direct Variant**
▲▲▲	18	97m	Tahune Face	**Cold Steel Dawn**
▲▲	20	165m	Tahune Face	**Groundrush**
▲▲▲	21	60m	North-West Wall And Environs	**La Grande Pump**
▲	20	50m	North-West Wall And Environs	**Deviant Imagination**
▲▲	17		North-West Wall And Environs	**Electra**
▲▲	22	110m	North-West Wall And Environs	**Thus Spake Zarathustra**
▲▲	20	50m	North-West Wall And Environs	**For Susan**
▲▲	19	160m	North-West Wall And Environs	**Culture Shock**
▲▲	12	103m	North-West Wall And Environs	**Teetering Tower Ridge**
▲▲	12	69m	North-West Wall And Environs	**Surf Slab**

Federation Peak

Federation Peak is a huge tooth of grey quarzite in the Eastern Arthur range, in south-west Tasmania's World Heritage Area. It is a real peak, unusual in Australia, and was first climbed in 1949. *Blade Ridge* ascends 300m from the scrub to the foot of the 300m North West Face and the 600m combination is possibly the longest route in the country (not counting traverses). Its remoteness (a 1–2 day walk in) means it sees few climbing visitors. It is more commonly ascended by daring bushwalkers, despite the incredible exposure on the ascent.

Geology/type of rock/quality: Quartzite.

Grades: 18+.

Height: Up to 600m.

Number of routes: Nearly 20.

Climbing style: Long, traditional protected face climbing. Some of these routes are amongst the longest in Australia and involve multi-day expeditions for access and ascent.

Brief history: Refer to guidebooks.

Season: Summer (Dec–Feb) is the best chance of finding a window of stable weather in this area. It can be miserable and can snow here even in the middle of summer. Be prepared for bad weather at all times.

Location/access: The quickest approach to Federation Peak is from Farmhouse Creek via Moss Ridge. This is reached from Hobart by heading south on the Huon Highway (A6) to Geeveston, west along Arve Road, and along Picton Road (1km short of Tahune Picnic Shelter) to Farmhouse Creek. The Bechervaise Plateau can be reached in one very full day of walking, or more reasonably in a day and a half. From Farmhouse Creek follow the well-marked and fairly easy track for 18km (7 to 10 hours) to Cutting Camp where good campsites exist. From here it is a very steep and muddy slog (4–6hrs) up Moss Ridge, to reach Bechervaise Plateau. From Bechervaise Plateau the Southern Traverse may be followed to reach the western campsites. **Note:** access may have changed. Check with the national park authorities.

Camping and local amenities: Supplies are best brought from Hobart. There are camp sites at Cutting Camp, on the Bechervaise Plateau, at the Hanging Lake on timber platforms **(camping beside the lake is now banned)** and on the north side of the Thwaites Plateau. Note that the World Heritage Area is a fuel stove only area.

Transport: Own vehicle.

Guidebook: There are no recent guidebooks. The old 1969 Climbing Club of Tasmania guide is online at Jonathan Nermut's excellent Tasmanian climbing web site (see Appendix 3).
Information: South-west National Park, tel: (03) 6288 1283.

Classics:

▲▲	18	220m	(8) 1979	The North West Face Direct
▲▲	17	330m	(11) 1961	The North West Face
▲▲	17	420m	(12) 1968	Blade Ridge
▲▲▲	18	600m	(20!)	The Blade Ridge/North West Face Direct

Mt Geryon and the Acropolis

Another remote area with incredible potential. These are two large dolerite peaks in the Cradle Mountain–Lake St Clair National Park. The incredible 500m east face of Geryon is another area that requires solid commitment.

Geology/type of rock/quality: Columnar dolerite, up to **
Grades: Up to 25.
Height: Up to 450m (on Geryon's West Face).
Number of routes: Less than 50.
Climbing style: Long, traditionally protected lines and cracks.
Brief history: Not recorded.
Season: Summer (Feb–March) is best.
Location/access: Cynthia Bay at the S end of Lake St Clair is about 2 hr drive W from Hobart along the Lyell Highway (A10). A ferry up the lake will get you to the start of a 3 hr walk to the Pine Valley hut. From here the base of Mt Geryon is further up the valley and up a scree shute.
Camping and local amenities: At the Geryon camp site, or there is a bivvy cave at the base of the East Face of Mt Geryon.
Transport: Own vehicle, or it is possible to get a Tasmanian Wilderness Network bus (Tues, Thurs, and Sat) to Derwent Bridge from where it is a 5.5km walk to Cynthia Bay. In summer the ferry runs from here to the head of the lake three times daily ($20 return).
Guidebook: 'Mt Geryon and the Acropolis', Rock magazine, 1984. This guide has been reprinted in Rock #38.
Information: South-west National Park, tel: (03) 6288 1283.

Classics:

▲▲▲ Geryon Traverse 17, Orion 17, The Shield 24, Black Man's Country 25, Old Wave Heroes 21.

Bare Rock (Fingal)

The locally named Bare Rock is obvious as you come through the Fingal Valley, on the Esk Main Road (A4) in the state's north-east, rising above the town. Its 200m face holds about a dozen routes, though the nature of the rock does not betray the lines.

The dolerite cliffs of Fingal have a mystique about them matched by few areas in Australia.

They are dark, brooding, sombre and, like the Edgar Allen Poe stories they resemble, they are more classic than fashionable. More recent bolted face routes such as *The Sapphire Rose* may show what the future holds for this cliff. The cliff is on private land and **permission must be obtained to climb**. **Closed in spring** for the peregrine nesting season.

Geology/type of rock/quality: Dolerite *. Loose rock, wear a helmet.

Grades: Up to 22.

Height: Up to 200m.

Number of routes: 13.

Climbing style: Long, serious, exposed, traditionally protected (just) natural lines on faces with one modern bolted face climb (*Sapphire Rose*).

Brief history: Refer to guidebooks. If interested, find Rob McMahon's classic article 'The Museum of the Mind' from *Peaks* 3 magazine, 1980.

Season: The cliff can get very wet and is best in the drier summer months of Dec–Feb.

Location/access: The locally named Bare Rock is obvious rising above the town as you come through the Fingal Valley, on the Esk Main Road (A4) in the state's NE. **You need to get permission to climb** from Mr and Mrs Spencer in Fingal, tel: (03) 6374 1002. Turn down Legge St from Fingal and continue until the road curves R and then L. Head for the cliff along a track until a locked gate (2.2km from Main Road). Continue on the track until a rocky road can be seen that leads up to another gate and into a paddock. From the gate on the other side of the paddock head L to another rough road which leads to the cliff. Best to walk from first gate.

Camping and local amenities: No camping at cliff. At St Mary's (21km E) there is a youth hostel and hotel.

Transport: Own vehicle or bus to Fingal, then walk.

Guidebooks: *Craglets 5* (5th Edition) Roger Parkyn and Matt Perchard, Climbing Club of Tasmania, 1997.

Information: Try Hobart or Launceston climbing shops (see Appendix 1) and web sites (see Appendix 3).

Classics:

▲▲	19	210m	(5) 1971	**Finn McCool**
▲▲	17	200m	(5) 1969	**MacDonagh**
▲▲▲	22	95m	(3) 1994	**The Sapphire Rose**

Note: There is an abseil descent that follows *The Sapphire Rose*, R (FI) of the middle of the cliff—(30m x 50m x 50m).

Freycinet

On the north-east coast of Tasmania, on the coastal granite of the Freycinet Peninsula, are some of the most scenically surrounded cliffs in the world, and the climbing is not bad either. Freycinet is like a beautiful tropical paradise, without palm trees and dancing girls—and it's not that tropical. It is beautiful though. In summer it is as close to a perfect climbing area as you could imagine. There are short, hard granite problems, 300m long slabs and the incredible 2km long *Hazards Sea-level Traverse*. The name of this climb is misleading as you get some height above the sea at times. Start at Sleepy Bay (a 50m swim or climb to get past Flowstone Wall, grade 16, 8hrs), thrash yourself senseless then cool off with a swim…

Geology/type of rock/quality: High quality granite. *** Slabs, faces and cracks abound.

Grades: Up to 28.

Height: Up to 250m but mostly one to two pitches.

Number of routes: Hundreds.

Climbing style: Predominantly traditionally protected climbs (slabs, cracks, faces) though newer routes have bolts. Some bolts are less than top quality stainless steel and have corroded badly in the coastal environment, so beware. Gracelands and the Underworld (mainly 22–27) are a couple of modern sport areas.

Brief history (by Pete Steane): Climbing at Freycinet first began in the late '60s and early '70s on the Hazards with Peter Jackson, Robert McMahon and Michael McHugh bagging most of the early routes including *The Crack of Pork*, and *Pearler*. Since then it has been hard to define any single 'era', with a number of climbers each contributing routes over the years. Ian Lewis, Lyle Closs, Kim Carrigan, Bryan Kennedy, and Doug Fife are a few of them. Kennedy's *Captain Goodvibes*, and *Fife's Boaring* are two middle-grade classics on Sow Spur. In 1975 Henry Barber freed Jackson and McHugh's 1970 line *Incipience* 22 on Mt Amos. It has never failed to impress the few successful leaders since, and legend has it as the scene of falls of up to 30m. During the early '80s the remote Flowstone Wall yielded several long and lonely routes by cunning climbers such as Kennedy and Phil Cullen, who understood that the heroic nature of the country justified the application of a secret weapon in the form of Adrian Herington. Sam Edwards and Rolan Eberhard used a somewhat less subtle weapon in the mid '90s when they bolted *Arocknophobia* near the L end of the wall.

The coastal climbing south of White Water Wall, including Cape Tourville, seems to have been dominated by members of the Climbers Union of Northern Tasmania and their visitors in the 1980s. Smith, Deka, McMahon, Maddison, and Fantini are names that often crop up. Their routes on Alchemy Wall are hard to match for good clean fun, while *La Grande Epoque* on Tourville has all the atmosphere you'd expect from a big sea cliff route. The White Water Wall area, the first coastal area discovered, saw action from Lewis, Kennedy, Closs, Dick Hain, and Carrigan from the mid '70s, with routes like *Lace Thunder, Ice Nine*, and *Harlequin*. Staszewski, Parsons and Bigg added some of the harder routes in the early '80s, such as *Heat of the Night* 24, the quintessential roof crack. And let's not forget Smith and Maddison's *Sweet Revenge* 22, or Cullen's immaculate *No Tern Unstoned* 19. The list goes on.

From the mid '80s to the early '90s Garn Cooper was active on the Hazards with several partners, mainly Alan Adams, but also Kennedy, Cullen, Steane and others. Their efforts include *Little Bits of Wire* on Amos, *It Aint Kosher* on Sow Spur, and *Don't Land on the Lunch* on Hazards Main Wall.

The '90s saw development of a number of craglets dotted around the Hazards, including Gracelands, Broadway, and the sport-climbers' Underworld.

Season: Like all Tasmanian crags, Freycinet can be good in the hotter months Dec–Feb, especially for the swimming, but the most settled weather is in Feb–Mar. Because of its sea-level position, Coles Bay offers year round climbing, something many of Tasmania's alpine areas don't offer.

Location/access: Freycinet is about halfway up the east coast of Tasmania, roughly 2hrs from both Launceston and Hobart. It is accessed from the Tasman Hwy (A3) that runs down the coast. Turn off to Coles Bay at the clearly marked junction 10km S of Bicheno, and from there take the road to Sleepy Bay and Cape Tourville light house. Turn L onto the White Water Wall Rd. You will arrive above the short, steep sea cliffs of White Water Wall (sign says 4WD). The long slabs of Main Wall are along the coast south from Sleepy Bay. Lassie's Wall and White Water Wall offer perhaps the best beginner (grades 10–17) climbing in the state. The cliffs of the Hazards main wall deliver longer, scarier adventure routes.

Camping and local amenities: There is a toilet and protected campsites above White Water Wall. National Park entrance fees apply. The campsites are fuel stove only areas. There is also camping and more luxurious accommodation in Coles Bay and this is the source of all amenities; food, fuel; etc. Book well in advance. There is a good bakery, a pub and fish'n'chips—what more could you want.

Transport: Own vehicle is best. Otherwise there are buses from Hobart to Bicheno (28km) and from there back down to Coles Bay. There is also a daily shuttle bus that will take you 5km to the national park car park (departs Coles Bay 9.40am and returns to Coles Bay from the car park at 10am).

Guidebooks: *A Climber's Guide to the Freycinet Peninsula*, CCT, 1996. This guide may now be difficult to obtain. Jon Tillar is currently compiling the new version of the guide.

Information: Freycinet National Park, tel: (03) 6257 0107.

Bouldering: There are granite boulders all over the place. No-one really bothers to record what they do on these except for the wee crags on the Hazards: Wave Wall, Talking Rock, The Kindergarten, Gracelands, Stealth, the Speaker Box, the Suzuki Complex, Lizard Rocks etc., and a bit of the coastal stuff like Rubik's Cube and Lego etc.

Bluestone Bay

Bluestone Bay is the most popular area due to its proximity to the campsite. It has good rock, good pro, steepness, shortness, easy access and morning sun (as opposed to the Hazards, Mt Amos, Sow Spur, and Cape Tourville which are longer, generally less steep, and slabbier). White Water Wall has the greatest concentration of long, easier climbs. There is a descent route at the L end of Harlequin Wall down a ramp. Follow the road S along the top of the cliff from where the road meets the campsite. A rough track can then be followed N to the ramp. These routes are described L>R from that access.

▲ **22** **45m** (2) 1982

Sweet Revenge — Starts at bottom of Harlequin Ramp where an easy broken wall meets a steeper wall with a roof at 15m, divided by a corner (*Crayfish Crack* 9). 1. (30m) Start at corner, climb 12m to roof, trav R, up to undercling then jam up and R to belay. 2. (15m) Up chimney and trav out under roof.

▲ **22** **55m** (2) 1977

Beaman's Route — Start as for *Sweet Revenge*. 1. (30m) Climb 12m to roof, trav R , moving down and across to finger and hand crack. Up this to belay. 2. (25m) L under roof to offwidth. Up this to top. *The Direct* 22 starts under the crack/flake climbing up past a BR.

▲▲▲ **18** **40m** 1975

Harlequin — Starts L up a V-corner on R-end of wall to rap station.

▲ **27** **20m** 1989

Granite Planet — R of *Harlequin* is an overhung buttress and R again a roof. Line through roof with FH.

▲ | 15 | 35m | (2) 1975

Ice Nine – Off the big boulder below a bottomless corner in middle of the R face Harlequin Wall.

▲ | 19 | 45m | 1982

No Tern Unstoned – On White Water Wall proper. L of *Apline*, a short shallow corner leading to a BR at 18m, then up R and up.

▲▲▲ | 12 | 70m | (2) 1975

Apline – The route follows the large aplite dyke which diagonally crosses the R-hand side of the White Water Wall face (L>R).

▲▲ | 10 | 45m | 1974

Ultimate Conception – Starts crack R of *Apline*. Up crack crossing *Apline*.

Lassie's Wall

Popular for leading and top-roping with good access. Lots of easy good lines. There are two N leading descent routes below and slightly to the S of the main White Water Wall campsite. Lassie's Wall is to the seaward side of the southernmost ramp.

▲▲▲ | 18 | 25m | 1982

Step Aside – The dyke/crack system at the L end of the Wall.

▲ | 15 | 25m | 1974

Cordon Bleu – The line through the small bulge just to the R.

Little Bluestone Bay

Alchemy Wall is the beautifully compact wall visible from the road. Head across Little Bluestone Bay. The distinct R leaning crack on the wall's L is *Hermes Trismegistus* 21. Access is by rap or a scramble down the northern end.

▲ | 19 | 20m | 1981

Coolibah Crack – The sharp arching crack on the L of the wall, around the corner from the main face.

▲ | 19 | 25m | 1981

Walking the Plank – The crack system R of *Hermes Tri'*. Cracks peter out at top. Trav R into *Blue-Eyed and Blonde*.

▲ | 19 | 25m | 1981

Blue-Eyed and Blonde – Crack to and through bulge R of *Walking the Plank*.

▲▲▲ | 21 | 25m | 1981

Alchemy – The next crack system R.

The Underworld

One of the sport climbing areas. Head down to the water from where the *Skyline Traverse* of the Hazards meets the Sea-level Traverse. There is an amphitheatre of pink granite undercut by a large cave.

Other classic routes in the area:

▲▲▲	20	15m		1981

Lightfingered Maddison – Lightfingered Maddison Wall (R of White Water Wall) – Up diagonals to sentry box and up wall.

▲▲	17	35m		1979

Beowulf – Deepwater Wall or Square Zawn

▲▲	18	20m		1980

Mithras – White Stack (abseil in to routes on White Stack and this route is the best easiest way out). Also here is the Dave Jones 28, *Holiday's in Bulimia* 15m from 1995.

▲▲	22	15m	1981, White Stack	**Whitesail**
▲▲	22	50m	(2) 1970 {1975}, Mt Amos	**Incipience**
▲▲	21	60m	(2) 1986, Mt Amos	**Little Bits of Wire**
▲▲	17	60m	(3) 1971, Mt Amos	**RH Negative**
▲	18	55m	(2) 1987, Mt Amos	**Babi Yar**
▲▲	20	42m	187-88, Sow Spur	**It Aint Kosher**
▲	19	55m	(2) 1982, Sow Spur	**Boaring**
▲	22	75m	(2) 1995, Sow Spur	**Silk Purse**
▲▲	17	50m	1986, Sow Spur	**Dive Between the Whirling Blades**
▲▲	18	50m	1977, Sow Spur	**Captain Goodvibes**
▲	19	45m	1977, Hazards Main Wall	**Full Sail**
▲▲	19	100m	(3) 1977 {later}, Hazards Main Wall	**Stud City**
▲	22	90m	(3) 1988, Hazards Main Wall	**Hootin and Jivin**
▲▲	18	95m	(3) 1988, Hazards Main Wall	**Kids on Skids**
▲	20	90m	(3) 1988, Hazards Main Wall	**Don't Land on the Lunch**
▲	20	150m	(4) 1977, Hazards Main Wall	**Cosmic City Flameout**
▲▲	16	230m	(5) 1974, Hazards Main Wall	**Japhilion**

Launceston

The climbers of Launceston have long been spoilt. There is so much quality rock close to, and in, their town. As a result there are well over 1000 named routes in the area. The weather is generally better here than the alpine crags. Most of the cliffs and climbs are on the South and North Esk and Tamar rivers, including Cataract Gorge, a 10 minute walk from the city centre. There are also areas like Mt Blackwood, Brady's Lookout, and Hillwood Volcano.

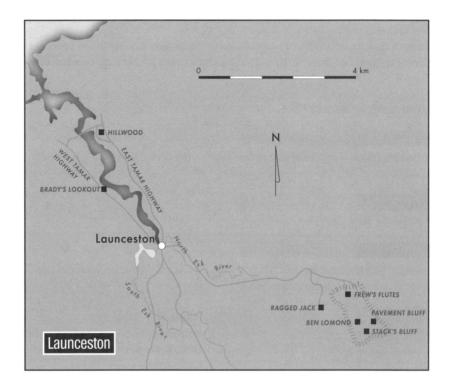

Launceston

Geology/type of rock/quality: Mostly dolerite. **

Grades: Up to 28.

Height: Up to 10–25m.

Number of routes: 700+, the Craglets Guide lists 50+ buttresses.

Climbing style: Mostly traditionally protected cracks but bolt technology is beginning to make its presence felt with bolted face and arêtes.

Brief history: Incredible evergreen local new router Rob McMahon started doing routes in Cataract Gorge in 1972 with Michael McHugh, but the area didn't take off until the early '80s when McMahon, with other locals, including Gerry Narkowicz, Simon Parsons, Neale Smith and John Fantini, started to do literally hundreds of new routes. Danny Ng bolted a couple of dozen classics in the late '80s before John Fisher and Michael Fox, in the mid 1990s, produced sport routes graded 23–26.

Season: Virtually all year round except for rainy days (see introduction, p. 196). The Gorge in Launceston is divided into a shady side and a sunny side.

Location/access: Head down Paterson Street for 5 mins from the centre of Launceston and park in the Penny Royal car park. Walk to the closest side of Kings Bridge and head up the Zig Zag track. Shortly you will start passing the buttresses. Generally the climbing is on the down side of the track—look for faint tracks to the more popular areas. For Duck Reach find any tourist map which will show you how to get to the old Duck Reach power station (along Corin St). Follow the river upstream to the buttresses. For the Riverbend, you need to drive out through St Leonards to Corra Linn. Walk from a gate on the L hand side of the road, a couple of hundred metres past the bridge. It is about 10min across the paddocks to reach the crags above the river.

Camping and local amenities: Launceston.

Transport: Own car, or Shank's Pony.

Guidebooks: For the 285 climbs within a kilometre of the suspension bridge there is a new guide: *Cataract*, Robert McMahon, Oriel, 2000.

Information: Try Allgoods Bush Hut, Launceston, for information, tel: (03) 6331 3644; Mick Fox, tel: (03) 6334 6633 or Mountain Designs, tel: (03) 6334 0988. There is some information online (see Appendix 3).

Bouldering: There is bouldering in the gorge, mostly on the shady side, off the tourist track

Classics: Feltham is one of the most popular buttresses in the Gorge with its concentration of classic climbs. Drop down from the Zig Zag track when its switches back L 50m after Trackside buttress. Abseil down the prominent corner of *Westham*.

▲	14	1972, Feltham Buttress	**Westham**
▲	18	1972, Feltham Buttress	**Lingham**
▲	16	1972, Feltham Buttress	**Feltham**

▲	17	1973, Gabriel Buttress	**Gabriel**
▲	18	1978, Gabriel Buttress	**Loose Money, Juice Money**
▲	20	1973, Traffic Fine Buttress	**Crux and Beyond**
▲	21	1980, Lady Midnight, Lower Tier	**Joan of Arc**
▲	22	1980, The Lost City,	**Double Dozen**
▲	22	1980, Ramona Buttress,	**Mac the Finger**
▲	17	Ramona Buttress	**Ramona**

Hillwood Volcano

This is the latest sport climbing venue in the area, with over 120 often fully equipped routes on steep basalt, 10–30m high. The cliff is on private land and access is delicate. Call Bob McMahon, tel: (03) 6394 4225 or Gerry Narkowicz, tel: (03) 6330 1435 to arrange access.

Classics:

22	**Long Kiss Goodnight**
23	**Dr Pepper**
23	**Ancient of Days**
24	**Sacred Stone**
27	**Throne of Judgement**

Sisters' Beach

Sisters' Beach and Rocky Cape are the main climbing areas on the north-west coast, further up from Burnie. There are a few good steep, pumpy sport routes here on quartzite buttresses, although some of the bolts have rusted badly so be careful. The beach is nice though.

Craglets 5 (5th Edition) Roger Parkyn and Matt Perchard, Climbing Club of Tasmania, 1997 covers Sisters' Beach. There is an old guide called *52 Climbs in the Rocky Cape Area* that covers Rocky Cape Wall.

Classics:

17	Superfly
27	The Dog's Coif
26	The Dog's Knob
25	Butcher's Dog

Ben Lomond

With its 30 kilometres of dolerite escarpment, perched high in north-eastern Tasmania, Ben Lomond is a baffling place. It is home to a history of epics and marvels, and long thin crack lines of the sort that mainland Australia doesn't offer. These cracks were the epitome of '70s climbing, when every surfie-like climber was looking for the perfect line, man. They are now less visited. The alpine environment and the associated bad weather, and the lack of a guidebook to the area, have not helped its cause. They still offer superb climbing if you are interested in experiencing all that the sport of climbing has to offer. There are few cliffs that offer such soaring regular cracks of all sizes. Hey, if you liked that move, why not repeat it for 100m?

The most visited cliffs are above Carr Villa on the northern end of the Ben Lomond plateau. These include the Pavillion, Robin's Buttress Frew's Flutes, Local Loser and Heathcliffe. More remote crags like Stack's Bluff, Pavement Bluff, Ragged Jack and Africa require more commitment.

Geology/type of rock/quality: Dolerite ***
Grades: Up to about 25.
Height: Up to 200m.
Number of routes: 100s.
Climbing style: Long cracks protected au natural (there is an anti-bolting ethic); take ten of whatever size crack you've picked! Taping up is recommended.
Brief history: Another of the Launceston areas that Bob McMahon and a cast of tens from the local area started to develop in the early '70s. McMahon has done many of the area's classics including firstly *Rock-a-day Johnny* 18 1974 and *Rigaudon* 18, 1976. UK climber Robin Thompson visited the USA, learnt the lessons of Yosemite jam cracks and brought his experience to Tasmania. In 1978, he put up several classics, including *Ramadan* 19. With the '70s obsession with cracks the cliff became de rigeur, with many climbers journeying to Tasmania to climb here. Notable first ascents include Keith Lockwood's *Rajah* 18 in 1978, John Fantini's *Aquilla* 21 in 1983 and Ken Rosebery's *Barbe de Vendetta* 18 1977. In 1981 locals Simon Parsons and Phil Bigg teamed up with Queenslander Rob Staszewski producing the stunning triptych of *Defender of the Faith* 21, *Master Blaster* 24 and *Dangerman* 21.
Season: The climbs are at an elevation of 1300m giving them an alpine feel. This means that the summer months are the best time to climb here. Expect bad weather anytime of year and be prepared. It snows here!
Location/access: From Launceston (in northern Tasmania) take the St Leonards Road (C401) to St Leonards and keep going. The name of the road changes to Blessington Road and winds along beside the North Esk River. After about half an hour, turn R at the clearly signposted junction and travel up the Ben Lomond road for about 10 km. Just before the ranger's hut turn R (signposted) and drive 1km

to Carr Villa. Park here. The Pavillion is about 20 minutes walk up to the L. Local Loser is straight above Carr Villa at the top of the scree and Frew's Flutes is the tall columnar cliff off to the R. A 30 minute walk across the scree, (stay high to avoid scrub) will get you there. Heathcliffe is the weirdly structured cliff further R of the Flutes.

Camping and local amenities: There is camping at the Carr Villa scout camp. Fees apply to enter the national park, but the collection booth is not manned in the summer (the mountain is most popular during the 'ski season'). Supplies are best purchased from Launceston if coming from the N.

Transport: Must have your own or arrange lift.

Information: Tel: (03) 6390 6279 for general enquiries about the national park.

Guidebooks: There is a very rough topo of the Flutes and Local Loser in *Craglets 5* (5th Edition) Roger Parkyn and Matt Perchard, CCT, 1997 as well as some info on Ragged Jack. There is some info online (see Appendix 3). A more extensive guide to the area is currently in formation.

Frew's Flutes/Robin's Buttress

Robin's Buttress is the L hand side of Frew's Flutes, with routes varying from 30–180m. There is a rough track that hits the cliff L of what is described as a 'donga-like protuberance of rock', a phallic projection of one of the columns down low (the abseil comes down here 47m and 24m). Watch the pull or perhaps walk down. L of this is a recessed column with a flaring corner (*Ramadan*) and L again a 20m high almost separated pinnacle. *Defender* starts on the R of this taking the offwidth that turns to a chimney. The rock quality deteriorates at the top so be careful.

▲ | 21 | 90m | (3) [19,21,-] 1984

Necromancer – The second major line L of *Defender*, about 20m. 1. (25m) Bridge and jam flared corner with black scoops in it, then around small roof to belay on top of square cut pillar. 2. (45m) Bridge corner to 1m roof. 3. (20m) L around roof then up crack which blanks out. Face climb to reach hand crack.

▲▲ | 22 | 75m | (2) [19, 22]

Black Celebration – Start as for *Necromancer*. 1. (25m) As for *Necromancer*. 2. (50m) Twin crack system.

▲▲ | 22 | 80m | (2) 1980

Die Nadel – A long and sustained (40m) thin hand crack up the wall 15m L of *Defender*, that finishes at that route's first belay.

▲▲▲ | 21 | 80m | (3) [19,21,18] 1981

Defender of the Faith – 1. (15m) Up offwidth in alcove that turns into chimney. 2. (35m) From the ledge atop the column take the crack on L, using face holds, to small ledge. 3. (30m) To top.

▲▲▲ | 20 | 80m | (3) [19,20,18] 1978

Rigaudon – 1. (15m) As for *Defender*. 2. (45m) The dihedral above belay ledge, R of *Defender*. 3. (20m) Up.

▲ | 19 | 80m | (2) [19,18] 1978

Ramadan – 1. (45m) Climb widening finger crack to R of *Defender*. At 35m take flake/crack to R and climb up to belay in line to R (*Rajah*). 2. (35m) Straight up through bulge, hand/fist crack to top.

▲▲ 18 80m (3) [18,17,18] 1978

Rajah — 1. (15m) Start off the phallus, climbing the 15m hand crack on L. 2. (30m) Hand crack (widens to offwidth at one point) to belay ledge atop *Ramadan* pinnacle. 3. (40m) Finish up *Ramadan*.

▲▲▲ 21 75m (3) [21,18,16] 1981

Dangerman — Start about 60m R of *Rajah*, to the L of four superb cracks L of block. 1. Up superb corner. 'The calf workout from hell'. 2. More of the same. 3. Wander to top.

▲▲▲ 24 80m (3) [24,20,17] 1981

Master Blaster — Start 3m R of *Dangerman*, beneath incredible crack that runs pure for 40m. (Green rap sling at top of 1st pitch) 1. Climb crack. Can rap from sling at 25m. 2. Continue up. 3. Up to top.

▲▲▲ 21 75m° (3) [21, 20,19] 1983

Aquilla — Start in finger crack in corner to R. 1. (25m) Stem up dihedral thankful for crack. Belay on ledge to R. 2. 20m. Crack to belay behind detached block. 3. (20m) Crack through bulge then up to top.

▲▲ 18 80m (3) [18,18,16] 1977

Barbe Di Vendetta — Start in handcrack R of *Aquilla* and L of column. 1. (30m) Crack past three steps. 2. (30m) Up corner, through small roof and up to belay. 3. (20m) Climb up the faces to top.

▲▲▲ 20 80m (2) [20,-] 1978

Rondeau — About 220m to the R there is a very 'obvious' line, a spearing crack (3 crack system) up the front of a 50m high recessed pinnacle. 1. (50m) Climb line to large ledge. 2. (30m) Continue to top.

▲ 22 85m 3) [22,21,17] 1985

Grim Reaper — Line up the face around arête to R. 1. (20m) Climb groove on L, traversing R at the roof at 17m, across two columns to large ledge. 2. (40m) Climb down a metre then back L. Over roof on finger locks and into crack which eventually leads to belay. 3. (20m) Slightly L and climb groove on arête..

Other classics on **Frew's Flutes**:

▲	20	90m	1981	**35mm Dream**
▲	22	75m	1985	**Powerdive Eliminate**
▲▲	18	180m	1974	**Rock a Day Johnny**
▲▲	22	10m	1981	**Warsaw**

Heathcliffe

Heathcliffe is the cliff to the R (W) of Frew's Flutes. It takes about half an hour by walking across the scree from Carr Villa, or about 40 minutes by walking across the top of the plateau, along the top of Frew's Flutes.

▲▲ 18   72m   2) 1979

Burma Shave — (The most uphill buttress of the cliff is very steep. This route begins on the L and goes straight up to join with the crux of *Highway of Diamonds*. 2nd pitch finishes up the airy prow.

▲▲ 18   72m   (2) 1978

Highway of Diamonds — Jam up L side of block at the base of the buttress. Step off and 'dance a highly cerebral waltz up the facets of the diamonds'. Trend L to turn the overhangs.

▲▲ 17   72m   (2) 1975

Madame George — R of *Highway of Diamonds* is an initially flaring corner with difficult bridging. Instead of continuing straight up it is easier to go R slightly and then come back L further up across the blank face under the block. 2nd pitch goes through the same prow as the previous two routes.

Flinder's Island

The large mass of granite on Flinder's Island in the Bass Strait is collectively known as Mt Killiecrankie. Its excellent rock holds more than 200 climbs up to 100m. Oddly, most of the development has been from mainland climbers. There is also climbing on the taller Mt Strezlecki as well as a few other crags on the island.

Geology/type of rock/quality: Granite ***
Grades: Up to 26.
Height: Up to 100m (Mt Strezlecki up to 800m).
Number of routes: 200+.
Climbing style: Granite face, crack, slab and flake climbs. Mostly naturally protected.
Brief history: Largely unrecorded. Try 'Killiecranking', Wayne Maher, *Rock* 26 or Mike Law's 'Disco In Furneaux', *Rock* 34.
Season: The weather here can be fairly wild, and as with most Tasmanian crags is probably best visited in the summer months (Dec–Mar). In winter, trust me, you don't want to go there.
Location/access: The cliff is on the north-west coast of Flinder's Island, the largest of the Furneaux group of islands in Bass Strait between Tasmania and the mainland. You can fly to the island from both Launceston and Melbourne and arrive in Whitemark on Flinder's Island. It is possible, though expensive, to hire a car on the island. Hitching around is easy though there is not much traffic. If hitching, it is probably easier to head for the town of Killiecrankie to the S of the cliff and walk N from there, although the walk is a fair bit longer. The cliffs are about a half hour walk from the end of the new road that comes into the N of them. Follow down the shore and the cliff is set back a little from the coast.
Camping and local amenities: You can camp on the shore below the middle of the cliffs. There are water soaks there apparently. There are also a number of accommodation options in Whitemark.
Guidebooks: Reportedly climber Steve Craddock is currently in the process of preparing and publishing a definitive guide.
Information: Try Melbourne or Launceston climbing stores (see Appendix 1) or web sites (see Appendix 3).

There are a cluster of good routes around the Chequerboard Buttress:

▲▲	18	80m	**Killiecranking**
▲	17	70m	**Cold Journey**
▲▲	20	50m	**Sunbeam**
▲▲	18	50m	**Over Balance**
▲	18	50m	**Blue Skies**

Also around the old campsite are some nice ones:

▲▲	21	50m	**Taipan**
▲▲	20	50m	**Sunset Boulevard**
▲▲	18	85m	**Adventures in Paradise**
▲▲	22	70m	**Norseman**
▲▲	23	60m	**Peppermint**
▲	22	70m	**Avalon**

But the best are a little further south around the pinnacle:

▲▲▲	18	50m	**Farewell Gesture**
▲▲▲	18	50m	**Far Away Places**
▲▲	18	70m	**Tendonitis**

APPENDIX 1: CLIMBING STORES

New South Wales

Sydney Metropolitan

Alpsport
1045 Victoria Rd
West Ryde NSW 2114
Tel: (02) 9858 5844 or 1800 803 680

Eastwood Camping Centre Pty Ltd
3 Trelawney St
Eastwood NSW 2122
Tel: (02) 9858 3833

Kathmandu Pty Ltd
Shop G12, Mandarin Centre
Cnr Victor St & Albert Ave
Chatswood NSW 2067
Tel: (02) 9410 0963

Kathmandu Pty Ltd
Shop 34A, Town Hall Arcade
Cnr Kent & Bathurst Sts
Sydney NSW 2000
Tel: (02) 9261 8901

Mountain Designs
Shop 16/9 Spring St
Chatswood NSW 2067
Tel: (02) 9415 4566

Mountain Designs
499 Kent St
Sydney NSW 2000
Tel: (02) 9267 3822

Mountain Equipment
72 Archer St
Chatswood NSW 2067
Tel: (02) 9419 6955

Mountain Equipment
106 George St
Hornsby NSW 2077
Tel: (02) 9477 5467

Mountain Equipment
491 Kent St
Sydney NSW 2000
Tel: (02) 9264 5888

On Rope
11 Nelson Ave
Padstow NSW 2211
Tel: (02) 9709 6299

Paddy Pallin
527 Kingsway
Miranda NSW 2228
Tel: (02) 9525 6829

Paddy Pallin
Shop 3, 74 Macquarie St
Parramatta NSW 2150
Tel: (02) 9633 1113

Paddy Pallin
507 Kent St
Sydney NSW 2000
Tel: (02) 9264 2685

Patagonia
497 Kent St
Sydney NSW 2000
Tel: (02) 9264 2500

Single Rope Technique
9 Nelson Ave
Padstow NSW 2211
Tel: (02) 9796 3455

Blue Mountains

Mountain Designs
190 Katoomba St
Katoomba NSW 2780
Tel: (02) 4782 5999

Paddy Pallin
166B Katoomba St
Katoomba NSW 2780
Tel: (02) 4782 4466

Rocksports Adventure & Travel Equipment
1A Ross St
Glenbrook NSW 2773
Tel: (02) 4739 3152

Summit Gear Pty Ltd
Shop 3, 88 Katoomba St
Katoomba NSW 2780
Tel: (02) 4782 3467

Point Perpendicular and Nowra
Paddy Pallin Adventure
Shop 5, 62 Owen St
Huskisson NSW 2540
Tel: (02) 4441 7448

New England
Mountain Designs
109 Dangar St
Armidale NSW 2350
Tel: (02) 6771 5991

Other areas
Mountain Designs
490 Dean St
Albury NSW 2640
Tel: (02) 6021 0133

Mountain Designs
Cnr King and National Park Sts
Newcastle NSW 2300
Tel: (02) 4962 3311

Australian Capital Territory

Belconnen Camping World
4 Oatley Crt
Belconnen ACT 2617
Tel: (02) 6253 2699

CSE Camping & Ski Equipment Pty Ltd
18–24 Townshend St
Phillip ACT 2606
Tel: (02) 6282 3424

Jurkiewicz Adventure Sports
47 Wollongong St
Fyshwick ACT 2609
Tel: (02) 6280 6033

Kathmandu Pty Ltd
20 Allara St
Canberra ACT 2601
Tel: (02) 6257 5926

Mountain Designs
6 Lonsdale St
Braddon ACT 2612
Tel: (02) 6247 7488

Paddy Pallin
11 Lonsdale St
Braddon ACT 2601
Tel: (02) 6257 3883

Victoria

Melbourne Metropolitan
Ajays Snow Country Sports
115 Canterbury Rd
Heathmont Vic 3135
Tel: (03) 9720 4647

Bogong
78 Oxford St
Collingwood Vic 3066
Tel: (03) 9415 7599

Bogong
374 Little Bourke St
Melbourne Vic 3000
Tel: (03) 9600 0599

Eastern Mountain Centre
654B Glenferrie Rd
Hawthorn Vic 3122
Tel: (03) 9818 1544

Kathmandu Pty Ltd
Warehouse Outlet
161 Smith St
Fitzroy Vic 3065
Tel: (03) 9419 1868

Kathmandu Pty Ltd
Level 2, 376 Little Bourke St
Melbourne Vic 3000
Tel: (03) 9642 1942

Mountain Designs
970 Whitehorse Rd
Box Hill Vic 3128
Tel: (03) 9899 1900

Mountain Designs
132 Smith St
Collingwood Vic 3066
Tel: (03) 9417 5300

Mountain Designs
654 Glenferrie Rd

Hawthorn Vic 3122
Tel: (03) 9818 0188

Mountain Designs
373 Little Bourke St
Melbourne Vic 3000
Tel: (03) 9670 3354

Paddy Pallin
8 Market St
Box Hill Vic 3128
Tel: (03) 9898 8596

Paddy Pallin
360 Little Bourke St
Melbourne Vic 3000
Tel: (03) 9670 4845

Paddy Pallin
88 Maroondah Hwy
Ringwood Vic 3134
Tel: (03) 9879 1544

Patagonia
370 Little Bourke St
Melbourne Vic 3000
Tel: (03) 9642 2266

Pinnacle Outdoors
55 Hardware St
Melbourne Vic 3000
Tel: (03) 9642 2955

The Wilderness Shop Pty Ltd
969 Whitehorse Rd
Box Hill Vic 3128
Tel: (03) 9898 3742

Mt Arapiles
Arapiles Mountain Shop
67 Main St
Natimuk Vic 3409
Tel: (03) 5387 1529

Other areas
Mountain Designs
Shop 1, Southside Central
37 Princes Hwy
Traralgon Vic 3844
Tel: (03) 5174 4877

Mountain Designs
9/171–181 Moorabool St
Geelong Vic 3220
Tel: (03) 5229 6000

Queensland

Brisbane
Kathmandu Pty Ltd
144 Wickham St
Fortitude Valley Qld 4006
Tel: (07) 3252 8054

K2 Base Camp
140 Wickham St
Fortitude Valley Qld 4006
Tel: (07) 3854 1340

Mountain Designs
105 Albert St
Brisbane Qld 4000
Tel: (07) 3221 6756

Mountain Designs
120 Wickham St
Fortitude Valley Qld 4006
Tel: (07) 3216 1866

Mountain Designs–Rocksports
224 Barry Pde
Fortitude Valley Qld 4006
Tel: (07) 3216 0462

Paddy Pallin
Adventure Equipment
138 Wickham St
Fortitude Valley Qld 4006
Tel: (07) 3252 4408

Torre Mountain Craft Pty Ltd
185 Moggill Rd
Taringa Qld 4068
Tel: (07) 3870 2699

Toowoomba
Mountain Designs
409 Ruthven St
Toowoomba Qld 4350
Tel: (07) 4637 8800

Townsville

Adventure Camping Equipment
11 Ross River Rd
Mundingburra Qld 4812
Tel: (07) 4775 6116

Cairns

Adventure Equipment Cairns
133 Grafton St
Cairns Qld 4870
Tel: (07) 4031 2669

It's Extreme
32 Spence St
Cairns Qld 4870
Tel: (07) 4051 0344

The Northern Territory

Adventure Equipment Darwin
41 Cavenagh St
Darwin
NT 0800
Tel: (08) 8941 0019

Western Australia

Perth

Mainpeak Pty Ltd
31 Jarrad St
Cottesloe WA 6011
Tel: (08) 9385 2552

Mainpeak Pty Ltd
415 Hay St
Subiaco WA 6008
Tel: (08) 9388 9072

Mountain Designs
Shop 3, Queensgate Centre
William St
Fremantle WA 6160
Tel: (08) 9335 1431

Mountain Designs
862 Hay St
Perth WA 6000
Tel: (08) 9322 4774

Paddy Pallin
884 Hay St

Perth WA 6000
Tel: (08) 9321 2666

Snowgum
581 Murray St
West Perth WA 6005
Tel: (08) 9321 5259

Bunbury

Mountain Designs
16 Stephen St
Bunbury WA 6230
Tel: (08) 9791 9888

South Australia

Acme Wall Company
171–174 West Tce
Adelaide SA 5000
Tel: (08) 8410 5448

Annapurna Outdoor Shop
210 Rundle St
Adelaide SA 5000
Tel: (08) 8223 4633

Mountain Designs
208 Rundle St
Adelaide SA 5000
Tel: (08) 8232 0690

Paddy Pallin
228 Rundle St
Adelaide SA 5000
Tel: (08) 8232 3155

Scout Outdoor Centre
192 Rundle St
Adelaide SA 5000
Tel: (08) 8223 5544

Tasmania

Hobart

The Climbing Edge
54 Bathurst St
Hobart Tas 7000
Tel: (03) 6234 3575

Mountain Designs
74 Elizabeth St

Hobart Tas 7000
Tel: (03) 6234 3900

Paddy Pallin
76 Elizabeth St
Hobart Tas 7000
Tel: (03) 6231 0777

Launceston
Allgoods Pty Ltd
71 York St
Launceston Tas 7250
Tel: (03) 6331 3644

Mountain Designs
2/41 York St
Launceston Tas 7250
Tel: (03) 6334 0988

Paddy Pallin
110 George St
Launceston Tas 7250
Tel: (03) 6331 4240

Devonport
Mountain Designs
217 Tarleton St
East Devonport Tas 7310
Tel: (03) 6427 8699

APPENDIX 2: CLIMBING SCHOOLS AND GYMS

New South Wales

Schools
Australian School of Mountaineering
166B Katoomba St
Katoomba NSW 2780
Tel: (02) 4782 2014

Australian Sport Climbing Federation Inc
NSW Branch
PO Box 1043
Artarmon NSW 1570
Tel: 0418 248 804

High 'n Wild Mountain Adventures
3/5 Katoomba St
Katoomba NSW 2780
Tel: (02) 4782 6224

Rocksports Adventure Training
1 Ross St
Glenbrook NSW 2773
Tel: (02) 4739 3152

Gyms
Australian Climbing Gyms Association
3/268 Victoria St
Wetherill Park NSW 2164
Tel: (02) 9609 5853

City Crag
499 Kent St
Sydney

NSW 2000
Tel: (02) 9267 3822

Climb Fit
Unit 4, 12 Frederick St
St Leonards NSW 2065
Tel: (02) 9436 4600

Hangdog Climbing Gym Pty Ltd
130 Auburn St
Wollongong NSW 2500
Tel: (02) 4225 8369

Mountain Designs
190 Katoomba St
Katoomba NSW 2780
Tel: (02) 4782 5999

Northern Beaches Rockhouse
19A Roger St
Brookvale NSW 2100
Tel: (02) 9905 6202

Summit Indoor Climbing Centre
Level 2, 40 Third Ave
Blacktown NSW 2148
Tel: (02) 9678 9635

Sydney Indoor Climbing Gym
59 Liverpool Rd
Summer Hill NSW 2130
Tel: (02) 9716 6949

The Cave
Village Fitness Leura
185 The Mall
Leura Village NSW 2780
Tel: (02) 4784 2163

The Climbing Centre
Unit 3, 16 Borec Rd
Penrith NSW 2750
Tel: (02) 4731 1130

The Edge Indoor Climbing Centre
9/10 Hudson Ave
Castle Hill NSW 2154
Tel: (02) 9899 8228

The Ledge Climbing Centre
Sydney University Women's Sports Association
Western Ave
The University of Sydney NSW 2006
Tel: (02) 9351 8115

The Pitch Indoor Climbing Centre
Unit 3, 268 Victoria St
Wetherill Park NSW 2164
Tel: (02) 9729 0212

The Quarie Climbing Gym
Macquarie University Sports Association
No 2 Gate Culloden Rd
Marsfield NSW 2122
Tel: (02) 9850 9494

Vertical Reality
377 Edward St
Wagga Wagga NSW 2650
Tel: (02) 6925 0069

Victoria

Schools
Adventure Plus Mountaineering & Rock
Climbing
PO Box 153
Natimuk Vic 3409
Tel: (03) 5387 1530

Arapiles Climbing Guides
16 Lake Rd
Natimuk Vic 3409
Tel: (03) 5387 1284 or 0428 504 460

Base Camp and Beyond
'Musbury'
Halls Gap Vic 3381
Tel: (03) 5356 4300

The Climbing Company,
117 Main St
Natimuk Vic 3409
Tel: (03) 5387 1329

Grampians Adventure Services Pty Ltd
Stony Creek Shops
Grampians Rd
Halls Gap Vic 3381
Tel: (03) 5356 4556

Grampians Central Booking Office
Main Street
Halls Gap Vic 3381
Tel: (03) 5356 4654

Gyms
Australian Alpine Institute
New Summit Rd
Mt Buller Vic 3723
Tel: (03) 5733 7000

Cliffhanger Climbing Gym Pty Ltd
Westgate Sports & Leisure Complex
Cnr Grieve Pde & Dohertys Rd
Altona North Vic 3025
Tel: (03) 9369 6400

Indoor Rockclimbing Gyms of Australia
Association
PO Box 431
Box Hill Vic 3128
Tel: (03) 9877 0377

The Climbing Mill
78 Oxford St
Collingwood Vic 3066
Tel: (03) 9419 4709

The Hardrock Climbing Company Pty Ltd
Unit 2, 16 Varman Crt
Nunawading Vic 3131
Tel: (03) 9894 4183

Queensland

Gyms
Rocksports
224 Barry Pde
Fortitude Valley Qld 4006
Tel: (07) 3216 0462

Rocksports
Cnt Bryants Rd & Cornubia Park Drive
Shailer Park Qld 4128
Tel: (07) 3209 8282

Western Australia

Gyms
Rockface
63 John St
Northbridge WA 6003
Tel: (08) 9328 5998

Tasmania

Schools
The Tasmanian Climbing Company
54 Bathurst St
Hobart Tas 7000
Tel: (03) 6234 3575

Gyms
The Climbing Edge,
54 Bathurst St
Hobart Tas 7000
Tel: (03) 6234 3575

Hobart Indoor Climbing Gym
7 Wilson St
North Hobart Tas 7000
Tel: (03) 6234 9544

APPENDIX 3: USEFUL WEB SITES
Australia

www.climbing.com.au
• a general guide to climbing in Australia, with news

www.arapiles.com
• general climbing resource

www.thecrag.com
• an index of 17 000 routes, grades etc.

http://homepages.tig.com.au/~rodw
• Crag X—general climbing resource

www.onsight.com.au
• Australian climbing photography

New South Wales

www.climbingmadness.com/default.htm
• info on Blue Mountains and Sydney climbing

www.cliffcare.org.au/blue_mtns.htm
• Blue Mountains Cliffcare, includes regular access updates

www.sydneyrockies.org.au
• Sydney Rock Climbing Club

www.geocities.com/Yosemite/Trails/8011
• The Sydney climbing site

www.geocities.com/Yosemite/8537
• Newcastle Uni Mountaineering Club

www.une.edu.au/~unemc/climb.htm
• University of New England Mountaineering Club

www.npws.nsw.gov.au
• National Parks information

www.thegong.com
• Online Wollongong rock

www.sydneyclimbing.com
• an online guide to Sydney craglets

Australian Capital Territory

www.act.gov.au/environ
• National Parks information

Victoria

www.arapiles.net
- all new route info for Arapiles, information and two climbing magazines

http://ariel.its.unimelb.edu.au/~mumc/mumc.html
- Melbourne University Mountaineering Club

www.parkweb.vic.gov.au
- information on Victorian National Parks

http://eurekabouldering.homestead.com
- bouldering in the Victoria Range, Grampians

www.geocities.com/Pipeline/Ramp/3904
- The Boulder Lounge, Grampians and South Australian bouldering and bouldering news

www.vicclimb.org.au
- The Victorian Climbing Club

http://unite.com.au/~u4264a/Main.html
- a guide to the Grampians, with maps, pictures and more

www.rockclimbing-guides.com/melb/Melb_e-guide/Melb_eGuide.htm
- Melbourne bouldering information

Queensland

www.immortal.net.au/climbing
- Lee Skidmore's website is one of the best climbing sites in Australia with excellent information and online guides to Queensland cliffs—it is indispensable for anyone planning a trip to Queensland

www.geocities.com/Yosemite/Rapids/1229/Code/boulderindex.html
- Queensland bouldering

http://members.dingoblue.net.au/~wakko100/
- an online guide to the bouldering at Townsville's Hervey Range

www.geocities.com/Yosemite/Gorge/6530
- Brisbane Rock Climbing Club

www.env.qld.gov.au
- National Parks information

http://www.geocities.com/Yosemite/Rapids/1229/Code/boulderindex.html
- includes Kangaroo Point Bouldering Guide

Northern Territory

www.nt.gov.au/paw
- National Parks information

Western Australia

www.calm.wa.gov.au
- National Parks information

www.geocities.com/yosemite/rapids/4933/CAWA_NS.html
- The Climbing Club of Western Australia

South Australia

www.sreynolds.net/index.htm
- Steve Reynold's home site contains, among other things, an online guide to Moonarie

www.denr.sa.gov.au
- National Parks information

www.geocities.com/Yosemite/Rapids/7291
- The Adelaide Hills, online guides

Tasmania

www.geocities.com/Yosemite/4161
- *Craglets* online with guides and information for Adamsfield, Coles Bay, Hobart and Launceston routes, and more

www.tassie.net.au/~jnermut/Climbing.htm
- excellent site with online guides to many Tasmanian areas

www.parks.tas.gov.au
- National Parks information with online permit forms

INDEX

H